William Bernard Ullathorne

Ecclesiastical Discourses Delivered on Special Occasions

William Bernard Ullathorne

Ecclesiastical Discourses Delivered on Special Occasions

ISBN/EAN: 9783337817312

Printed in Europe, USA, Canada, Australia, Japan

Cover: Foto ©Lupo / pixelio.de

More available books at **www.hansebooks.com**

ECCLESIASTICAL DISCOURSES

𝕯𝖊𝖑𝖎𝖛𝖊𝖗𝖊𝖉 𝖔𝖓 𝕾𝖕𝖊𝖈𝖎𝖆𝖑 𝕺𝖈𝖈𝖆𝖘𝖎𝖔𝖓𝖘.

BY

BISHOP ULLATHORNE.

LONDON:

BURNS AND OATES,

17 & 18 PORTMAN STREET, AND 63 PATERNOSTER ROW.

1876.

PREFACE.

——◦——

THESE Discourses are called Ecclesiastical because
they were either addressed to ecclesiastics or treat
on ecclesiastical subjects. They form a volume embracing certain points of pastoral theology, a subject
on which we have very little that is Catholic in our
language, if we except the excellent little book by
Canon Oakeley. Some few of these Discourses have
been published before, and have now been carefully
revised. The Instruction on Mixed Marriages has
been extended for the purpose of exhibiting the early
discipline of the Church on this important subject.
The three discourses on Science and Wisdom, addressed to the clerics of St. Bernard's Seminary, have
for their object to show the moral and religious value
of philosophic science and thought, when employed
· in the service of religion, a subject too much neglected

among us in days when it is so much demanded. The discourse on Counsel, although addressed on a solemn occasion to a congregation of religious women, forms a sequence to the one on Wisdom, and its principles are equally applicable to ecclesiastical deliberations. In this discourse I am much indebted to the notes of Cornelius à Lapide on the text. Although these Discourses are chiefly addressed to ecclesiastics, I trust there is that in them which may offer a solid instruction to thoughtful Catholic laymen.

BIRMINGHAM, *March 25th,* 1876.

CONTENTS.

(viii)

ECCLESIASTICAL DISCOURSES.

I.

The Discourse

Delivered at the Conclusion of the First Diocesan
Synod of Birmingham, in the year 1853.

OUR first Diocesan Synod, Brethren and Sons in Christ, is drawing to a close. Let us thank God for so great a blessing. How beautiful and joyful for brethren to dwell together in unity! Here is no conflict of new opinions, no clashing of mortal passions. The order of our assembly is a transparent reflection of the order of that universal Church of which we form a part. The laws to which we have listened are no new experiments, taken up with hesitation, or advanced with doubt: they are brought forth from the great stores of ecclesiastical tradition. The greatest pontiffs and prelates conceived them, and the saints have practised them. How many who have won their seats in the great hierarchy of heaven, through their observance of laws like these, have them traced in their spirits with the light of the divine

A

glory. May the Holy Spirit trace their wisdom out most deeply in our lives. You have before you the first fruits of hierarchical government. And blessed are the eyes that see what you see, and the ears that hear what you hear: yea, blessed are you if you keep them and are grateful for them.

For our part, we are overwhelmed with consolation. We already anticipate the good which must arise from our more perfect entrance into the spirit and the constitution of the Church. We will confess to you, that, from the moment the sacred mitre was placed upon our head, so unworthy of it, a sense of the want of this more perfect organisation grew upon us, increased with experience, and never left our mind. Nor can we say that the hope we entertained that we should live to witness it was ever a hope against hope. We had seen too many of the beautiful manifestations of Divine Providence in our missionary life to have any fears on the subject. We looked forward then, with confidence, to what we this day see with a grateful heart.

Let us glance back for a moment. The hierarchy arose at a time when greater and more illustrious Churches were breaking from those iron bonds with which, for ages, the temporal powers had bound them: and in the freshness of their freedom they greeted us as arisen from the dead. And no sooner had the apostolic hands of Peter removed our swathings and set us free, than a certain glory of persecution came upon us, which deeply fixed the fact of our restoration in the minds of men, and inscribed it in broader characters for the page of history. Can we doubt but that this was a counter-stroke of our Heavenly Father's policy? It has already become too clear to admit of doubt in reflecting minds. We cling more closely than ever to the Holy See. We embrace the hierarchical order with a warmer faith and a firmer constancy. "Quare fremuerunt gentes, et populi meditati sunt inania, adversus Dominum et adversus Christum ejus; qui habitat in coelis irridebit eos, et Dominus subsannabit eos."

And now, what does this hierarchy mean? It means that the hour which our fathers longed to see is come. They saw it not in their lives; it is amongst their *glorioles* to witness it from heaven. O Milner! how wouldst thou have rejoiced to see this day, and with what a grateful heart wouldst thou have presided over this assembly. And, my venerable predecessor! whose large apostolic heart anticipated the coming wants, and provided for them. The hierarchy! which arose amidst so wild an opposition; it means that fertile organisation which the Holy Ghost breathed into the Church from her earliest beginnings. It means the restoration of that discipline by which the saints awakened and directed the energies of pastoral solicitude. It means an episcopacy and a clergy imbued with the deep wisdom of the Sovereign Pontiffs, of the Fathers, and of the Councils. It means the regulation of ecclesiastical government by subordination of authorities, under the influence of that unity which is the secret of all strength. It means subjection to precise rules both for bishops and for their clergy, and obedience for those who govern in the

Church, as well as for those who are governed. Study well that Provincial Council in all its features, or any similar one, and you will see that the prelates of the Church bind themselves more strictly far than they bind their subjects. And never yet did any portion of the Church imbibe more vigorous discipline, but there burst out from it more copious fruits;—a holier clergy, a more pious laity, a greater harvest of souls. The Church expects to see in us these fruits of renovation. Pius IX. expects it vehemently. When last we stood in his presence, that holy Pontiff said to us, "Whatever defects there are amongst you, we look for their correction through the hierarchy." And shall it not be? Shall it not be, when saints have prayed for us in so many lands. Long and much have they prayed for us. All the Churches have prayed for us, and have cheered us on in our long fight of patience. The blood of our martyrs, whose bones lie dishonoured, though angels watch over them; the works and tears of our confessors; the pure prayers of our virgins; and the sufferings of our faithful poor, all have cried to God for our cause. Can we, to whom God has given the work for which they have prayed and suffered, be alone found wanting? When the vintage is ripe for the gathering, shall any of it perish through the slackness of those who, at this eleventh hour, are called into the vineyard. Oh, blind indeed are they who see not how open is God's hand over us; how rich His gifts unto us; how little *we* have deserved them; how much He requires at our hands!

For we are not as they who have a certain work

traced out, with exact limits, which done, their work
is over. We are not like those shepherds who are
set to watch a certain and a numbered flock. We
have others also to feed with the celestial food. We
are missioners. O name, rich with the most noble
and generous associations! Our work is that of
apostles. Other sheep must we bring into His fold,
that they may hear the voice of the Prince of Shepherds, and know it from that of aliens. The missioner is one who has as much work before him as
by the utmost stretching of his strength he can accomplish ; and seeing an undefined amount of labour
beyond, he prays the Lord of the harvest to send
more workmen to his aid. He is a devoted man, a
man of sacrifices. Unless he make himself a sacrifice, as an apostle would, for the souls of his brethren,
he may be a priest, but he is unworthy to be called a
missioner. A missioner is a priest, laborious, patient,
not easily discouraged, ingenious by the force of that
ardour which the spirit of his position enkindles to
meet wants as they arise. And when he sees some
want before his eyes, so great that it haunts his mind
like a vision, then he may begin that work with an
assured faith ; let him only use the ordinary rules
of ecclesiastical prudence, and he may ever be
well assured that God will carry him through its
difficulties.

You are "the salt of the earth, and the light of
the world." You are the light of the world, if you
constantly imbibe the most pure wisdom of the Holy
Ghost ; you are the salt of the earth, if you inhale
and breathe forth the piety of Christ. St. John

indentifies the sacerdotal with the angelic life. And when St. Paul enjoins that women veil their heads in the church because of the angels, he insinuates reverence for the purity of her ministers. Humility is the first of all the conditions of your influence. And "proud priest" is the keenest of all reproaches. In that degree in which you diminish in yourselves will you rise in favour both with God and men. Your force, after the manner of that of the Son of God made man, is found in meekness. All the strength of your soul is gathered up in the long endurance of a patient heart. And the flame of sacerdotal life, and its sweet unction, charity—charity, which sees only God and souls—charity, which energises our wills to every sacrifice for their sakes—charity, which can do more than all cleverness, than all genius, than all learning, than all eloquence—charity, which draws souls with a heavenly persuasiveness,—charity is the fruit of recollection, and of pure interior prayer. The man of God well furnished to all good works is the man of prayer, the man of the Holy Ghost.

If the soul of every faithful man is formed in the image of Christ by the character of baptism, yours is formed in the image of His priesthood by the seal of ordination. He was both Priest and Victim. So must you be. So will you be, if, with all His saints, you love His companionship ; a victim for the sins of men, a victim for your own. If, indeed, you love His company, it is sweeter than the conversation of men ; and you will seek Him in the tabernacle, you will seek Him in your chamber, you will seek Him in

the Scriptures and in the Saints, you will seek Him
in your Breviary. In those wonderful psalms, in
which in the days of His flesh He poured out His
inmost soul to His Father, you will find Him as
perfectly as in the Gospels which so divinely record
His outward words and actions. You will seek Him
in your own heart, you will seek Him in the hearts
of the poor.

Why is the layman so quick to see the failings of
the priest? And why, if we except certain circumstances, is he commonly so accurate a judge? It is
not that any predisposition whets his criticism to
sharpness, but his faith has given him an exalted
idea of the priestly character. All his sense of that
dignity is delicate. Anything mean, anything sordid,
anything passionate, anything selfish, anything not
most pure, most perfect in its modesty of word, of
look, of demeanour, wounds and blots that beautiful
and chaste image of the priest which the layman's
faith has raised up in his mind. He knows that his
atmosphere is not yours,—that God has separated
you from him,—that you are the angel of his soul,—
that nothing worldly should breathe out of you.
He knows well that the Spirit of God is most calm
and simple, and he expects in you a simple heart
and a single mind. Any affectation, aught of vanity,
the laity cannot endure in the clergy. They know
that the man of the world is not the man of God.
Let the priest but indulge himself a little freely
beyond the reserve of his state, let him but show
an inclination to bask in the favour of laymen, and
he becomes but too soon and but too much in their

estimation like the rest of men. As you are separated by sacred order, so will they say, should you be separated in life from the common lives, even of faithful and pious men. Let them but see you out of the line of your duties, taking relish a little keenly for such enjoyments as they can give you, and quick will be the conclusion that your resources are not within yourself, nor your sweetest converse with your Lord.

You, Brethren, whom we have constituted our Vicars, whether Vicar General or Vicars Foran, remember that you are both the eye and the hand of episcopal authority. You are to observe where our eye may not reach, and you are to execute what by our ministry is resolved upon. And as the responsibility of your acts rests upon us, keep well in your minds how great a responsibility that is.

You, Brethren, who are raised to the honours of the Chapter, remember that you are the senate of the diocese and our council. As you are placed before your brethren, so let your light shine before them. Seek wisdom more precious than gold. Study the laws and ordinances of the Church to the best of your opportunities, that you may give us such enlightened counsel as we may with security adopt.

Venerable Superiors of Venerable Orders and Institutes; of whose value they know best who have tasted of them most; to you and to your brethren we look for the more perfect examples both of piety and of discipline. If the laity, with that ideal of the priest in their consciences, cannot abide the shortcomings of the priest; so the priest has his ideal of the religious man, as in a state tending to perfection, and his judgment is not satisfied if he can only say that you are not unlike himself.

Priests of the Seminary, oh, what a charge is yours! The future of the diocese is in your hands. Not only the priests, but the future prelates of the Church, must arise from under your labours and your pious influence. Be more intent on sacred wisdom than on profane learning, though that is not to be neglected, and know that its seat is in the heart more than in the head. God destined, indeed, the spoils of the Egyptians for the adornment of His tabernacle, but He put the wisdom of His own Spirit into the hearts of those whose duty it was to adapt them to His service.

Priests of the Mission, called to a part of our solicitude, our joy, and our crown. Be holy as your work is holy. Often retire within yourselves. Beware of offering the Holy Sacrifice through custom. Prepare yourselves for that tremendous action. Let not the dust of the world, in which you work, ingrain itself in your own souls, but wash them often in the streams which flow from Calvary. Cleanse the motes from the eye of your own souls, that you may have spiritual discernment into the souls of other men. Be familiar with the saints, and read their holiest books. Adorn the sanctuary of God more than your own house, and let its order and propriety show that your faith is both alive and effective. Next to your church love your school, and be often in it. Visit your people from house to house. St. Paul found time for this amidst his care for all the Churches; and if that truth rebounds on us, let it rebound to our confusion. Remember that you are missioners, and that the Son of God was a missioner, and reflect in the light of His example what that office implies. Preach Jesus crucified, and not yourselves. But how can you preach Him except as you know Him, and how can you know Him except as you live and converse with Him ; you will find Him more in prayer than in books, though in them He also speaks to you. The power of preaching is in unction, the power of unction is in divine love, the power of divine love is in prayer from a pure heart. Behold our Lord, the Missioner of His Father, how He blesses and instructs the little children, and is simple with the simple. Win their hearts, and gain them to our Lord, and they shall win His heart threefold to you.

In fine, Brethren and Sons in Christ, receive the decrees which the Fathers of the Provincial Council have enjoined, and our own, as of the will of God, and be ever mindful of that strict account which we shall all have to give of them in the day of the divine judgment.

And may God Himself, and our Father, and our Lord Jesus Christ exhort your hearts, and direct you in the holy way of obedience, and confirm you in all good works and words, that you may walk in all things worthy of the calling in which you are called, being in all things pleasing to Him ; that, approved in the holy advancement of your virtues, you may appear before God our Father, adorned with the graces of His Spirit, at the coming of our Lord Jesus Christ, with all His Saints. Amen.

II.

The Discourse

*Delivered at the Third Diocesan Synod of Birmingham
in the year* 1864.

MY VERY REV. AND REV. BRETHREN,—The
prayers, consultations, and solemn rites with
which the Church brings us into Synodical order, are
designed in the wisdom of the Holy Ghost to awaken
the bishop to the sense of his responsibilities, and to
dispose him for his acts and utterances; whilst they
are equally intended to incline the hearts of the
clergy to the spirit of ecclesiastical renovation.

Hundreds of voices in our conventual choirs, and
tens of thousands in our churches, have joined their
prayers for this object. Old men bent towards their
graves, young men and maidens who send sighs to
God amidst a corrupt generation, the virgins of Christ
prevailing by their purity, the children blooming in
their innocence, and the penitents low-voiced in
shame and sorrow, all these have prayed for us.
The saints, ever responsive to our call, and prompt
to second our acts of piety, have sustained our supplications where they stand before the throne of

grace. The faithful children have prayed for their spiritual fathers, to our Father who is in heaven, that, looking upon the face of His Son, on His Cross and in His Passion, He would please to unite their hearts in one, and make them the pure reflections of His light ; that He would augment their sacerdotal grace and virtue, and consolidate their lives in the laws of canonical discipline.

And what has our Lord promised to an assembly like this, that is called in His name and with a view to His glory ? It is after speaking of the duty of obedience and of the terrible consequences of dis-obedience to the prelates of His Church, that He says : " *Verily I say to you ; whatsoever you shall bind on earth shall be bound in heaven ; and whatso-ever you shall loose on earth shall be loosed in heaven. Again I say to you, that if two of you shall agree upon earth concerning anything whatsoever that they shall ask, it shall be done for them by my Father who is in heaven. For where two or three are gathered in my name, there am I in the midst of them.*" Let then our faith pierce through all mortal obstructions, that we may look towards the Lord and Master of our souls, who, having descended in the Sacrifice, comes with us into the midst of this assembly. The desire of His heart is to make us wise and energetic builders up of His mystical body. Opening then our hearts to His sacred influences, can we do better than to recall that first impression of our sacred character and that sacerdotal sense which came upon us in the day of our ordination, and to stir up the grace that is in us by the imposition of hands ?

What a day was that! purified by prayer and by
eternal light, and washed even to the soles of our
spiritual feet in the bath of repentance, we knelt in
our white robes within the shadow of the altar, and
received the unction from the Holy One, and the
word of power. How we felt the glow of that new
creation! How the gale of the new spirit breathed
through us! How we were humbled beneath the
sacred dignity that came upon us from the High
Priest who sits at the right hand of God. His seal
upon our hands was as tender as mercy. His fire in
our hearts was as the burning of a holocaust. And
when the pure Host and the cup with the blood of
the grape were delivered into our hands, with what
awe did our ears receive the sacramental words:—
"*Receive the power of offering sacrifice to God, and of
celebrating masses both for the living and the dead, in
the name of the Lord.*" Was not each breath of pride
hushed to silence in our hearts? And did not each
selfish aspiration in our nature give place to some
holier movement born of grace and charity? Sub-
dued with that sense of God's infinite condescension,
and melted with that ray of His goodness, had we
any other resolve than this, that that sacrifice should
be our life, and that we would patiently bear the
stigmas of that sacrifice to the end of our mortal
existence? Was it not our vivid conviction that we
had nothing left us but to show forth the death of
the Lord, and this not from the altar alone, for that
would be a shocking inconsistency, but in the un-
earthly character of our lives? The mystical exhortation with which the Church had just addressed us

through the mouth of the bishop, seemed already to
have entered into our will past revocation. But let
us hear those words once again :—" Keep your lives
spiritually healthy, pure and holy. Understand
what that is which you offer unto God. And do you
imitate that victim which you hold in your hands.
As it is the death of your Lord which you so often
celebrate, take care that you die yourself to your
own vices and concupiscences. Let your teaching
be a spiritual medicine to God's people ; and let the
odour of your life breathe like a fragrant perfume
in God's Church ; that so, by your deeds as by your
words, you may build up that house which is the
family of God." And then the prelate, bearing outwardly the staff of authority, and inwardly his dread
solicitude, concluded in these words :—" So be it, that
neither we, for having advanced you to this sublime
office, nor you, for having received it at our hands,
may suffer damnation from the Lord, but rather
receive His reward, which may He grant us through
His grace."

Consider, my brethren, what this priesthood is,
what a call : what a gift : what a sublime communication of the sacerdotal character of Christ! It is the
prerogative of mercy which the Incarnate Son hath
won over the justice of the Eternal Father, yet without defeating justice ; it is the power which God
exerts over God for the pardon of the human race ;
it is the very function of grace and mercy, and it is
committed to human keeping. The acts of this
power are efficacious even unto the portals of hell,
and even to the gates of heaven ; nay, they go be-

yond the gates, and reach that golden altar which
is before the face of God, on which stands the Lamb
for ever slain, and for ever pleading mercy. The
priest is chosen from among men, and is appointed
for men, in the things that are of God, that he
may offer gifts and sacrifice for sin. He is the agent
of the Incarnate God, and the dispenser of His grace,
His truth and life. "*Let a man so account of us,*"
says St. Paul, "*as the ministers of Christ, and the
dispensers of the mysteries of God. Here now it is
required among the dispensers, that a man be found
faithful.*" If there be other motives for leading a
holy and abstracted life, there can be none higher or
more sovereign than this, that we are the priests of
the Most High God ; and that it is the priesthood of
Christ which we indelibly hold, and which indelibly
holds us, and that we are called to the care of souls.
In this are we called to be like the angels of God,
that we stand before God in our ministry of eternal
things, and that we are sent of God to men to be His
messengers of pardon and peace. Can we have a
diviner motive for a life of high thinking and of
lowly feeling ? Can any distinction between this and
that class of priests, furnish higher arguments for
an unworldly life and a close union with God, than
the character of the priesthood itself, and the work
to which you are called ?· Can the servant of grace
be also the servant of this blind and sensuous
world ? Even the votaries of this world say—no,
and they expect him to be altogether unlike themselves.

Let me offer a passing comment on that word

Secular, as far as it applies to that great body of clergy whose title of ordination points to the cure of souls. Let me rub off the rust of ambiguity from that term, lest it dim the brightness of that order of which our Lord Himself was the founder. *Secular* and *Regular* are not opposed, as if they of the latter designation inherited a holier priesthood than yours of the former ; but because the same divine priesthood is held in different spheres. The Regular seeks that sanctity through the help of a special rule which you seek in the common wisdom of the Church and in the graces of your ministry. The word *Secular* in this construction has nothing to do with a secular spirit, but it marks out the field of your labours. Our Lord says: —" *The field is the world*, ... *and the good seed are the children of the kingdom*, ... *and the reapers are the angels.*" So the angels, who have nothing secular in their spirits, have a secular work to do in the field of human life. It was to the Secular clergy that our Lord first said :—" *Ye are not of the world.*" Why then did He send them into the world ? He tells us —" *Ye are the light of the world.*" But the lights of the world, the sun by day and the stars by night, are set above the world, or how could they illuminate the world ? Has God then ordained His spiritual lights to walk in the earthly or in the heavenly system ? Should they shine with the corruption of the earthly or with the purity of the heavenly ways ? And if our Lord calls you the salt of the earth, it is for the purpose of reminding you, that if the body of salt being mixed with earthly elements grow vapid and lose its virtue, if the man of God lose his spirit in the man of the world, there is nothing left with which the earth can be salted.

Remember well, my brethren, that God has put no other well-spring of light and grace in that church and congregation of yours but yourself—no other authoritative witness to His brightness and purity but yourself—no other index pointing His way of truth and holiness but yourself. And "*if the salt lose its savour, with what shall the earth be salted.*"

An army has many distinctions in its array, of rank, uniform, and discipline ; but valour is expected to be the attribute of every soldier without distinction. There are many grades and orders in the army of God's priesthood, and each one finds his own special strength in that grace which awaits him on the path of his vocation ; but sanctity is the attribute that is looked for in every priest. And the very idea of sanctity involves detachment from profane, that is, from worldly, pursuits and pleasures.

In the hour in which our Lord consecrated His priesthood—and it was the secular priesthood which He personally consecrated—after initiating His disciples into the mysteries of His Body and Blood, He spoke of the detachment which He had wrought in their hearts—" *You have not chosen me, but I have chosen you, that you should go, and should bring forth fruit ; and your fruit should remain. . . . If you had been of the world, the world would love its own : but because you are not of the world, therefore the world hateth you. Remember the word I said unto you : the servant is not greater than his master. If they have persecuted me, they will also persecute you : if they have*

B

kept my word, they will keep yours also." The conflict between the world and the priesthood arises òut
of the opposition of their natures. And by the world,
of course, we mean all those who put God second to
themselves, and His cause second to their own cause.
Now the haughty and clever men of the world cannot
even in imagination endure a power so high and
exacting as that of the priesthood, claimed by men
who put forth no palpable pretensions, nothing that
can be visibly grasped in its sources or calculated in
it effects. For it is he who hath the spirit of God who
sees the things of God ; but the sensual man seeth
not these things, they are foolishness in his eyes,
and because they are spiritually examined his eyes
cannot see them. And the dull men of the world
follow the judgments of their quicker guides. The
very demeanour of one who dares, and that on the
ground of his spiritual character, to stand aloof from
the world's ways of thinking and acting, is resented
as an assault on its habits and a disdain for its
opinions. He would not be more provoking who
should obtrude the costume of five hundred years ago
upon the fashions of the hour. And to say the truth,
the presence of an unworldly priest does challenge
the interior habits of the man, even unconsciously.
Our Lord says as much in that very discourse, where
He declares that when the Spirit of Truth, which He
promised to send His disciples, shall come to them,
*" He will convict the world of sin, of justice, and of
judgment."* It was far then from our Lord's intention
to offer us maxims like these :—that you may win the
world, be like the world : or, that you may conciliate

the times, be like the times. For the more you are
like the world, the less are you the witness of God.
And St. Paul found that if after their own fashion he
pleased men, he would cease to be the servant of
Christ.

But it is not in man's nature to deal much with the
world and not inhale its spirit into his own; and
therefore our Lord provided a remedy for this human
infirmity, and an antidote against the peril of it. In
that selfsame hour in which He constituted the
priesthood in the Apostles, He made a solemn prayer
to His Father that its members might be kept from
the evil of the world : and He sanctified Himself from
the world that they might be sanctified in Him.
Turning from them to the Father, He said—"*I pray
for them, I pray not for the world. . . . Holy Father,
keep them in Thy name. . . . I have given them my
word.*" O luminous, uncreated, and creative Word!
O Word which is Thyself!—"*I have given them my
word, and the world hateth them, because they are not
of the world ; as I also am not of the world. I pray
not that Thou shouldst take them out of the world, but
that Thou shouldst preserve them from evil. They are
not of the world, as I also am not of the world. Sanctify them in truth. Thy word is truth. As Thou hast
sent me into the world, I also have sent them into the
world. And for them do I sanctify myself, that they
also may be sanctified in truth.*"

Why does our Lord interpose that hour between
His mystical and His bloody sacrifice ? Do we not
begin to see that it was to breathe this ordination
discourse into the breasts of His Apostles, and to

leave it for the daily meditation of all who share their priesthood ? The fire of the eucharistic grace caused their hearts to burn within them ; and whilst thus ductile and impressible through the tenderness of His charity and the contemplation of His departure from them, He reiterates upon them, stroke upon stroke, as with the sword of His Spirit—" *Ye are not of the world.*" He puts the word of His power into them ; He sanctifies Himself for them ; He prepares in Himself that sacerdotal grace which He gives to them as the principle of the sacerdotal virtues ; and He sends them into the world encompassed with the adamantine shield of that imperishable prayer, in which He asks the Father to keep them from sin and secularity. Need we wonder, then, that the grace of the priesthood is so strong a grace, and that it takes a long course of inward neglect and decay, or a violent course of rebellious resistance, before it is absolutely broken down, before the world is scandalised with a fall like that of Satan ? In sanctifying that grace for us the God Incarnate resisted the world unto death, and asked the Father that He would give unto that grace a preservative strength against the world. Ah then, my brethren, let us not let in the world upon that grace, and upon the fruit of that prayer ! For He would have us be the light of the world, unmingled with its darkness ; and the salt of the earth, untainted with its corruption. And as we have freely received, so would He have us freely give to the world, whilst we only inwardly receive from His fountains.

Why did our Lord refuse to pray for the world ?

He prayed for them whom in the strength of His grace, He sent into the world, and for all those whom they should draw in their mystical nets out of the foaming floods of its iniquity, but there His prayer stops and goes no further, because He would have all men to come to Him through their ministry. And so our Lord says—"*I pray not for the world, I pray for them. . . . And not only for them do I pray, but for them also do I pray who through their word shall believe in me; that they may be one, as Thou, Father, in me, and I in Thee; that they also may be one in us: that the world may believe that Thou hast sent me. And the glory which Thou hast given to me I have given to them: that they may be one, as we also are one. . . . And the world may know that Thou hast sent me, and hast loved them, as Thou hast also loved me.*" Oh, my brethren, what a light is here! The glory of the Son is to be loved of the Father, and to be one with the Father. Love is the life of unity. The glory of God is the perfection of unity in the society of three Persons. Towards that unity every spirit of grace is tending. In that unity all science from every intelligence culminates, all love terminates, and all desires find repose, even the desires that ascend from the remotest nooks of the spiritual creation. Unity is the prime witness of God. It is proof work, showing the hand of the divine workman. It is work cast in His likeness, like the individual human soul. It reveals the operation of His Spirit, like that soul when at one with herself. Amidst the strife of human thoughts and the din and discord of opinions, when a man seeks for the signs of God in earnest, he seeks for what will solve all discords into unity. And hence our Lord prays for the unity of all who believe in Him, through the word and the union of them whom He has appointed, that they may show forth His work to the world, and the divinity of the Workman. To secure that unity, He generates His priesthood from one, and generates the Church from the unity of the priesthood. And He plainly indicates that as this work of unity goes on, extending over time and space, and through the tribes and races of the earth, resisting change and casting out division, the proof of the divinity of His work will rise higher as the base of unity extends farther, and is more rudely buffeted by the surges of division that are weltering beyond its confines. It is the master miracle of the Eternal Word : a miracle of no transient kind, but coeval with the ages. And He tells us that as the glory of God in heaven is the unity of the Persons in one, so His glory on earth is the unity of the members of the Church in one. And as God is one in substance, one in knowledge, and one in love ; so the Church is one in authority, one in the Word of Truth, and one in the bond of charity. It is in the likeness of its Author, and bespeaks the presence of His Spirit, of which also our Lord said in that same discourse—"*I will send Him unto you. . . . He shall receive of mine, and show to you. All things whatever the Father hath are mine. Therefore I said, that He shall receive of mine, and show to you.*"

Here, then, is the true spirit of the priesthood, to think and feel with the great soul of the Church—

sentire cum ecclesia. To have that thought in us which was in Christ Jesus. To enter into His Word, which will transform our own, and to cultivate the charity of the brotherhood. So shall we be truly solicitous "to keep the unity of the Spirit in the bond of peace." Therefore the Apostolic Fathers, on whose spirit the words of our Lord were so fresh and vivid, are instant with the clergy that they be of one mind and heart with their prelates. St. Ignatius the Martyr almost wearies them with the injunction that they do nothing without their bishop, that nothing be done out of unity, nothing outside the Spirit of God. St. Clement, in his great Epistle to the Corinthians, carefully defines each one's station in the Church, and says to each and to all—"Step not out of your rank, for that is not just, that is to go counter to the will of God."

A long course of responsibility in ecclesiastical government cannot fail, my brethren, to give a certain facility of observation, a sort of ecclesiastical sense, I might almost say a *gratia gratis data*, an instinct acquired by contact with the Church on many points, the result of which becomes a vivid comment on the gospel. Let us instance the exercise of sacerdotal grace on the mystical body of Christ. One and the same order of priesthood is equal in all priests, and it may be said that, as the soul is all in all the body and all in every part, so is the priesthood all in all the body of priests and all in each one of their number. And yet with what a different force and attraction do we see the same sacerdotal power put forth by one as compared with another in the selfsame

ministry. I am speaking, of course, not of the
efficacy of sacraments, but of the efficacy of ministration, an efficacy that does not depend, beyond a certain moderate limit, on natural ability or on human
culture. No, it depends on the way in which the grace
that is in you by the imposition of hands is stirred
up by your cultivating the sacerdotal virtues. Let
me take some single-hearted missioner, intent on the
one thing needful : he has imbibed a deep impression
that, as a man of God, he need not take much time in
dressing out his mind for this world's sake, and prefers to nourish the fountains of his heart on habitual
recollection and prayer. You may know such men
at a glance. They draw crowds to their confessional.
You find the type of such men in St. Vincent of Paul,
and in the late Curé of Ars. What is their secret ?
It is this—they abide in Christ, they draw their light
from His word, they penetrate into the spirit of the
great High Priest, they cherish His operation in their
hearts. And has He not said in that ordination
sermon—" *The branch cannot bear fruit unless it
abide in the vine*" ? Hath not He who has engrafted
us into His eternal priesthood said this truth so dis-
tinctly that there is no escape from it—"*I am the
vine, you the branches : he that abideth in me, the same
beareth much fruit ; for without me you can do nothing.
If you abide in me, and my words abide in you, you
shall ask whatever you will, and it shall be done unto
you. In this is my Father glorified, that you bring
forth much fruit, and become my disciples. As the
Father hath loved me, I also have loved you. Abide in
my love*" ?

And no sooner has that black sheep of the flock, the sacrilegious apostle, gone on his traitorous errand,' than our Lord bursts forth to His newly-created priesthood in these tender and ardent words—"*A new commandment I give unto you, that you love one another, as I have loved you, that you also have love one for another. By this shall all men know that you are my disciples, if you have love one for another.*" He would weld His priesthood into compact unity in the flame of His eternal charity; and would have all who offer one and the same victim of love to give to each other the charity which He gives to them. What higher motive can a priest have for love and reverence of his brother priest, than that he also is a priest of God, and that in him the power of Christ dwells? Especially is this love and reverence required where two or more priests are placed together in one ministry. There let the order of Christ reign. Let it be remembered that he who is the first has the care of souls, and the administration. And that whilst his co-operators share his solicitude, the chief responsibility rests with him. Now, every degree of responsibility implies the same degree of authority. Let nothing be done in the church, in the school, in the congregation, in the house, nor in your own conduct, independent of his knowledge and approval. For it must not be lost sight of that the chief responsibility is with him who has the care of the mission, and that the bishop will not only exact an account from him of the flock, but also of the clergy who are placed under him. There is a maxim, thank God it is as rare amongst us as it is detestable, that says—Let him who has the responsibility and the credit have the labour, I will keep to my own lines. But, O ungenial man! unfit for confidence, you are put there not merely for a line of work, but to learn wisdom and to imbibe charity, and to know that "brother helped of brother is as a strong city." The second should never absent himself for a day without knowledge of the first, or how can he provide for the contingencies of duty that may arise? Nor should he remain out, as a rule, beyond regulated hours, or, independent of higher considerations, derange such other regulations as are essential to a sacerdotal household. On the other hand, the first priest should treat his co-operators as his brethren, with open confidence and with cordial affection; not lording it over the brethren, but being a pattern to them from the soul. In a word, let charity abide in that fraternal love which our Lord has asked His Father for you, and love will suggest whatever is becoming, and whatever is of good report.

What, my brethren, is that fruit of which our Lord speaks so much, and in which He seeks the glory of His Father? It is the precious fruit of souls of which He says, If you abide in my love, you shall bring forth much fruit. It is impossible to love Christ and not love to save souls. A soul among created things is the noblest, and when pure is nigh unto God. What is the diamond of purest ray serene compared with the lustre of that ray of light in which God constitutes a soul and brings it into relationship with His intelligence? And what is all created sense compared with that touch of the divine finger on the conscience,

instinct with the sense of His eternal law? If we
go to the skilful for a true valuation of the jewel, God
has appraised the soul of man, and has redeemed it,
not with gold and silver, but "*with the precious blood
of Christ, as of a lamb unspotted and undefiled.*" And
this soul, so dearly redeemed—I use the words of St.
Gregory Nazianzen—God has placed on the earth to
be *alter angelus, cultor sui.* If that soul has turned
away from God, you are its illuminator. The more
need have you that the light of God's countenance
should shine upon you. If Satan would blow his
pestilence on that soul, you are its protector from his
fiery breath. If it hath sunk into unclean mire, you
are to rescue and redress that soul. The more need
have you to be clean of heart. If, like the light straw
or idle feather, it is tossed to and fro in the eddies of
human opinion, your office is to bring that soul into
the stability of truth. Oh, what a mission is ours!
And what a prize we have in view to keep our
courage up to earnest work! What a life it is to
rescue souls from the everlasting pit, and to send them
off rejoicing on their way to heaven! God despises
no soul, however degraded, because He sees its capa-
bilities. And let us ever remember what is the sum
of all the divine history as it looks towards man; it
is the expression of that sublime Attribute—that
Attribute which we are called to imitate and to
second—that mercy and magnificence with which
God "*lifteth up the needy from the dust, and the poor
from the dunghill, to make them sit with princes,
even with the princes of His people.*"

For this went forth the Master of the household

into the byways and the hedges, and brought the
destitute and forlorn into His banquet. For this the
great Shepherd left the fold in tranquillity, and followed the lost sheep, carrying them, when rescued
from the thickets, on His shoulders back to safety.
For this did He who holds the keys of life and death
cause the publicans and the harlots to go before the
learned scribes and the haughty Pharisees into His
kingdom. Love, even the divine love of souls, has in
it a quality so humble, that it can only deal with
spirits that are humble ; nor can anything that is not
humble pass into the sphere of eternal love.

The ways of God in souls are open to you, my
brethren, in the sacred confessional. It is a wonderful
experience that is closed to all other men. It would
seem as if God had almost as much ordained that
tribunal for the illumination of the pastor as for the
healing of the penitent. And how many an arrow
sped unconsciously—some pointed with compunction,
some with remorse, some with light and some with
fire, and others imbued with sweetest unction—is shot
into the heart of the judge from that of the penitent.
And have you not found that it is the humblest spirit
that most awakes your own tenderness ? That it is
the soul most lost to self, be it in contrition or in
gratitude, that most impresses your heart with the
truth, that " *God knows the proud afar off and the
humble near at hand.*" Blessed is that priest whose
heart is open to the sacred influences that flow from
the commerce of God with souls in the hour of their
self-humiliation.

But in that moral science which prepares us for

the tribunal there is a subtle peril, not always understood. I am not speaking of the morbid anatomy of
certain vices, for here all spiritual guides support the
instincts of piety in guarding the outward door of the
imagination ; but I speak of a peril that is too real
though less noticed. The man who is strong, healthy,
and generous in his piety is always inclined to carry
his devotedness into that free atmosphere which lies
beyond the rigid prohibitions of sin and anathema.
In his case love and zeal are ever amplifying the
circle of duty, and his motto is *Latum mandatum tuum
nimis*. But the scientific habit of reducing laws to
their lowest degree of obligation, and of contracting
obligation within its narrowest limits, the very skill
of running the lines of the precept with sharp definition round the verges of sin, has in it, like skill in
most arts and sciences, a peculiar charm and fascina-
tion for its possessor. Valuable as this science is in
guiding and relieving souls, though in its development
it is of recent ages, it has this peril for him of whose
mental habits it forms a strong feature, that he may
be led, even unconsciously almost, to guide his own
conduct in the race by the signal-posts of danger.
And, not to speak of the contraction of heart and
abatement of generosity that must follow, we all
know that he who coasts along the lines that divide
right from wrong must often run beyond them
through sheer infirmity. Hence there are few sounds
that pain my ears more than certain questionings if
they come from clerical lips, asking, Am I bound
to do this ? and, Am I bound to do that ? And I
love to hear the chimes of that sacerdotal heart which

ring in clear notes of self-sacrifice, asking, Is it best
to do this ? or, Is it more wise to leave that alone ?
Counting it all honour and benediction to do the
most for every one in every case that a good and
faithful servant of God can do.

My brethren, I conclude. When our Lord committed His flock to His chosen Shepherd, three times
He asked him, *Peter, lovest thou me?* so that at the
third interrogation Peter's heart grew sad. But our
Lord knew the love which was in Peter's heart, and
He drew from him the confession of his vehement
love, once, twice, and thrice, that He might fasten
the care of His sheep upon that love. And then
Jesus told His disciple how that care of feeding souls
for love of his Divine Master would fasten him upon
the cross. To feed Christ's flock is the work of love ;
and love, but above all love that suffers, is that which
saves what Love has died to redeem.

III.

The Discourse

*Delivered at the Opening Session of the Second Pro-
vincial Synod of Westminster, in the year 1855.*

MOST Eminent Cardinal Archbishop, Brothers
in the Sacred Episcopate, and Brethren in
the Priesthood,—Synods are of Apostolic origin ; the
principles on which they rest are plainly delivered
by our Lord in the gospel, and their first exercise is
clearly recorded in the Acts of the Apostles. And
who can doubt, even after our own short experience ;
who can doubt, after that description of the fruits of
our own first Synod, which we heard from the lips of
his Eminence but yesterday ; who can now doubt,
more than St. Charles Borromeo, whose words have
been echoing through the Church for the last three
hundred years, that "the Holy Council of Trent,
amongst its other acts for the Church's renovation,
was especially inspired to re-establish that discipline
of holding Provincial Synods which had been so long
going to decay."

These Synods breathe a wisdom of order and raise
up a life of discipline throughout a province such as

the several bishops, working by isolated efforts in their respective dioceses, might strive in vain to accomplish. There is a divine sentence which says, that "in multitude of counsel there is safety." And certainly what is accomplished by the common counsel of the bishops, helped by their learned and experienced advisers, brings a higher light to bear upon the subjects placed before us from the concentration of so many individual lights into one focus. Where our several lights are found from the first to accord, their united force grows into admirable strength and authority : where they exhibit a difference of view, through the process of discussion what is less accurate becomes rectified, until the right illumination gains the ascendancy, and finally rules the whole assembly. Then, for the sifting out and separating of what may possibly find its way into our deliberations of human infirmity, of individual temperament, or of shortsighted personal interest, the Church has provided her Synods with most wise rules and cautious methods of proceeding. Let us briefly review them. The first thing published to the members of the Synod is the rules of life to be observed by them while it lasts; for the discipline of a Synod has much of the character of a spiritual retreat, as well with respect to good order as with respect to exercises of devotion. Looking more to the light of the Holy Spirit than to their own, the assembled Fathers seek that light through the Sacrifice, through prayer, and through solemn supplications.

The drafts of their proposed decrees pass from

their hands into the special congregations of theologians, canonists, and other ecclesiastics, experienced
in their subjects, and by them they are freely sifted,
discussed, and annotated, after which process they
return to the bishops, who revise them by the light
thrown upon them in the congregations. After this
third process the decrees are brought before the whole
Synod, assembled in the church in general congregation, where, after each has been read out by the
proper official, those of the Synod who had not a
previous opportunity are called upon for their remarks
and criticisms. After this more solemn examination,
they return to the bishops for their second revision.
And after this is accomplished, they are prepared for
the public session. In that session, after the solemn
Sacrifice and supplications are concluded, all withdraw except the bishops, who, after a final revision of
the decrees, give the suffrage of their decisive votes
as to what shall or shall not be enacted into a law of
the province. Meanwhile, in the repeated discussions
as well by the bishops as by the representatives of
the clergy and of the religious orders, by the intervals
that pass between one examination of the decrees
and another, by the solemn religious rites and devotions that intervene, and by the fraternal charity that
pervades the members of the Synod, every opening
is given for the escape of what may possibly have
entered into our discussions from mere human sense,
frailty, or shortsightedness, and what is of the prudence of the Holy Spirit has become manifest to
all.

There is in Synods a venerableness of authority,

C

an efficacy of influence, and a fruitfulness of order, that descends into them from Heaven. They have received the especial promise of divine assistance ; and it is this which makes the union of bishops in their Synodal order so blessed and fertilising to the Church. Their joint action, the genuine simplicity with which they leave themselves open to consider the suggestions of the second order of the clergy, and their combined decisions after so much thought and protracted prayer, give to provincial legislation a weight and an authority so far above that of each single prelate, that each bishop becomes sustained in the regulation of his diocese by the joint strength of all his comprovincials.

Our episcopal liberty is held unimpaired, whilst our canonical obedience calls us together—that obedience, I mean, which we solemnly swore at our consecration. For with our hands upon the Holy Gospel of truth, among other things we solemnly declared, that, "*called to the Synod, unless canonically impeded, I will come.*" And when we have come together at that call, the Holy Spirit dwells in our midst, to enlighten and energise our councils, and to hold us together in the bond of charity and peace. Wherefore, confident of His coming on our invocation, before all our proceedings with believing hearts we repeat this prayer—" *We are here, O Lord Holy Spirit, we are here in Thy presence ; detained, it is true, in the exceedingness of our sins, yet specially gathered together in Thy Name. Do Thou come unto us ; do Thou be present with us ; do Thou vouchsafe to descend into our hearts. Teach us what we must do ;*

show us the way in which we should walk; work Thou the work we are to bring about. Do Thou suggest, do Thou accomplish our judgments, who alone, with the Father and the Son, dost possess the Glorious Name. . . . Join us efficaciously to Thy gift of grace alone, that we may be one in Thee, and may in nothing swerve from the truth; that, being gathered together in Thy Name, we may in all things hold fast to justice tempered with piety. So that here our judgment may in nothing contend with Thee, and hereafter we may obtain the eternal reward for what we have well done."

We may now ask the question, What is a Provincial Synod? Speaking with the accuracy of the canonists, a Provincial Synod is the congregation in council of the bishops of some one province of the Church, called together by him who has the legitimate authority—that is, by the Archbishop or Metropolitan of that province—to which all those are likewise called who by right or custom possess the claim to be called. But whilst the other members enjoy the deliberative voice, the bishops alone possess the judicial or decisive voice. The scope of Synodal action is described by the Council of Trent as extending to "the regulation of morals, the correction of abuses, the settling of controversies, and such other purposes as are allowed by the sacred canons."* Among these purposes, one of the most vital and important is that of regulating ecclesiastical discipline, by the prudent application of the principles of the Church's common law to our own especial circumstances and requirements. And besides its legislative authority,

* Con. Trid. Sess. XXII., c. 2, De Reformat.

a Provincial Synod is also a judicial tribunal to examine and decide in certain ecclesiastical causes defined by the sacred canons.

Two things our Lord has promised to these ecclesiastical assemblies, on condition that they be gathered together in His Name. But to comprehend the
force and application of these divine promises, it is
essential to observe that they were spoken with
express relation to the judicial authority of the
Church, and to the power of binding and loosing.
Our Lord is speaking to the disciples—that is, to the
future apostles and bishops of the Church—when He
enjoins on them to rebuke the offending brother, and
if he will not hear, to take with him one or two more,
and then He adds—" If he will not hear them, tell the
Church ; and if he will not hear the Church, let him
be to thee as the heathen and the publican. Amen
I say to you, whatsoever ye shall bind upon earth
shall be bound in heaven, and whatsoever you shall
loose upon earth shall be loosed also in heaven."
Here is the judicial power of the Church. Then our
Lord makes these two promises—" Again I say to
you, that if two of you shall consent upon earth, concerning anything whatsoever they shall ask, it shall
be done to them by my Father who is in heaven.
For where there are two or three gathered together
in my name, there am I in the midst of them." The
General Council of Chalcedon, and other great councils, have pointed out the special application of these
divine promises to the Synods of the Church.

How are we to understand the condition attached
to these promises, that we be gathered together in

the name of Christ? How, except that we come together in communion with His personal representative, with His Supreme Vicar upon earth? For they who gather not with Christ's Vicar are they who scatter and divide from Christ. First, then, you are assembled in the Holy Ghost; secondly, Christ is in the midst of you; thirdly, at your prayer the Father will accomplish your work.

The apostles received the Holy Spirit with an abundance that brought all things to their minds whatsoever Christ had taught them, and each of them was infallible in his teaching; yet when grave contentions arose in the Church, they assembled in Synod with the seniors or presbyters, and after discussion gave their joint doctrinal decision, and to that decision they attached a law of discipline. Thus they not only set an example to the Church for her future Synods, but by their combined authority augmented the vigour and effect of their ministry. The First General Council, that of Nicea, standing upon earlier tradition, enjoined that the Provincial Synods be assembled twice in every year. And if we ask the cause of such frequent assemblies, it was because in those times almost all ecclesiastical causes were determined in Synod. In the Sixth General Council, Synods were required to meet but once in the year. But as ecclesiastical causes came more and more to the diocesan tribunals, and in other points the discipline of the Church changed with the development of her position in the world, the Fifth Council of Lateran allowed an interval of three years between one Provincial Synod and another; and the Council of Trent

reinforced the law of triennal Synods in more strenuous terms.

And oh! exclaims St. Charles Borromeo to one of
his Synods of Milan—" Oh that this method of
Synods, as practised by those most holy men, and
delivered to posterity for the saving of the Church,
oh that it had been as constantly retained and as
piously followed to the present time I All their
counsel and goodwill would then have acted upon
our diligence even to this day, and would have instructed our piety. It is impossible to say to what
an extent the interruption of this custom has afflicted
the world with calamities. For," continues the Saint,
"when the fear of judgment is removed, when no one
is left, none but the Supreme Pontiff alone, to take
account with the shepherds of the Lord's flock as to
how they have kept the deposit, as to how they have
dispensed the wheat, as to how they have cultivated
the vineyard, as to how they have done the steward's
duties, there is no one besides to exact the loan with
interest, no one who, according to the law of the
Fathers, will bring those many and weighty obligations, laid upon each one of us, to examination.
Thus the institutions of ecclesiastical discipline begin
to fail and to sink into a miserable condition ; thus
they whose office it is to keep the rest in the course
of duty become themselves conspicuous for their
swervings from the path of duty."

To the testimony of the Saint whose Synods have
been the models to all subsequent times, let history
bear witness with her thousand voices. Let her bring
her multitudinous facts from every province of the

Church, and tell us truly, Was there ever in any
province of the Church a lengthened period, in which,
whether through the calamities of the times, through
the oppression of princes, or through the lukewarm-
ness or shortsightedness of the bishops, those holy
assemblies suffered interruption and went into obli-
vion, and the Churches of that province did not
grow in various ways remiss? Was it not a consequence that the episcopal authority became weak-
ened? Did not the ecclesiastical laws languish
and become relaxed? Were not the joints of organisation slackened and loosened? Did not the high
maxims of Church polity go down, and in their lower
level become infected with the secular atmosphere?
Did not the quick and fine-wrought nerves of discipline pine away from their healthy freshness, and
begin to exhibit the process of decay? Hence the
learned Bellarmine has not hesitated to maintain
that, although General Councils are not absolutely
essential to the Church's preservation, yet to maintain the good government of the Church, Synods,
whether general, local, or particular, are altogether
indispensable.

When the discipline of a Church is relaxed, the faith
itself is put into more or less of danger. How long
had Synods been laid aside in our own country before
that great catastrophe called the Reformation laid
her Church prostrate in the dust? How long had
they been omitted in Germany before a like calamity
overtook them there? And to glance at more recent
times, how long had Synods ceased in France before
the hour of her Church's desolation? Heresies arose,

indeed, in the ages when Synods flourished the most ;
but, by the instrumentality of her Synods, how vigorously did the Church hold her ground or recover it.
Then came the tide of barbarous invasions, and the
day of barbarous populations, sweeping away a large
portion of the Church from the soil of Europe, and
her Synods together with it, until by conversion she
recovered her ground. But in the more recent ages,
marked by such dire calamities to the Church, had
kings and statesmen been resisted in their early
attempts to creep into the vitals of the local Churches ;
had the torpifying chill of secular intrusion been re-
pelled in time ; had there been more men with the
spirit of St. Thomas of Canterbury ; could Synods
have been held in substance, though divested of their
legal formalities ; had the bishops of the nations held
together in the Holy Spirit, despite of all sufferings ;
had they put forth their strength with united vigour ;
had they contended for the freedom of their Churches
to the end in the spirit of St. Athanasius, even in meek
defiance of the overbearing powers of the world—who
can doubt but that those Churches would have either
stood erect, or have revived after awhile, however
shorn of their material splendour ? Yes, they would
have stood on, however dimmed of outward lustre,
rich within, amidst those debased systems of government, and those ruins of fallen states and prostrate
dynasties, the fall of which they might in sundry
cases have prevented.

I have but expanded the maxims, my brethren, of
a great Pope of the fourteenth century. Urban V.
writes to the Archbishop of Narbonne in these words—

"The authority of the sacred canons bears witness, that formerly the holy Fathers, whether Roman Pontiffs or Bishops of other Churches, were prompt in their care of the Lord's flock. They were most intent on the celebrating of those Synods, in which they were devoted to the extirpating of vices and the planting of virtues, both in the clergy and the laity, and to the direction of the Churches and the pious institutions. The ecclesiastical state took much growth from their labours, as well in its spiritual as in its temporal concerns. But what a grief to reflect that in proportion as the prelates grew remiss and these Synods ceased to be upheld, vices pushed forth apace, indevotion spread among the people, the aforesaid liberty was lessened, and the divine worship neglected!"

Let us consider more closely how a Provincial Synod is constituted. An assembled province of the Church reflects a striking resemblance to the Universal Church herself. This resemblance is not a mere figure, it is an actual presence of all the ecclesiastical elements of the Church exhibited in a limited portion of the whole. I do not merely allude to the canonical order that reigns among us, nor to the subordination of that order in its several gradations to the one head presiding. Nor again, to those solemn rites of the Church, however magnificent, her holiest prayers, and the great Sacrifice of the Living Lord Himself, sanctifying the deliberations that we hold within this holy temple. But I speak of the personal elements that constitute this Synod.

Let us go back for an instant to that hour when the creation of the Church was completed. Let us take

one of those pictures in which men of faith in older
times have from their mystic hearts portrayed the
mysteries of that wonderful moment in visible form
before our eyes. Behold, then, that *cœnaculum* of
Jerusalem, where the Holy Ghost breathes the fire of
life into her youthful frame. Peter is presiding in
that assembly. The apostles are seated in their order.
The disciples stand reverently behind them. Mary
is there, and her look inspires encouragement. The
Holy Ghost has come in fire upon them, and the
place is filled with His light. A wonderful illumination rests on the head of Peter. Tongues of fire
send forth their light from the head of each apostle.
The mystic rays that fill the breast of Peter stream
out to all. Other streams pass from the breast of
each apostle to His brethren, and again in minor
radiations to the disciples. All their faces beam
with light and love. And the place of Judas alone is
vacant, dark, and untouched by grace.

But the apostles, after constituting the episcopal
succession, departed, and their apostolate departed
with them from all except one. To Peter was given
the plenitude of the entire apostolate, to continue in
his successors, the Roman Pontiffs, and that apostolate
reigns over the Church this day in Pius IX. And
what have we here, my brethren ? First, the episcopate, instituted by the apostolic power, in our union
with which lies the force of our authority. Then the
order of the episcopate, of which the ancient Council
of Milevis says—" Let each one know the order
decreed to him by God, and let the less ancient defer
to the more ancient, nor presume to act without their

counsel." To which the bishops of the Council, sixty
in number, replied—"This is the order from the
Fathers. This was observed by the ancients." Then
there are the representatives of the ancient presby-
teries, those senates of the bishops which we have
here in the delegates from the chapters. Then there
are those heads of colleges or seminaries, who, as
delegated by us, represent the training of our clerics
to the ministry. Next there are the superiors of the
various religious orders, who represent the mystic
portion of the Church, and the call of God to the
counsels of perfection, whilst the theologians of the
bishops may be also taken to represent the seventy-
two disciples, those seniors, as St. Luke calls them,
who joined in the deliberations of that Apostolic
Synod whose acts we have in the Holy Scriptures.

But does this enumeration give the whole personality of the Synod? Far from it. If this were the
whole, we could not produce the reflected resemblance
of the entire Church in this assembly. Nay, we should
be powerless to produce even one valid act. There
is one more, one whose power to call us together,
one whose right to preside and direct our action, one
whose archiepiscopate, as distinguished from simple
episcopacy, according to sound canonical doctrine
and order, is a constitutional delegation from the
Supreme Apostolate of Peter. And of the fact, that
pallium bears witness which your Eminence so honour-
ably bears upon your breast. It is this participation
in the apostolic authority, so derived and so dependent, that gives its unity and force to our assembly,
and completes the resemblance, the living reproduc-

tion of the elements that enter into the constitution of the Universal Church. Hence the 27th of the Apostolic Canons says—" The bishops of each province must recognise him who stands the first amongst them, and account him their head, and do nothing of great moment without his intervention." And hence that remarkable sentence in the 4th Canon of Nicea, that "the firmness of those things which are transacted in each province is to be attributed to the metropolitan bishop."

A delegated authority is ever open to modification, and with the change of times and conditions the great and ancient powers once delegated to archbishops have undergone considerable modification. From the wisest motives the Holy See has long since resumed various powers of that delegation, and the Sovereign Pontiff acts more directly in the affairs of each particular diocese. Amongst other reasons for this change these two are obvious—that communication from all parts with Rome has become greatly facilitated even for ages past, and that each see is found to be stronger by resting directly upon the Apostolic See. But this is worthy of remark—that in whatever concerns the calling together, the presiding over, and the enforcing of Provincial Synods, the authority of the archbishop remains unchanged.

But our Synod reflects the character of the universal Church in another feature. Its decisions and decrees must come before the Apostolic See for its revision of them. Without that revision and approval they would remain inactive, void, and lifeless. Without that sanction they cannot go forth, they cannot be

received, they can do nothing for the life and salvation of those for whom they are intended. No great
thing finds sanction even in the local Churches unless
the Apostolic Power intervenes. This is one of the
oldest practical traditions of the Church. Pope St.
Innocent I. bears witness to this in the beginning of
the 5th century, where, in his letter to the Archbishop
of Rouen, he states that it has ever been the custom,
that "all things be referred to us as the head and
summit of the episcopal order, so that, through
consulting the Holy See, what is certain and suitable
to be done may be separated from things that are
doubtful." And replying to the Fathers of the Synod
of Milevis, held in 416, the same Pontiff says—
" Among the other cares of the Roman Church and
employments of the Holy See are those in which, with
faithful and healing examination, we reply to those
consultations that come to us from so many quarters."
And he recalls to their certain knowledge that " from
the Apostolic fountain replies to consultations go forth
through all the provinces."

" The whole order of this Synod," says the holy
Archbishop of Milan to one of those he had assembled—" The whole order of this Synod exhibits
the form of Apostolic mission. For," he continues,
" whilst with mutual charity we confer on our affairs,
the and on what belongs to the Churches ; whilst we
discuss the most chastened cultivation of the sacred
offices; whilst we investigate the discipline of both
clergy and people ; whilst we inspect the execution of
our own decrees and visitations ; whilst we set before
our eyes whatever things are found to be defective in

their institution ; whilst we are consulting how best we may restore them ; whilst, under the authority of the Holy Spirit, we are intent on framing other constitutions, whereby we may aptly repair whatever demands our care—the whole object and end at which we aim is no other than that by these helps our minds may be illuminated, our charity enkindled, our hearts inflamed with the love of souls, and that the episcopal force and ardour in our own souls may be more and more burning; that, by the authority of our decrees, a certain new spirit may be stirred within us, to reduce the turbulent to order, to drive away the pestilence of vices, to heal each spiritual sickness, and to bring to the people beneath our care whatever remedies they need. Oh, salutary labours of Episcopal Councils ! . . . And we, even we, who are the teachers and physicians of the Church, we also are taught, built up, repaired, refreshed, and raised to a better life."

If the bishops are the legislators of a Synod, the first they bind are themselves, restricting their own discretion even more than that of their subjects. For their ecclesiastical laws are in restraint of their own freedom, and bring on them a constant solicitude in watching over their execution. Perhaps there is nothing more worthy the admiration of a reflecting mind watching the progress of a Synod in its deliberations than this : you see the leading minds and authorities of a province come together, each with his own individual lights, experiences, and aspirations; but in the calm contact and open discussion, devoid of personal susceptibilities, with other enlightened minds, the limits and peculiarities of the individual mind recede, and a breadth and clearness of view is gradually opened to the assembled Fathers that probably no single mind could have reached, and the final results are set forth with a brevity, precision, and harmonious adaptation to their objects that no single mind could have accomplished. From what can this arise, my brethren, but from the vivifying and unitive force of the Holy Spirit, under whose constant invocation we proceed in our deliberations? From what can it arise, but from those secret influences with which the Holy Spirit seconds our human efforts, as the Church has taught us to confide?

The chief materials of our legislation are already prepared to our hands. For we possess the treasury of the Father of the family, and we draw forth from that treasury laws new and old. Wonderful is that treasury! that inexhaustible store of Synodal laws and Pontifical constitutions, which form the patrimony of the Universal Church—that accumulation of maxims, of precepts and of laws, which have emanated from the highest fountains of authority, and each of which has its history of successes and of failures, its decisions in explanation, and its attendant train of learned commentators—that unlimited supply of practical wisdom, which has gone forth to rule the Church in her endlessly-varied experience of time, of place, of men, of their institutions and their manners, through all their multitudinous fluctuations.

Rare, indeed, is that case that can in any province of the Church arise and ask for a remedy, but in the

treasury of the Father of the family there is found
some authentic law already tried, some prescription
already well proved, which only requires to be
brought forth, moulded judiciously to the case in
hand, enforced through Synodal action, and then all
that is needed is a bishop's vigilance to watch over
its operation, and the remedy is found, and the evil
in most cases gets its cure. I say in most cases, for
we must still take into our calculation the resistance
of perverted wills. Thus, whilst from the ocean of
the Church's law, through the channel of Synods, we
pour the reinvigorating streams with sound discretion, and neither more nor less than the local want
requires, they support that Church all round, just as
the water sustains the floating ship, and that too
with the whole power of the ocean from which it
flows.

But whilst the doctrines of the Church, as being
eternal facts, are of their very nature unchangeable ;
whilst the Faith can admit of no modification, except
so far as, for us mortals, new light is thrown upon its
articles, and new expression and new definition is
given to what has ever been believed, the laws of
discipline have in them this difference of character,
that they are at the same time both changeable and
unchangeable. They are unchangeable in so far as
they arise out of the unchangeable constitution of
the Church. They are unchangeable in their principles and their · foundations, for these are of the
divine and eternal law and of the essence of reason.
They are unchangeable in their spirit and their final
end, which is to secure the order of God, through the

order of His Church, amidst the continual disorders
of men. In what, then, are the laws of discipline
made changeable? They change in their continual adaptation to new objects. For nothing is so
changeable as man. Nothing is so full of mutabilities as the shifting elements of this world of man.
And in order to reach man still, through all his
endless mutabilities, the great principles of ecclesiastical law have continually to be drawn forth in
new applications and new conclusions. The one
pole of the law is fixed, and its root is in the eternal
justice of the heavens; whilst the other, turned
towards the creature that it directs and saves, must
ever move and adapt itself to the unceasing changes
of man and of society. Just as the eye of man is one
and the same, but the direction of its axis changes;
it opens and it closes, it contracts and it expands,
as its objects change and the light of the time
demands. Or, if you will pardon a quainter image
for its aptness—just as on the face of some old cathedral clock, whilst with one extremity the pointers
are fixed upon their unchangeable centre, with the
other they gravely move on the circumference, and
point to the hours, the seasons, and the epochs
as they rise into existence.

This is one of those wonders of the Church that
deserve our profoundest meditation—one of those
great evidences that show how full she is of life
and rejuvenescence—this inexhaustible spirit of law
within her bosom; which acts or reposes, slackens or
quickens in vigour, and spreads abroad her radiations,
according as the wants of each portion of the Church,

D

of her prelates, of her priests, and of her people, may demand her universal care.

You, my brethren, who are called to aid the Fathers of this Synod with your light and your experience — Procurators of Chapters, Heads of Colleges, Superiors of Religious Orders, Theologians—permit me to address to you a most earnest but affectionate word apart. You here represent the sentiments and views of your brethren. You give valuable aid to our deliberations. But you also carry back amongst your brethren the lights derived from our Synodal deliberations. And certainly it is a great instruction to assist at the fountains of ecclesiastical discipline. You will naturally be looked to by the rest of the priesthood, not indeed as authorised interpreters, but still as having held a better position with greater opportunities for comprehending our disciplinary decrees. This influence for good is too precious to be thrown away. And many of you hold offices that imply the delegation of some degree of jurisdiction in your hands.

But as without adequate knowledge of the principles of theology you could have but an uncertain knowledge of its particular decisions; so without knowledge of the principles of ecclesiastical law you can make but faint and insecure handling of the decrees that emanate from this magnificent science. Let me then recommend to you, and that earnestly, the study of the canon law. Even for practical purposes it has become not only important, but for some of us, almost indispensable. And if indeed you would have one of the noblest enlargements of

the human mind; if you would thoroughly understand the constitution of the Church and the action
of her government ; if you would have that true key
to her history, the knowledge of her laws; if you
would comprehend what has been the continuous
action of her Pontiffs on her destiny; if you would
know the Church's most vital operations for her own
internal harmony; if you would learn the great
lesson of what have been her gratuitous graces of
that nature which St. Paul calls *helps* and *governments*, these lights will arise for the illumination of
your minds from the study of the canon law.

And is it not strange, when we come to reflect on
it, that in these our times, and it may or may not be,
in this very place, there are more learned Churchmen
who are acquainted with the constitution, the laws and
the government of the old pagan empire of Rome—
than there are Churchmen who hold in their minds
the elements of the law and policy of the great
Christian empire of which they form a component
part ; and that there are more who are learned in
the government and economy of that Jewish Syna-
gogue which has passed away, than in that of the
Catholic Church, of which they are both the members and the ministers?

The triple knowledge which the Fathers so much
commended, as forming the training and true accomplishment of an ecclesiastic, was the Scriptures, the
traditions, and the canons. They considered no one
fit to hold a place of influence above his brethren
who did not competently know the canons as well
as the Scriptures. Nay, it is a precept of the law

to this day, for that law is essentially conservative of itself, that no one shall be chosen to exercise jurisdiction, whether primary or delegated, who does not know the canons. It is a maxim of the law, expressed in the words of Pope Celestine, that "it is not lawful for a priest to be ignorant of the canons."

A canon who has his chapter duties must not be unacquainted with chapter laws, and he who has to counsel his bishop in ecclesiastical government, should know the principles of that government. A vicar-general, to be the eye and the hand of his bishop, must not himself need guidance at every step. A religious superior, who has to regulate the relations of his brethren with the other ecclesiastical authorities, must know both in what those relations consist, and where the boundaries of the two authorities are marked and divided.

Theology teaches us the great features of the Church, the basis of her structure as it were, and the bones of her organisation. That science tells us also of the precious blood that circulates in her veins. It will say much to us of the Holy Spirit who breathes His life within her soul. The saints and holy writers make known to us the most interior sentiments of her great heart. And by the light of history we may comprehend the grace and beauty of her way across the gulf of time. But those nerves and ligatures, those sinews and those muscles in which lie the sources of her harmonious movements, of her vigorous and independent action, for the knowledge of these, we must go to the science of the canons.

Let me, in conclusion, pass for a single moment to our great exterior work. Great, indeed, is the harvest of souls, and few the labourers. But what is it compared to that field of the whole world, sunk in the grossest of vices, dark with the vilest superstitions, and putrefying in the corruptest of civilizations, when those twelve apostles began their wondrous mission? Give us, O God, apostolic hearts. Detachment, prayer, charity, love of souls. Oh yes, love of souls, and that generous spirit of labour which that love inspires! I recognise your virtues, my brethren, and I confess my own failings. But oh! remember that charity can do all things, and that the man of God is a man of prayer. That we must not think of what is useful for ourselves, but of what is profitable to many souls. And that the love of souls is the most unselfish love of God. Apostolic men are raised up from age to age, and whole peoples are drawn to them with hearts converted. These are our models. It is not so much by force of intellect or learning, it is not by refinement and polish, if we except that high refinement which holiness gives; but it is by a great apostolic heart, it is by a heart detached from every selfish object, and burning with the love of souls, it is by a heart truly simple and humble, and the fire of the Holy Ghost flaming and burning in that heart, that a priest becomes an apostle to convert a multitude of souls. And how is the Holy Spirit attracted to that heart? His fire is conceived in prayer, enkindled in love, brought forth in zeal, made perfect in suffering. This is the whole secret of the formation of apostolic men.

Let us strive in our degree. And let us not despair of our England! God, who commands us to labour, requires us to hope in its results, and to confide in Him for the issue of our labours. With Abraham, the patriarch of faith, let us go on hoping even against all signs of hope. Our fathers hoped and laboured on, though they had neither our signs nor our encouragements. For are there not signs? Signs there are on the earth beneath and in the heavens above. But the greatest sign is in the heavens. O Immaculate Mother, from the brightness of whose glorious origin every cloud has disappeared, remember that our fathers in their ancient liturgy were wont to cry to thee that England was thy dowry! Remember that they were amongst the first of the zealous who gave festive honours to thy Immaculate Conception, and forget not now their children. But do thou so intercede for them, that the clouds may be removed from their eyes, and they may see thy Son and thee in that inseparable glory. Let those rights over thy dowry so long withheld revive, and let the people of this kingdom give their worship to thy Son and honour to thee, to their peace and to their joy. And for us, my brethren, let us hope in the Lord, and do good ; and we shall be filled with His riches. Let us delight in Him, and He will give us the desire of our heart.

𝕬𝕟 𝕴𝕟𝕤𝕥𝕣𝕦𝕔𝕥𝕚𝕠𝕟 𝕠𝕟 𝕸𝕚𝕩𝕖𝕕 𝕸𝕒𝕣𝕣𝕚𝕒𝕘𝕖𝕤,

Delivered on occasion of the Fourth Diocesan Synod of Birmingham, in 1869.

THE number of mixed marriages that we are called upon to celebrate increases to an alarming degree. And the mischief to souls, and the not unfrequent apostasies from the faith, that come of these unions between Catholics and persons who are not Catholics, call for the gravest reflections both from the clergy and the laity. Would to God some means could be devised that would effectually discourage these unholy unions! Knowing from long observation and experience the troubles and sorrows that in most cases follow from them, knowing how many Catholics lose their faith through them, well aware how many others slacken from their religious duties, or grow indifferent to them, and how many, alas! incur the awful responsibility of seeing their children lose the faith, I seldom receive an application to grant the Church's dispensation for such marriages without suffering an anguish of heart which the custom of doing so tends rather to increase than to diminish. The conditions which the Church attaches to these dispensations are laws of salvation, without which the Catholic's conscience can have no security; yet granting that such conditions are accepted, how often are they fulfilled? In most cases, our only justification in dispensing is to prevent worse evils from the beginning of them; and if at that time we may have some faint hope that the conditions attached to these dispensations will be carried out, how often is that hope defeated!

You know well, brethren, that to grant such dispensations, under any circumstances, belongs not to our ordinary power. For a Catholic to form a union so intimate as that of marriage with one who is not a Catholic, has been at all times and in all places forbidden by the Church, as not only perilous to sanctification but even to salvation. You also know that with the universal law common to the whole Church no local bishop has authority to dispense. The Vicar of Christ, as visible Head of the Church, and he alone, moved by sufficient reasons, can dispense with the Church's universal law. It is solely, then, in virtue of a special delegation from the Sovereign Pontiff, which is granted for a limited time, and on the conditions which he prescribes, that a bishop can exercise dispensing power with respect to these mixed marriages. But the very fact that in granting these dispensations a bishop must act not as an ordinary but as a delegated judge, and in face of the universal law, must of necessity deepen the sense of his responsibility.

In an instruction addressed by the Holy See, in the

year 1858, to all the archbishops and bishops of the
Church, it is explicitly taught that the Church "has
always reprobated these marriages, and has held
them to be unlawful and pernicious; as well because of
the disgraceful communion in divine things, as because
of the peril of perversion that hangs over the Catholic
party to the marriage, and because of the disastrous
influences affecting the education of the children."
And then the Holy See reminds us that the most
holy canons forbid these marriages, and that if "the
more recent constitutions of the Sovereign Pontiffs
relax the severity of the canons in some degree, so
that mixed marriages may occasionally be allowed,
this is only done for the gravest reasons, and very
reluctantly, and not without the express condition of
requiring beforehand those proper and indispensable
pledges which have their foundation in the natural
and divine law."

Ten years later, in the year 1868, the Sacred Congregation of Propaganda issued a new instruction,
expressing surprise "that there should be some who
seemed still to think that the principles so clearly
laid down in the former instruction, principles which
the Holy See had ever taught, could in any way be
derogated from." The Sacred Congregation then
enjoins upon the bishops that "lest perchance from
misconception of that instruction, the people confided
to you should suffer any harm, you are earnestly
exhorted to take proper occasions, studiously to
teach and to inculcate, both on the clergy and the
laity committed to your care, what is the true doctrine
and practice of the Church respecting these mixed

marriages." The instruction concludes with these most earnest words—" Wherefore we earnestly request of your charity, that you strive and put forth your efforts, as far as in the Lord you can, to keep the faithful confided to you from these mixed marriages, so that they may cautiously avoid the perils which are found in them. But you will gain this object the more easily if you have care that the faithful be seasonably instructed on the special obligation that binds them to hear the voice of the Church on this subject, and to obey their bishops, who will have to give a most strict account to the Eternal Prince of Pastors, not only for sometimes allowing these mixed marriages for most grave reasons, but for too easily tolerating the contracting of marriages between the faithful and non-Catholics, at the will of those who ask it."

These are very solemn words, reverend brethren, and they point to exceedingly grave responsibilities that you largely share with me. They demand, in the name of the Sovereign Pontiff, that we thoroughly enlighten ourselves as to the character and tendency of these marriages, and as to the way in which the Church looks upon them. They call upon us, having first thoroughly instructed ourselves, to do our best to enlighten the faithful about them, and to do our utmost to discountenance and discourage them. It is impossible to deny that the principal cause of the frequency of mixed marriages is to be found in the inadequate instruction that the faithful receive respecting them, and especially in their dangers not being pointed out in early youth, before the passions arise and interfere with the calm judgment of the question. Of this I have strong proofs, having known pastors here and there so zealous in teaching the faithful the dangers of these marriages, and so firm in warning all persons to be prudent in the control of their affections, that an application from these zealous priests for a dispensation is a rare event, and never made unless upon the strongest reasons.

Exceptional cases there undoubtedly are, where the marriage proceeds happily; and that, not merely in the complete fulfilment of all the pledges given, but even in the conversion of the non-Catholic party. Still the overwhelming majority of examples stands on the opposite side ; and who shall venture to predict that this or that marriage will turn out happily for the faith, and not for its destruction ? Even in those exceptional cases where the marriage proves happy in the final result, we must guard against letting them blind us to the fact that in the very far greatest number of cases such marriages end unhappily.

I am not ignorant of the fact that this deficiency of instruction arises in part from an apprehension of wounding those who have already contracted mixed marriages. No doubt it is a subject that demands the use of prudent, grave, and measured language ; yet where the salvation of souls is at stake, the Church knows neither reticence nor false delicacy. If youth are taught the law in their catechism, they will be prepared to hear it enlarged on from the pulpit. If the prohibition and its causes are made known to them before their passionate fancy gains its development, they will have the Catholic sense and instinct within them to guard and withhold them before they get entangled in engagements. If parents are taught to reflect on the perils that are intrinsic to these marriages, on the practical disadvantages in a religious sense that attend even the best of them, and the strong sense of the Church against them, they will be more careful in keeping their children from the immediate occasion of them, and will be less disposed to encourage them.

Hard and stern as the prohibitory law may seem to the lax or indifferent, or even to better-disposed Catholics who have never really thought the subject through, it is, in fact, both a reasonable, a merciful, and a charitable law. And, like all laws resting on divine and unchangeable foundations, and preventive of great evil to human souls, it has been in force in all ages, even from the time when man was ejected from the earthly paradise for the sins of the first married pair.

The sixth chapter of Genesis shows how large a share mixed marriages had in bringing about that universal corruption which led God Himself to say that He "repented that He had made man." For the sons of God, that is to say, the sons of Seth, who represented faith on the earth, married the daughters of men, that is, the descendants of Cain, who carried on the traditions of unbelief. Reckless of spiritual considerations, the sons of faith married the daughters of unbelief from sensual motives, "because they were fair." And the inspired Scripture points to these unions as to the original cause of that universal corruption in remedy of which God sent the purging

deluge. When the generations after the deluge had
sunk anew into corruption, and idolatry had stifled
faith and the true worship of God, God chose the
patriarchs to worship Him in faith ; and that their faith
might be preserved in their descendants, He inspired
them to shun the daughters of the unbelieving races
around them, and to seek their wives even from a
distance, from the more religious race of which they
were descended. And when God, through Moses,
gave His divine law to His chosen people, stern and
uncompromising was the prohibition against their
mingling in marriage with the children of unbelief.
Indeed, the whole drift and provision of God's law was
directed towards preserving the faithful from alliance
with the populations that were devoid of faith, and
the whole history of that people from the time of
Solomon, and after his sad example, goes to show
that mixed marriages in defiance of God's law, and
despite of the warnings of the prophets, were amongst
the chief causes of the infidelities, the impieties, and
sacrileges that forfeited for God's people the protection of God, brought heathen worship into the very
palaces of their kings, and to the gates of the Temple,
and brought unutterable calamities on the people.
It is impossible to read the Old Testament with
attention, and not see that the divine prohibition of
marriage between believers and unbelievers was a
most benign and merciful dispensation, and that the
neglect of it was ever accompanied with evils of the
gravest description.

If we turn to the Church, and the law of Christ, we
shall find St. Paul laying down a rule for married

converts from paganism that clearly shows it was never contemplated that Christians should marry unbelievers. The apostle tells the Corinthians—"*If any faithful woman hath an unbelieving husband, and he consent to dwell with her, let her not put him away.*" "He is not speaking of those who are not yet married," as St. Chrysostom explains, "but of those who are already married ; he does not say, if any one wishes to take an unbeliever, but if any one hath an unbeliever, that is, if any one has received the faith whilst the consort remains in unbelief, and the other party consents to cohabit, let no separation be made." "*But,*" says the apostle, "*if the unbeliever depart, let him depart; for the brother or sister is not under bondage in such cases, but God hath called us in peace. For how knowest thou, O woman, whether thou shalt save the husband ? or how knowest thou, O man, whether thou shalt save the wife ?*" The apostle intimates that if the unbeliever refuses to live in peace with the converted believer, or wantonly deserts her, the marriage bond is dissolved. Hence the ecclesiastical law leaves the Christian free in such a case to contract a Christian marriage. But this is limited to the case of an unbeliever who is unbaptized. St. John Chrysostom says to the Christian party in explanation of St. Paul's words—" If he orders you to sacrifice to his idols, or to join him in impious acts in your marriage, or to depart from him, it is better the marriage be dissolved than that piety should suffer." But the whole instruction of the apostle implies, if it does not express, that a marriage between a Christian who is free, and an unbaptized pagan or an unbeliever, cannot be thought of. And accordingly such marriages, although no natural or divine law positively forbids them, have been always forbidden and treated as invalid by the Church from the earliest to the latest of her laws, because of the extreme peril of perversion as well to the Christian party as to the children. And rarely, and only for reasons of extreme gravity, is this law dispensed with.

The Council of Eliberis, in the year 313, expresses the whole spirit and intent of this law in few but most significant terms. "Even although the young unmarried women may be numerous," says the Council, "yet Christian virgins are on no account to be given in marriage to heathens, lest in that fresh, elated, and florid age they should dissolve into adultery of soul." Adultery of soul is infidelity to God, and this is the tremendous peril attached to such marriages. It was the ground of the law delivered by God to Moses against the marriage of His people with the Gentiles around them. In the seventh chapter of Deuteronomy it is commanded—" Neither shalt thou make marriages with them. Thou shalt not give thy daughter to his son, nor take his daughter for thy son ; for she will turn away thy son from following me, that he may rather serve strange gods, and the wrath of the Lord will be enkindled, and will quickly destroy thee." And mark well the touching reason which follows, and which cannot fail to come home to those Catholics who dwell in small numbers among multitudes who are strangers to their faith—" Because thou art a holy people to the Lord thy God. The Lord thy God hath chosen thee to be His peculiar people of all peoples that are upon the earth. Not because you surpass all nations in number, is the Lord joined to you, and hath chosen you, for you are the fewest of any people ; but because the Lord hath loved you, and hath kept the oath which He swore to your fathers, and hath brought you out with a strong hand, and redeemed you from the house of bondage."

Can a Catholic have realised what it is to have the high and noble privilege of being one of God's chosen people, of being a child of the Church of Christ, and a member of the household of faith ; and yet prefer to become one flesh, and to live in one spirit, with an alien from God's Church, rather than with one of God's chosen people ?   Even to this day, a Jew who, in defiance of his law, contracts marriage with one who is not of the children of Israel, is held in abhorrence by his brethren.   If Joseph married Asenath, and Moses Sephora, it was before the divine law against such marriages was delivered, and we may justly presume that their wives accepted the faith of Israel.   In the case of Booz and Ruth the Scripture makes it clear, and records the previous conversion of Ruth in her own words—" Thy people shall be my people, and thy God my God."

The very learned canonist Cardinal Pitra has not hesitated to say, after other distinguished canonists, that as a general rule, more danger hangs over the marriage of a Catholic with a heretic than over the marriage of a Catholic with a heathen. For in the case of marriage with a heretic, he observes, the union is a great sacrament, representing, as St. Paul teaches, the union of Christ with His Church; for which reason it ought not to be profaned by union with one who is rejected from the membership of Christ and of His Church. To this searching argument Cardinal Pitra adds this pithy remark from Zonaras, the Greek commentator on the canons: "How the married pair, with their minds taking opposite directions about the faith, can agree well in other things, let any one consider. Having no feelings in common about religion, which is the chief object and the ruling principle of life, how shall they communicate with each other on equal terms upon the subordinate concerns of life?"*

A Catholic must naturally hold marriage with a heathen in greater abhorrence than marriage with a baptized person. And if, in an evil hour, such a marriage were contracted, the dread of heathen influence would be far greater, and the desire and solicitude for that heathen's conversion far more earnest. But a daily familiarity with heresy removes half the dread of it; and weak Catholics, who are ill instructed, are apt to lose sight of the immeasurable distance between faith and heretical opinion, between the security of the Church and the absence of all safety outside the Church. And where the non-Catholic party to the marriage possesses kindly and attractive qualities either by nature or from culture, or where the character of the non-Catholic party is the stronger of the two, and where the Catholic is drawn away from Catholic influences and associations, and brought under the anti-Catholic influences

* Pitra, in Constitut. Apost. vol. iv., Constit. Joannis XXII. n. 5.

E

of those with whom the non-Catholic consort habitually associates, it must of necessity require an extraordinary and special gift of grace for that Catholic to hold to the faith, and the duties of faith. We know that many who are placed in such circumstances fall away from the faith, and too often carry distressed and tortured consciences to the end of their lives.

There was a time, not later in date than the middle of the fourteenth century, when to marry a heretic furnished legal suspicion of either an inclination to heresy or to foster heresy. The civil law defined marriage to be a perpetual life in common between the contracting parties, and a mutual communication of Divine and human rights; and it was argued that for a Catholic to enter of free choice into a lifelong union of so intimate a nature with a heretic, furnishes a grave presumption of sympathy with heresy.*

There is a notion abroad that the law of the Church against mixed marriages is of comparatively recent date. To remove this grave error, I shall prove from grave and authentic documents that, from the very earliest down to the latest period of her history, the Church has always reprobated these marriages and accounted them unlawful. Our first authority is that of the Holy Apostles, who prohibit all social intercourse with heretics. In his Second Epistle, St. John says: " If any man come to you, and bring not this doctrine, receive him not into your house, nor say to him, God speed you. For he that sayeth to him, God speed you, communicateth with his wicked works." If the Apostle forbids the faithful to receive

* Pitra, in Cons. Apost. vol. iv., Constit. Joannis XXII. n. 4, 5.

heretics into their house or to greet them on the way, how could they be allowed to marry them? St. Paul gives the same rule to Titus: "A man that is a heretic, after the first and second admonition avoid." And to the Corinthians he says of one whose husband is dead: "She is at liberty, let her marry whom she will, only in the Lord." But to marry in the Lord is to marry in the Church, and to unite herself with a member of Christ; and so the Fathers interpret the passage. Tertullian says, that "when the Apostle says, Let her marry only in the Lord, he is no longer advising, but strictly commanding; so that in an affair of this great moment unless we obey we perish."*

In the year 313, the Council of Eliberis in its 16th canon decrees: "If heretics will not enter the Catholic Church, the daughters of Catholics must not be given to them in marriage. They are not to be given to Jews or to heretics, because there can be no society between believers and unbelievers. If parents act against this decree, let them abstain from communion for five years." †

In the year 372, the Council of Laodicea decreed in its 10th chapter, that "Those who belong to the Church ought by no means to ally their children indifferently with heretics in matrimony." ‡

In the year 451, the General Council of Chalcedon, in its 15th action, 14th canon, decreed: "Neither ought one who is marriageable to contract marriage with a heretic, a Jew, or a Pagan, unless such a one

---

* Tertullian, ad Uxor, L. 2, c. 1.
† Harduin's Concilia, vol. i. col. 252.   ‡ Ibid., vol. i. col. 783.

promise to join the orthodox faith; so that an orthodox person may be united with one who is orthodox. If any one shall transgress this definition of the Holy Synod, he shall be subject to canonical correction." *

In the year 506, the Council of Agatho in its 67th canon decreed : "It behoveth not that Catholics be united in matrimony with all sorts of heretics; they may accept them, nevertheless, provided they profess themselves about to become Christians and Catholics." †

The substance of these laws was embodied in the *Corpus Juris;* and in the 14th decretal of the Sext, *De Hæreticis,* it was enacted that a woman marrying a heretic should be deprived of her dowry.

The law prohibiting mixed marriages continued to be re-enacted in the Middle Ages; and in the year 1309, the Council of Posen, presided over by a Papal Legate, and confirmed by Pope Clement VI. in 1346, decrees as follows : "That the Catholic faith, which spurns the rending spirit of any error whatsoever, may not be stained with the ferment of any schism or heretical depravity, with the counsel and consent of this present Council, we, by a perpetual edict, prohibit that any one subject to our legation, who desires to be held and accounted a Catholic, shall presume to give his daughter, niece, or other relative, in marriage to a heretic, to a Patarene, to a Garane, to a schismatic, or to any other person who is opposed to the Christian faith, so long as they remain in error ; because this brings no small injury and loss to the aforesaid faith. For, as we have learnt from experience, men who through the devil's instigation are

* Harduin's Concilia, vol. ii. col. 607.   † Ibid., vol. ii. col. 1005.

separated from the Catholic faith, draw their wives, however Catholic, to the error of unbelief, instead of their wives drawing them." *

In the year 1583, the Council of Bordeaux, approved by Pope Gregory XIII., in its 15th title on Matrimony, decrees as follows : " Let the faithful Catholics be frequently admonished by their parish priests, that they give not their sons and daughters in marriage to heretics, or to men who are aliens from the Catholic faith and religion ; for by such marriages we grieve to say that very many have made shipwreck of the faith."†

After such a chain of Synodal authorities, it would seem to be unnecessary to quote the Fathers, unless to exhibit the motives that moved them to hold these mixed marriages in abhorrence. I shall limit myself to St. Ambrose and St. Augustine.

In his book on Abraham, St. Ambrose says : " With the holy thou shalt be holy, and with the perverse thou shalt be perverted. If this be true in other things, how much more is it true in marriage ? How can there be accord of charity where there is discord as to faith ? . . . Differing with respect to faith, they cannot believe, they cannot think that His grace is imparted to their marriage whom they do not worship together. Reason teaches this, but examples give us far more proofs of it. Often does the seductive influence of woman circumvent even strong men, and make them fall from their religion. And for this reason ought you to hold your affections under admonition, and guard against error. The first thing

* Harduin's Concilia, vol. vii. col. 1300.   † Ibid., vol. x. col. 1351.

therefore to be sought in marriage is religion."* And
writing instructions to his suffragan, St. Vigilius of
Trent, for his guidance in the Episcopal office, St.
Ambrose says again: "There can be scarcely anything more grave than a marriage with one who is
an alien from the faith. For these incentives kindle
to uncleanness, and to discord, and to crimes of sacrilege. And as marriage ought to be sanctified by
the sacerdotal veil and benediction, how can that be
called union in which there is discord as to faith?
They ought to communicate in prayer, yet how can
they have the love of God in common who are
separated from each other in devotion?"†

In writing to the Donatist Bishop Maximinus, St.
Augustine thus reproves the marriage of Catholics
with schismatics: "These miserable people, believing
in Christ, have their food at home in common, but the
table of Christ they cannot have in common. Must
we not weep at so often seeing the husband and wife
vowing to each other in Christ to have their bodies
faithfully united in one, whilst they rend the body of
Christ through being attached to different commu-
nions? Great is the scandal, great the devil's triumph,
great the ruin of souls."‡

In Venerable Bede's History of our Saxon forefathers, there is a letter of the year 645, addressed
by Pope Boniface V. to Queen Ethelberga, congratu-
lating her in that she "had received the wonderful
sacrament of Christian faith, and continually excelled
in the performance of such works as are pious and

---

* St. Ambrose, De Abraham, L. 1, c. 9, n. 84.
† Id., Ep. 19, ad Vigil.   ‡ St. Aug., Ep. 23, n. 5.

acceptable to God." The Pope then exhorts her to do her utmost to bring her husband, King Edwin, from Paganism to Christianity ; and the maxims to which he gives expression, respecting the married state of a Catholic Christian, are so applicable to our subject, that I quote them, as well for that reason as because they lay the first basis of tradition in this country. "It causes us no small grief," says the Pontiff, "that part of your body still remains a stranger to the knowledge of the supreme and undivided Trinity. Whereupon, in our fatherly care, we did not delay to admonish your Christian Highness, and to exhort you that, with the help of the Divine inspiration, you will not defer to do that which, both in season and out of season, is required of us ; that, with the co-operating power of our Lord and Saviour Jesus Christ, your husband also may be added to the number of Christians, to the end that you may thereby enjoy the rights of marriage in the bond of a holy and unblemished union. For it is written, 'They shall be two in one flesh.' How can it be said that there is unity between you if he continue a stranger to the brightness of your faith by the interposition of dark and detestable error ? Therefore, applying yourself continually to prayer, do not cease to beg of the Divine mercy the benefit of His illumination ; to the end that those whom the union of carnal affection has made in a manner but one body, may, after death, continue in perpetual union, by the bond of faith." *

For the schools of theology, which are unanimous

* Bedæ Histor., L. 2, c. 11.

on the question, it will be sufficient to quote St. Thomas. He says: " If one of the faithful contract marriage with a baptized heretic, the marriage is real, although, if he knows her to be a heretic, he sins in contracting it ; just as he would sin who should marry one who is excommunicated. Yet this does not destroy the marriage." *

When we compare the doctrine and language of the early Councils and Fathers, in respect to mixed marriages, with that of recent Popes, it at once becomes evident that the recent Pontiffs, even in their most energetic deprecations of such marriages, have but repeated the doctrine and language of the earlier Church. Where there is a difference, it is to be found in the greater leniency of the recent Pontiffs, who, however reluctantly, have inclined more to the human weakness of the times, in granting dispensations for very grave reasons, and especially to prevent worse evils ; although they never cease to deprecate them, to deplore them, and to do all in their power to put a stop to them.

We may now bring the motives advanced by the earlier Church for the condemnation of these marriages together in one view, that by their juxtaposition we may see their irresistible force. The Apostles exhort the faithful to hold no communication with heretics, or with those who make divisions, and to avoid all such persons. And St. Paul enjoins them to marry only in the Lord, that is, in the Church. The Councils forbid Catholics to marry heretics, because there can be no society between

* St. Thom., 4 Sentent., d. 39, 9. 1, a. 1.

believers and unbelievers. They subject the Catholic
who so marries to privation of communion and to
canonical penance. Later on, the ecclesiastical law,
whose sanction was enforced by the civil law, deprived the woman marrying a heretic of her dowry.
It was legally declared that Catholics marrying
heretics or schismatics contracted a stain, and became suspected of heresy or of fostering heresy
or schism. The proofs of experience were brought
to show that these marriages injure faith, and often
cause shipwreck of faith. St. Ambrose tells us that
these marriages are incentives to sacrilege, to unclean
conduct, and to discord ; that they cause the loss
of the Church's blessing and of matrimonial sanctity ;
and that, instead of uniting in soul and through
Christ, there is union neither in faith nor in prayer
nor in the Holy Communion ; but the husband and
wife are rent from each other in the worship of God.
St. Augustine adds, that they vow their bodies
to each other, whilst they rend the body of Christ,
and become a scandal, a triumph to the devil, and
ruin to souls. And St. Thomas tells us that it is
as if a Catholic married an excommunicated person.
There is not one of these motives that does not still
hold, and of the force of which we have not had
trying experience in our days.

To enable us to enter more completely into the
mind of the Church in her condemnation of mixed
marriages, we must distinguish the different kinds of
marriages that are celebrated. Marriages are either
natural, or civil, or religious. A natural marriage
commonly takes place outside of civilised society

and its provisions, where the two persons accept each other for life according to the law of nature. A civil marriage is one in which the parties are united according to the civil laws of the country, but without any religious rite or ceremony. Many Pagan marriages were of this kind, although others were celebrated with some religious rite. Such are the marriages performed in the registrars' offices of this country in the presence of a Government officer. They are purely civil marriages. The civil marriage includes the natural marriage. The religious marriage is either Catholic or it is not Catholic. In this country, a religious marriage that is not Catholic is celebrated in some place of heretical worship and before an heretical minister ; and as it is accepted by the law of the State, it includes the civil marriage and also the natural marriage. But however valid, if celebrated between two persons who are baptized, it is unlawful even to the extent of mortal sin, and that for the grave reasons that I shall presently give.

Catholic marriage is a marriage in the Catholic Church of Christ. It was founded by Christ upon the natural law, which is not solely natural, for God Himself ordained it in Paradise, and by His own Divine act united our first parents, and pronounced upon them His Divine benediction. Although in course of time the original law of marriage became corrupted, although even under the law of Moses God tolerated many things because of human weakness, our Blessed Lord, in clear and express teaching, brought back the law of marriage to its original purity. He raised up the natural to the character of a supernatural marriage, making it a sacrament, giving grace to the married pair; so that they may be united not merely in the order of nature, but in Christ, in union of soul, of faith, and of a love whose final end is God, and of which the love of God is the ruling principle. This sacramental grace is further given to the married pair to help them through the duties, difficulties, and responsibilities of married life. When St. Paul tells us that marriage is "a great sacrament," he adds the condition that it be "in Christ and in the Church." As the State with us permits the Catholic marriage, and makes it legal by the presence of its own representative, a Catholic marriage in this country includes the civil as well as the natural marriage.

It is the supernatural side of the Catholic marriage which shows how grievous is the sin of a Catholic in marrying outside the Church, and without her benediction. The Divine revelation teaches us, in the words of St. Paul, that the sacramental union of the married pair is representative of the union of Christ and His Church. Nor is this a mere symbolical representation, for it has an actual foundation in the sacramental grace which constitutes the supernatural principle of that union. The Catholic marriage, therefore, when entered upon with religious dispositions, reflects a profound mystery, and one of the greatest mysteries—that of the union of Jesus Christ with our human nature in the membership of the Church. The principle of Christ's union with the Church is grace; and the supernatural principle of marriage in Christ and in the Church is grace.

Again, the principle of Christ's union with His Church is charity. He loved the Church and gave Himself for it, and the end of all His love is the final union of the Church with Him, in the Father, in the kingdom of heaven. And the supreme principle of the marriage union between two devout Catholics is charity, which purifies natural love from its rudeness, and raises it to a love in Christ, according to His unblemished law, that looks to a final union in the kingdom of Christ and of God. Then, as St. Paul teaches, Christ is the Head of the Church, which obeys Him and is subject to Him as her Lord and Master. And, in like manner, the husband is the head of the wife, who is subject to him in obedience, and that not only because of nature's law, but for Christ's sake. And as Christ is the Saviour of His mystical body the Church, and nourishes and cherishes it; so is the husband bound to protect, nourish, and cherish his wife, who is to him as his own body, and who, like himself, is a member of Christ, and is therefore to be treated with reverence. Such is the supernatural side of Catholic marriage, as based upon the exposition of St. Paul.*

Again, as the union of Christ with His Church is fruitful in bringing new children to God through His blood, so the union of the Catholic husband and wife is fruitful, not only in bringing forth children to the world, but in bringing them by faith to Christ and to His Church. Thus the sublime end of their marriage is to add members to Christ, and to increase the kingdom of God. This it is that brings

* Ephes., c. 5.

upon them the sacred duty and high vocation of training up their children in the faith of Christ and in the fear and love of God. To this end also is the sacramental grace of marriage given to them. As we thus contemplate the Catholic marriage on its supernatural side, and the sublime ends to which it is ordained, we see in the clearest light why it has been raised to the dignity and perfected by the grace of a sacrament, and why it can only be thus dignified and graced in Christ and in the Church.

There is one point more in a Catholic and sacramental marriage most significant of its whole character. In the other sacraments, the bishop or the priest is the minister; but in marriage, the parties themselves are the ministers, and the office of the priest is to witness and to bless their union, and to place it on the records of the Church, for a perpetual remembrance of what has been in the Church accomplished and in heaven ratified.

We have heard St. Ambrose speak of "the sanctification of the sacerdotal veil and benediction." The veil extended over the married pair, whilst the benediction of the Church is given, is one of the ancient rites of the Church. It was used by the Jews, and is still used by them; and in many countries it is still used by the Church. It is a symbol of the intimate union of marriage under the benediction and protection of God.

We may now understand more clearly why St. Ambrose calls the marriage of a Catholic with one who is not a Catholic *sacrilegious*, and why Benedict XIV., and other Popes after him, have judicially applied to it the same awful term. Sacrilege is a violation offered to something sacred in that in which it is sacred. And Christian marriage is, in the first place, a communion in sacred things. But, as St. Paul teaches, there can be no communion between light and darkness; that is, there can be no religious communion between one who has the faith, and one who has not the faith. They cannot communicate in faith, in worship, or in sacraments. And for one without faith to communicate in a sacrament is sacrilege, because it is the violation of a most sacred thing. Yet marriage in the Catholic Church involves this sacramental communion. Secondly, the parties to the marriage are the ministers of the sacrament, and, in a mixed marriage, one of the parties ministers in that solemn act of religion, having neither Catholic faith nor belief in the sacrament. Thirdly, the Catholic marriage is a communion in the grace of Christ, and in the benediction of the Church; and therefore the spouses prepare themselves by purifying their hearts in the Sacrament of Penance, and partake together of the Body of the Lord. But in a mixed marriage, although the baptism of the heretical person secures the validity of the marriage, and although, to prevent worse evils, the Church may very reluctantly grant such a dispensation as to prevent the unlawfulness of the marriage, yet she withholds her blessing, and forbids the holy sacrifice, and mourns over a union which is neither a communion in faith or in grace. Fourthly, we have seen from Divine revelation how a Catholic marriage represents and signifies the nuptial union between Christ and His Church, the profound meaning of which sacramentally affects the spiritual relations of the married pair in Christ, and gives them great united responsibilities as members of the Church. But how can the union between a member of the Church and one who is not a member of it express the union between Christ and the Church? And how can they fulfil united duties towards the Church? For such grave reasons as these has the Church called these mixed marriages sacrilegious.

What, then, must we call them when a Catholic puts the Church altogether out of the question, cares for no dispensation, and, doing the utmost violence to the sacrament, celebrates his or her marriage with an heretical person outside the Church, before a civil officer or an heretical minister?

In his vision of the Heavenly Church, St. John hears the voice of a great multitude crying out: "The marriage of the Lamb is come, and His wife hath prepared herself. And it is granted to her that she should clothe herself with fine linen glittering and white. For the fine linen are the justifications of the saints." And an angel said to him: "Come, and I will show thee the Bride, the wife of the Lamb." And then the angel exhibits to the Apostle the glorified Church in its multitudinous splendour and array. But does a marriage such as we are contemplating reflect, even in an earthly form, the spiritual unity of that Divine marriage? Can the Catholic espousing an alien from the body of Christ expect to prolong the union into that celestial marriage where all are one in Christ, and the Divine vision of the celestial marriage is the unveiling of faith?

Finally, Christ generates the children of the Church through His blood, and by faith and love conducts them to His kingdom. And it is the sublime office of the married pair to present their children to Christ, and with united solicitude to guide them on the path of faith and heavenly love. Yet how is their united strength, authority, and devout influence to accomplish this, as God intends, when one parent contends for the faith and the other contends against it? How can they accomplish this when, as it so often happens, all promises and pledges are broken, and the children are refused either a Catholic baptism or a Catholic education? How can either a Catholic man or a Catholic woman contract a marriage with a secure conscience, where, granting the influence to be on both sides equal, the parent without faith must neutralise the influence over the children of the parent blessed with faith? The Councils, Fathers, and Pontiffs of all times but proclaim the experience of which we ourselves have so many proofs, that these marriages are injurious to faith, and often cause the loss of it both to the Catholic parent and the children. In the very hour of marriage, when, as St. Augustine says, bodies are united and Christ is divided, the souls of the children who may be born are put to this fearful hazard. How can the Church bless such marriages, or do otherwise than, with half-averted face, reluctantly grant a dispensation, in the bare hope of saving the Catholic from worse evils?

Let us now turn to the doctrine and disciplinary decisions of the Holy See, which has ever held one uniform language on this subject. Especially have the Popes been instant against mixed marriages since the rise and spread of Protestantism. And although in his Treatise on Diocesan Synods the illustrious Benedict XIV. has vindicated the right and authority of the Holy See to grant dispensations for very grave reasons, and to prevent worse evils, yet in his Constitution addressed to the Bishops of Poland, the great Pontiff affirms " the antiquity of that discipline with which the Holy See has ever reprobated the marriage of Catholics with heretics." He quotes a letter of Clement XI., in which, replying to a petition for dispensation for a mixed marriage, the Pope says —" We hold it of greater moment not to overpass the rules of God's Church, of the Apostolic See, of our predecessors, and of the Canons, unless the good of the whole Christian Republic require it." And in another letter Pope Clement says—" For the Church in truth abhors these marriages, which exhibit much deformity in them and but little spirituality."

Benedict XIV. next quotes his own earlier decree referring to Holland and Belgium, in which, after the Sacred Congregation of the Council had discussed the question in his presence, he had pronounced with supreme authority. In that decree he declares his " extreme grief that Catholics can be found who, disgracefully deluded by an unhealthy affection, neither abhor these hateful marriages nor abstain from them, even although the Catholic Church has always condemned and forbidden them." And he

F

"greatly commends those prelates who strive, even with severe penalties, to restrain Catholics from joining themselves in this sacrilegious bond with heretics." He seriously exhorts and gravely warns all bishops, vicars apostolic, parish priests and missioners in Holland and Belgium, "to do their utmost to deter and hinder Catholics from entering into this kind of marriage to the damage of their own souls." And where a mixed marriage has already been contracted, " the Catholic party, whether husband or wife, is to be sedulously brought to repentance for the grievous sin committed, and to ask pardon of God, and to strive their utmost to bring the party erring from the faith into the bosom of the Church, which will contribute greatly towards obtaining pardon for the sin committed.".

The Pontiff adds that it was extremely rare for his predecessors to dispense in these marriages except on condition of the heresy being renounced, and even then only in the case of the marriage of sovereign princes, and to prevent great evils to the commonwealth ; yet never without the condition of the Catholic being left free in the exercise of the Catholic religion, of the children being educated in Catholic holiness, or without the promise of making every effort to draw the heretical consort into the Church.

In the year 1858 the reigning Pontiff issued the instruction on dispensing in mixed marriages, signed by Cardinal Antonelli, to which we have already referred, and addressed it to all archbishops and bishops, in which he exhorts them "to keep the holy teaching of the Catholic Church respecting these marriages most religiously, and in all its inviolable integrity." With "the ardent zeal of their pastoral office must they turn away the Catholics intrusted to them from these mixed marriages, and exactly teach them the doctrine of the Catholic Church, and its laws as affecting these marriages." He is convinced they will "keep for ever before their eyes the Letters and Instructions of his predecessors, and especially of Pius VI.,* of Pius VII.,† of Pius VIII.,‡ and of Gregory XVI.,§ which they addressed to many bishops of the Catholic world concerning this most grave and momentous subject." "All know," says the Pontiff, "what the Catholic Church has always felt about these marriages between Catholics and non-Catholics, as she has always reprobated them because of the disgraceful communion in divine things, the peril of perversion impending over the Catholic, and the perverse training of the children." His Holiness insists that "if anything of the severity of the Canons is relaxed, in dispensing by authority of the Holy See in mixed marriages, that can only be done for grave reasons and with very great reluctance," and only on express condition of exacting all the prescribed conditions to guard against perversion, and to protect the Catholic education of the off-

* Pius VI.   Epist. ad Archiep. Mechlinien. et Episcopos Belgii, 1782.
† Pius VII.   Epist. ad Archiep. Moguntinum, 1803.
‡ Pius VIII.   Epist. ad Archiep. Colonien. et Episcopos Treviren., Monasterien., et Paderborn, 1830.
§ Gregory XVI.   Epist. ad Archiep. et Episcop. Bavariæ, 1832. Instructio ad eosdem, 1834.   Epist. ad Archiep. et Episcop. Hungariæ, 1841.   Instructio, 1841.   Instructio ad Archiep. et Episcop. Austriæ in Germania, 1841.

spring. There is to be no mass, no blessing; and whatever rite is allowed arises from the necessity of legalising the marriage and preventing worse evils. The main reason for thus treating mixed marriages, the Holy Father tells us, is, "that Catholics may never forget, nor the Church's law let it out of mind, with what earnest endeavour our Holy Mother the Church has never ceased to warn her children, and deter them from contracting these mixed marriages to their own and their children's undoing."

In the year 1868 the Sacred Congregation of Propaganda followed up this instruction with another that we have previously quoted, every sentence of which calls for the careful study and reflection of the missionary clergy. Amongst other things, it is urged upon us in this instruction that the precautionary promises exacted of the contracting parties are by no means a warrant of themselves for obtaining a dispensation. Reasons for the dispensation must be assigned that actually arise out of the individual case, and that are "altogether just and grave." For "the precautionary conditions are exacted by the natural and divine law, and that for avoiding the intrinsic dangers inherent in mixed marriages; but there must be some grave difficulty impending over the faithful, that cannot otherwise be removed, before they can be allowed to expose their faith and morals to grave risks."

These last words sum up the judicial responsibility resting on the person who grants the dispensation. There must be grave risks impending over the faithful that cannot otherwise be removed to justify its

being given. Will it justify the soul of any Catholic
to make these risks, or bring them about, with the
view of pleading them as a ground for dispensation ?
This would be in fraud of the law; and no one has a
right to profit by his fraud, or to claim an indulgence
or a privilege whose plea is set up in a fraud. Can
there be a greater fraud than for a Catholic to go and
engage himself to marry one who is not a Catholic,
and then to come and plead the engagement as a
ground for dispensation ? This is but a cunning way
of trying to wrest from the Church both her law and
her judgment ; it can be followed by no blessing.
Where a marriage is canonically unlawful in itself,
there can be no espousals, and no engagement binding before the Church, until the legal impediment is
removed. No Catholic is justified in contracting
such an engagement until a dispensation has been
previously obtained. The farthest extent to which the
Catholic should go is to have it clearly understood
that everything must depend on the condition that a
proper dispensation is obtained, and he or she should
make no irrevocable engagement until it is obtained.

Our blessed Lord has given us this imperative
rule—" He who will not hear the Church, let him be
to thee as the heathen and the publican." And St.
Paul exhorts us to have one mind with Christ. " Let
this mind be in you, which was also in Christ Jesus,
who humbled Himself and became obedient, even
unto death." On what is the Church built, except
upon obedience ? Who has a right to expect unity
and happiness in marriage if he begin it in opposition to the mind of the Church, and in disobedience

to her voice? Who can expect union in marriage if he will not have her blessing and her grace to cement that union? It is more difficult, by far, for a Catholic and a Protestant to have a complete union in marriage than it is for two Protestants, because the seeds of division are sown between them from the beginning, however much this may at first be concealed from their eyes; and happy is it for the Catholic when conscience is not sacrificed to secure an outward peace.

The Pontiffs, having all these evils in view, even when, for the purpose of preventing greater evils, they grant their dispensations, declare not only that they do it "with extreme reluctance," but that they do it "as it were dissembling certain things." Of this both Benedict XIV. and Pius VI. made a solemn declaration at the feet of the crucifix. To any faithful soul contemplating such a marriage this is awful to reflect upon. It is awful to the bishop who has to exercise his delegated power in the granting such dispensations. It is awful to the priest who has to deal with the case.

There is another maxim of the Eternal Wisdom that must not be omitted from the account. It is expressed in these words, " He who loveth the danger shall perish in it." What the perils are that beset these marriages we have already seen. But let us look a little more closely. To a true Catholic, religion is the first of all things, the very law of life. The house of a Catholic should be a Catholic house. It is a little church, second only in sanctity to the consecrated Church where the sacred mysteries are celebrated and the Adorable Sacrament reserved. It should be pervaded with a certain religious tone, and more especially so in the private apartments of the family. As the house contains a family of God's children, it should be under the benediction of God. There should be nothing in it to offend the Christian sense, to awake temptation, or to cause disedification. The crucifix should be found in the place of prayer, and devout pictures should speak of God and heaven from the walls. In this little private church the words of our Lord should be fulfilled at all times, and especially in the hour of family prayer, "Where two or three of you are gathered together in my name, there am I in the midst of you."

The father is the authority of the family, the mother the model of its piety. The children grow in faith as in stature, under the combined influence of their parents, and never retire to rest in the peace of their well-guarded innocence without receiving their benediction. Where the house is not one of humble condition, in choosing domestics, faith, and the life of faith, is looked to as well as capability, that the house may be a truly Catholic house, that there may be nothing 'of a divided spirit in it, and nothing of injurious example to the younger members of the family. There marriage shows itself to be "in Christ and in the Church;" there are seen the fruits of its sacramental grace; there, where faith has married faith, and grace is joined to grace, there is interchange of both corporal and spiritual goods, or, as St. Augustine puts it, "there is union of two souls in one religious mind and will."

In a mixed marriage how much of this beautiful
life disappears! The house is not Catholic. The
family is not Catholic. The atmosphere is not
Catholic. The symbols of the faith are not visible.
The souls of the husband and wife are locked up
from each other; they have no communion of
thought or feeling in the chief concern of life.
Think what it is to be never able to speak or act
together in what concerns God, the soul, the Church,
or the life to come. Think what it is to have no
joint counsel or community of feeling in what concerns the spiritual welfare of a family. Think what
it is to have one's faith shut up in the breast, there to
pine and faint for want of full and open exercise in
the household, and the family duties. How often are
the visible tokens of religion removed to avoid offence,
whilst the faith is kept hidden from sight like some
dangerous secret. Where are the family prayers?
Where is the communion in the sacraments? Happy
is the Catholic wife when she is not thwarted in her
ways to the Church. How often must she stay at
home when she would gladly seek some consolation
there, until her devotion grows feeble for want of
exercise! Happy is she when her faith and her
Church are left unassailed, and when she is not teased
with sectarian importunities, if not by her husband,
by his relatives and friends, and even by their assiduous ministers—always assiduous where a Catholic is
concerned. Perhaps (for this often happens) she is
much isolated from her Catholic friends, and] from
those who, in the hour of need, could give her support.
Happy is she, then, if at last she does not sacrifice

her inward conscience to human respect and to a
shallow exterior tranquillity. She has chosen the
peril, and blessed is she if saved by a miracle of
grace. Yet has she no right to expect such a miracle. Happy is the Catholic husband whose sectarian wife neither oppresses his weaker religious will
by her zeal, nor undermines his faith by the more
subtle influences which she can bring to bear upon
him. Even if faith be held to, peace will go. The
inspired Ecclesiasticus says—" Where one buildeth
up and another pulleth down, what profit have they
but the labour? Where one prayeth and another
curseth, which voice will God hear ? "

It would be as unjust as ungenerous not to admit
that there are Protestants who loyally keep the promises they have made in marriage with Catholics,
and who truly respect the faith and religious exercises of their Catholic spouse, and fulfil their pledges
respecting the education of the children. But prudence looks to what generally happens, and not to
the exceptional cases. And wisdom never runs any
serious risks in matters of the soul. The individuals,
and even the families, that have fallen from the
Church through mixed marriages, amount to numbers incredible to those who have not examined the
question thoroughly ; and the number of Catholics
bound at this moment in mixed marriages, who live
in a hard and bitter conflict for the exercise of their
religion, for that of their children, and in certain
cases for the soundness of their moral life, could they,
with all the facts, be known, would deter any thoughtful Catholic from contracting a mixed marriage.

The Catechism of the Council of Trent teaches that "the dignity of a sacrament is given to marriage for this end, that a people may be procreated and brought up to the religion and worship of God, and of our Lord Jesus Christ." Nature looks in marriage to the earth, and grace leads in the sacrament to heaven. Nature looks to peopling the world, and grace to raising up souls to God. From the sacramental point of view, therefore, must we estimate the obligation of Catholics to bring up their children in the Catholic faith and worship. No Catholic can in conscience enter upon marriage without having the fullest guarantees on this subject. Yet what guarantees can be held secure when experience shows that the most solemn pledges are being constantly broken. In some cases they are treated with absolute contempt and scorn. Severe as these words are, they are the severity of truth ; for, alas ! not few are the persons who hold to no point of honour where the Catholic religion is concerned.

The contest not unfrequently begins when there is question of baptizing the first child. The Protestant husband will have the boys baptized and brought up in his way. The Protestant mother will have the girls to follow her way. And to the eyes of the world there is a semblance of equity in this arrangement ; but the world cannot take into consideration the Catholic's conscience provided for before the marriage, the sacramental obligation, and the free pledges on the other side that have been made as essential conditions to the contract. Sometimes, again, the Protestant father is for leaving the children free, without being taught any specific creed, until, as he says, they are able to judge for themselves, and on this ground the Catholic mother is restrained from teaching them their religion. It is not so unusual for the Protestant father to declare that no child of his shall ever enter a Catholic Church, or be taught the Catholic catechism or prayers. Sometimes, wearied with the contest, the weak mother will at last exclaim, like the woman before Solomon's judgment-seat who was not the true mother—" Let it be neither mine nor thine, but let it be divided." And as there is no Solomon to settle the point of justice, a compromise is effected.

Again there is the benumbing influence of human respect, so potent over weak souls, and the fear of offending those who may benefit the children in a temporal point of view. Then there are those terrible trials to the child's heart, who, loving both parents equally, finds them opposed to each other in all that concerns God, the soul, and the religious life. To one dear parent the question of religion as between parent and child is a forbidden topic ; and happy is it when the child is not the troubled witness of a contest about the guidance of its soul, of a contest that cannot fail to wound parental influence as well as filial reverence.

I know that the passion of human love is often fanciful, accompanied with little of solid reflection or forethought, and regardless of religious considerations, especially in young persons. And I know that the responsibility of these marriages often falls with its heaviest weight upon the Catholic parents, who either take not due provision as to whom their children associate with, or who put temporal advantages before those of religion. I know, likewise, how difficult it is, in certain cases, to find suitable Catholic acquaintances for their children. But I likewise know that, in a number of cases, little trouble or consideration is taken to seek such proper acquaintances for them.

In a sermon by St. John Chrysostom on the choice to be made in marriage, there is a passage which I will quote for its bearing on the main point of this instruction. "Those of you," he says, "who have set your hearts on marriage ought not to venture on a matter so grave without mature deliberation. If you buy a house, you carefully examine its condition, and whether it will suit you. Before you engage your servants, you take every means to know about their health, their good sense, their mental qualities and moral dispositions. And if the house prove defective, you can sell it again; if your servants are useless or unmanageable, you can free yourself from them. But you cannot dispose of your wife; she is joined to you for life, and is always with you in the house. Whenever, therefore, you think of marrying, look well to the laws of the Church as well as to the laws of the country; because it is by the laws of the Church that God will judge you. Where you offend the civil laws, your punishment is but temporary, perhaps a fine in money; but if you trample upon the laws of the Church, it is your soul that will be punished, and there is the fire that is everlasting." *

* St. J. Chrysost. Serm. Quales ducendæ uxores.

I conclude this instruction with an admirable passage from the Synodal address published by the Hierarchy of Australia. "The frequency of mixed marriages," say the Right Rev. Prelates, "is a terrible blot upon the character of our Catholic community. It is sad to think with what facility Catholic parents consent to such irreligious connections, and with how little caution they expose their young people to social intercourse, where passionate fancy and the thoughtlessness of youth are certain to entail the danger of mischievous alliances. It is in the main the fault of the parents more than of the children, who hear so little warning against mixed marriages—so little denunciation and deprecation of their dangers and miseries. If young people did hear from the clergy, and from parents, as often and as explicitly as they ought, the sense and doctrine of the Church concerning such marriages, they would be a far rarer calamity than they are. The generosity of the young would revolt from such unions if they saw them in their true light, as a danger and a disgrace. Yes, a disgrace; not, perhaps, always in the eye of the world, but always in the eye of the Church. How are they to be interpreted ? On one side there is the Church teaching that matrimony is a sacrament—that the married life has its own great duties, its own difficulties, for which special graces of God are necessary, and which are provided by Him—that the state is to be entered upon thoughtfully and solemnly—with careful preparation of mind and heart—that spouses are to be of mutual help and encouragement in the grand end of all human life, the life for God and the

next world.   This is on one side ; and on the other,
what is there ?   A mere fanciful or passionate attachment, with little enough of worth about it, even when
pure with the utmost natural purity it can have; a
mere passionate attachment, overlooking, or at least
most certainly undervaluing, the great considerations
we have just stated.   Is not this a disgrace?   Or if
the motive to mixed marriage be an advantageous
alliance in respect of money prospects, is it not even
more disgraceful to soil a sacred thing with the sordid calculations of a commercial bargain ?   Or, if
the mixed marriage be coveted because one of the
parties possesses some little higher worldly standing
of fashion, or connection, or style ; why, is not the
thing still more contemptibly disgraceful, at least for
the Catholic, with his or her belief about the one
Church, the holiness of sacraments, the preciousness
of God's grace, and the true end of life ? "

V.

𝕮𝖍𝖊 𝕯𝖎𝖘𝖈𝖔𝖚𝖗𝖘𝖊

*Delivered at the Consecration of the Bishops of Salford
and Amycla, October 28, 1872.*

"Take heed to yourselves, and to the whole flock wherein the Holy
Ghost has placed you bishops, to rule the Church of God, which
He has purchased with His own Blood."—ACTS xx. 28.

M Y BRETHREN,—Although these were the parting words of St. Paul to certain bishops of Asia
Minor in an age long past, they are not dead, their life
has not even faded ; for the grace that enters the
heart of each bishop at his consecration reanimates
the inspired words anew, enkindling in him the sacred
fire that gives life and vigour to the apostolic words.
The Holy Ghost exhibits to his mind, through its
text, the form and features of the episcopal office ;
and we who have grown grey beneath the responsibilities of that office can well understand, and deeply
feel, how the light and the divine energy of these
words have penetrated the hearts of these our brethren
elect ; who in solitary meditation and silent prayer
have for some time been preparing themselves
to receive the awful responsibility of the episcopal

office through the Holy Ghost from the Throne of
the Eternal Trinity. Take heed to yourselves, says
the Holy Spirit, that living in God, and resting on
His strength, you may have heed to the whole flock,
and may rule the Church which Christ has purchased
with His own Blood. Nor are the words of St. Peter
of less searching power. In that first Epistle, first of
the long series of apostolic letters with which the
Vicars of Christ have illuminated the Church, the
Prince of the Apostles says to the bishops of Asia,
" The ancients I beseech, who am myself an ancient,
and a witness of the sufferings of Christ, and a
partaker of the glory that shall be revealed. Feed
the flock of God which is among you, ἐπισκοποῦντες,
exerting the episcopal office, not by constraint, but
willingly, according to God : not for filthy lucre, but
cheerfully : nor as lording it over the clergy, but
becoming a pattern of the flock from the heart."

Nor does the Sacred Scripture fail to define the
duty that binds the flock to the shepherd. For these
are the words of St. Paul to the scattered people of
God—" Obey your prelates, and be subject to them ;
for they watch, as having to give an account of your
souls, that they may do this with joy, and not with
grieving. For this is profitable to you."

In lines of light the inspired words mark out the
whole form and order of a diocese. The bishop
watches over and feeds and rules the flock, and is
accountable to God for their souls : the flock is
subject to him, and is obedient to his voice, and this
is profitable to them.

What is a bishop considered in himself? What

is he to his diocese? What is he to the Universal
Church?

It is obvious, my brethren, that a bishop must
first be all that in himself which he is afterwards
to become to other men. And well has this been
expressed by that type of a great bishop, St.
Ambrose. " The life of the whole flock," says the
Saint, " must first be found in the bishop. For he is
elected from all men to preside over all, and being
exalted into the calm estate of peaceful judgment, he
is the healer of all men." * His power is in the Holy
Ghost; and Christ Himself, as the Divine Founder of
the Church, has ordained the channels through which
that power comes upon him. But whilst his episcopal
light and energy through sacramental consecration
are derived from the Holy Ghost, his commission as
a successor of the Apostles must come in an unbroken
line of succession from these same Apostles; even as
they derived their mission from Christ Himself.

But where, in this nineteenth century, shall we find
the apostolic authority except in the chair of Peter,
and in the line of the Roman Pontiffs? Twelve
hundred years ago that divinely-constituted authority
sent Augustine to found the See of Canterbury, and
Paulinus to found the See of York. But those Sees,
with their suffragans, have long departed from the
Catholic faith, and with the loss of communion with
the Apostolic See they have lost their Catholic jurisdiction, and even their Catholic orders; whilst the
same apostolic authority that founded those sees of
old, has founded sees anew; and amongst others it

* Epist. 82, ad Vercell. Eccles.

G

sent your late venerable bishop to establish the See of Salford, and has appointed his successor, who is now presented to you. The votes of the Cathedral Chapter commended him to the attention of the Pontiff, the suffrages of the bishops sustained their commendation; the 259th successor of St. Peter has called him to the episcopal office; and notwithstanding his reluctance, has given him his institution, his jurisdiction, and his flock.

You may well understand, my brethren, how mortal men should tremble at the call to an office of such high and vast responsibility; a responsibility that ends not with time and the world, but extends up even to eternity; a responsibility so great, that as the saints have said, even the shoulders of angels would dread to receive its burden. Be not surprised, then, when you hear that these Right Rev. Prelates have each, after their call, made their humble representations, but that, after being reassured, following the maxims of the saints, each has bent himself to the burden. For the angel of the schools and summit of theology, the ever-venerable St. Thomas, lays it down as a principle derived from the saints, that if after representation made the call to the episcopal office is renewed, it would be against charity to refuse the great labour for souls, as it would be against humility to refuse obedience to the call of the Church.

Through the Vicar of Christ comes the call; whilst acting on the apostolic commission, through the sacramental ministry of the Archbishop and assistant bishops here present, the episcopal ·character and order are conferred. But whilst they minister the solemn rite, the Holy Ghost is the interior consecrator; exalting the priest to the high priesthood, extending the sacramental power, consolidating the grace of government, conveying to the consecrated prelates the plenitude of sacerdotal power, imprinting on their souls in light and unction that highest character and most indelible which constitutes the bishop in the image and likeness of the one great High Priest—that High Priest who has entered with His Blood into the eternal sanctuary, and is the Bishop and Shepherd of our souls. For although every priest, from the Supreme Pontiff to the humblest missionary, is invested with one and the same power as respects the Divine Sacrifice and the Sacrament of Christ's Body, yet the order of the episcopate extends to other sacraments and to other consecrations beyond the powers of the simple priest.

The bishop it is who alone ordains, and so creates, the clergy. The bishops they are who alone raise the priest to the episcopal order. The bishop it is who alone consecrates the chrism, that "holy and divine chrism," to quote the Dyonisian Books, which is the visible sign of the invisible unction of the Holy Ghost in so many sacraments and consecrations. It mingles in the waters of Baptism; it seals the brow of the confirmed Christian; it sanctifies the hands of the priests; it consecrates the heads of the bishops; it strengthens the shoulders of emperors and kings; it makes holy unto God the walls of churches in their sanctification; it embalms their altars, and it consecrates the sacred vessels for the

Christian sacrifice. The bishop it is who perfects the Christian character and grace in the Sacrament of Confirmation. The bishop it is who consecrates the churches to God. And to him, as the representative of Christ, is committed the care of the sacred virgins, and the reception of those vows by which they bind themselves to Christ.

This highest plenitude of sacerdotal power the bishop derives from his consecration ; and with it, as we have said, that implanted character from Christ's eternal priesthood, which neither his will, nor his weakness, nor the violence of men, nor time, nor eternity, can ever erase or blot out ; because it is the indelible seal of the high priesthood of Christ.

Yet though divinely marked off from other men, and even from his brethren of the priesthood, by the episcopal character, and though filled with spiritual power by the sacramental extension in episcopal ordination, this power would remain for ever locked within his individual breast ; it would be incapable of being brought into lawful exercise, and of bearing fruit according to the will of God, but for that jurisdiction and authority which presents him to a diocese and assigns to him a flock. And this jurisdiction comes not to the bishop through his episcopal consecration, but is conveyed to him by the apostolic authority of the Holy See. For it is one thing to be a bishop, it is another thing to be sent by the Vicar of Christ with a commission to rule a diocese, and to shepherd a flock.

To the Apostolate was given the exclusive power of defining the local churches, of constituting them into dioceses, and of appointing bishops over them. The apostolic authority might appoint certain delegates of its authority to appoint bishops to certain portions of the Church, and such were the Patriarchs of the East; but the same authority which gave the delegation could, for that very reason, withdraw that delegation when this was judged expedient, and has long since withdrawn it.

When the Apostles departed from the earth, the apostleship did not depart. It was concentrated in the See of Peter, and in the successors of the Vicar of Christ. "On this rock," said its Divine Founder, "will I build my Church, and the gates of hell shall not prevail against it." Hence it is that he who sits in the apostolic chair can alone form dioceses, can alone constitute cathedral churches, can alone appoint bishops to them, can alone invest them with jurisdiction to feed and rule the flocks. Without this divine provision, what would the Church be but an endless entanglement and confusion of jurisdictions? What flock would know its shepherd? What shepherd would know his flock? How should we realise that maxim of St. Cyprian, that "the Church is in the bishop, and the bishop in the Church?" Where would be the sense of St. Paul's exhortation, "Take heed to yourselves, and to the whole flock, wherein the Holy Ghost has placed you bishops to rule the Church of God?" A learned and skilful lawyer has all the capacities of a judge within him; but a judge he is not, until he receive his commission from the supreme power of the sovereign, and is exalted to the bench, and has some specific court or circuit assigned him in which to exercise his judicial authority. A soldier may possess the most consummate qualities of a general, but a commander he cannot be until the sovereign invest him with his commission, and assign to him a division of the army. Without these royal commissions, marking out the limits of jurisdiction or of command, what perplexity would there be in the administration of our laws! what confusion in the command of our armies!

And so in the Catholic Church. The most holy and enlightened bishop ever consecrated can neither put forth the graces of his ministry nor his powers of ruling until the sovereign authority of the Church has assigned to him the chair of jurisdiction in a cathedral church, and the circuit of a diocese wherein that jurisdiction can be exercised. Hence the charge of St. Peter to the local bishops, to feed the flocks that are among them. Hence the canonical words of St. Cyprian, that " to the several pastors a portion of the flock is assigned, which each one rules and governs." Hence the 38th Apostolic Canon, that " he is the bishop to whose faith the people are confided, the account of whose souls will be exacted from him." Hence the invariable form of the apostolic brief, appointing each bishop to some one cathedral church. Hence the canonical requirement of appointing even an auxiliary or coadjutor bishop to some specific see, even though that see be placed *in partibus infidelium*, as the Right Rev. Prelate here consecrated to the See of *Amycla*. For no bishop is consecrated without a title, and the see it is which gives that title.

No temporal sovereign or state can give this

jurisdiction. It is not of earthly, but of heavenly creation. It is emphatically a power from God. It is the spiritual jurisdiction of the spiritual kingdom which Christ Himself founded, and which He declared was not a kingdom of this world. The channel of its derivation is through the Apostolate. The cause of its power is the sufferings of Christ; its giver the Holy Ghost. For "the Holy Ghost has placed you bishops to rule the Church of God," says the Apostle St. Paul. For the temporal power to attempt the giving of episcopal jurisdiction is to usurp the Apostolate. For any one to attempt receiving this jurisdiction from the temporal power is to deny the ordinance of Christ, and to sin against the Holy Ghost. As if spiritual power could spring out of the earth; as if it could be the birth of the human will; as if this power, descending through the Holy Ghost, could be passed from hand to hand as a product of human revolutions!

Once clothed with his jurisdiction and invested with his mission, the bishop is the ruler of the churches, the guardian of the revealed truth, the witness and the judge of faith, the custodian of God's law, the enforcer of the Church's canons, the father of his clergy and their judge, the pastor of his people, the chief preacher of the Word of God to the flock, and the guide of souls. All other ministries are exercised in dependence on him. Whoever are gathered into the flock are gathered unto him. For the Church is in the bishop; and should the dire necessity arise, it is the bishop who cuts off the faithless and unbelieving member from the flock. It is the

bishop who deprives the contumacious of his communion, which is the communion of the Catholic Church.
And that he may bear these tremendous responsibilities with less fear of human frailty, the Church assigns
to him a senate of advisers in the reverend Chapter
of his cathedral. Without their counsel, there are
many things he cannot legally do. Without their
consent even, there are several things in which his
hand is stayed from action.

Beyond his sacramental grace, where, my brethren,
are we to look for the light, strength, and support of
a diocesan bishop? What is the security for the
wisdom of his rule? It lies in this, that the Church
has left nothing to his arbitrary disposal. In his
government of others, he is himself governed by a
law. In every act of his ministry, he is subject to a
precept and a rule. At every step and turn in the
exercise of his office, whether it regard the churches,
the sacraments, the visitation of his flock, the temporal administration of his diocese, the discipline of the
clergy, or the conduct of the people, he is guided by
law, and is obedient to law. He is the living, moving, and speaking expositor of the Church's canons
and provisions of discipline. No man has such a
laborious life of subjection and obedience to law and
rule as a Catholic bishop. He has a double duty of
obedience, so to speak—one to the Church's laws;
another in the adapting of his judgment and his conduct to the exigences and requirements of the souls
confided to him, and that in grave cases under pain
of being in the wrong, and of an appeal to higher
authorities. Whilst through the bishop's obedience,

and enforcement of obedience, to her teaching and her laws, the whole flock obeys the voice of the Church.

There was a time, and the time ran through long ages, when the bishops of the Church were surrounded with secular splendour; when, as feudal barons, as councillors of the sovereign, as ministers of state, or as administrators of the king's equity, they combined a temporal power from the state with the spiritual authority of the Church ; when, as large dispensers of charity and hospitality, they were endowed with considerable, in some cases even with princely revenues ; when, in short, for their services to the world they were glorified by the world. This state of things began in the fourth century with the Emperor Constantine. No sooner was Christianity seated on the throne of the world than the emperor discovered that, in compliance with the injunction of St. Paul, the Christians had abstained from the civil courts of law, lest they should be contaminated by the idolatrous rites that accompanied the pagan's oath to his gods, and that the bishops had become extensive arbitrators of the disputes that arose between the members of their flocks. Seeing this, the emperor invested the bishops with judicial power in civil cases, thus giving legal sanction to their decisions in temporal questions ; but the diadems of honour which the emperor likewise offered them they refused to accept. And when Charlemagne, in the eighth century, became the founder of a great empire based on Catholic principles, he gave to the bishops of that empire a secular power and position that consummated the union between Church and State, and became the pattern to other Catholic nations. In our England, for example, the Catholic religion was held to be part and parcel of our common law for well-nigh a thousand years ; but the bishops alone could be the interpreters and judges of that part of the common law. In those days, the Catholic faith and law of conscience were the guarantees of the duty both of the sovereign power to the people and of the people to the sovereign power. When the people were oppressed, they looked mainly to their bishops to obtain redress, and clamoured for the return of the laws of good King Edward—king and saint in one.

Except in what concerned the faith, the law of God, and the Church's constitution, the Church in her bishops made great sacrifices for the welfare of the state, looking above all things to the general good of the people. And the result has been summed up in a brief sentence by a great living statesman and historian. After a full survey of the facts, the Protestant Guizot concludes that the kingdoms of Europe and their civilisation were mainly the work of the Catholic bishops. But for the Church to accomplish effective work of this kind, it required the condition, that either the kings with their people were rising from the degraded state of paganism to the faith, or that from the rulers to the people the body of a nation remained united in the faith. When the state was Christian, and the people were Christian ; when the Christian and Catholic faith and moral teaching were recognised as the sound and secure basis of civil law and social happiness ; when, in a word, the kingdom bowed down to God, and worshipped Him in the unity of one truth, one Church, and one Sacrifice, under the supreme authority of one apostolic pastor, then were the bishops invested with temporal powers from the state, as well as with spiritual powers from the Church, for the greater good of the people and the state. But the division of minds and separation of hearts that come of heresies, schisms, and unbeliefs, rend a nation down to its deepest foundations, and unnerve the power of its rulers by the loss of the radical unity of its people, and thereby fails the essential peace and happiness of a kingdom. For what peace can there be without religious peace? and how can we have religious peace among men without unity? and how can we have unity without a principle of unity? or how can we be held together without obedience to that principle?

There came the revolt predicted by St. John and by St. Paul—the revolt which was to be the calamitous period of the Church of Christ—a revolt the result of sensuality and pride; of sensuality discarding self-denial; of pride refusing submission to the ordinances of God; and thirsting, like the fallen angel, for the calamitous joy of independence. Then fell great avalanches of men from the rock of faith; and having no principle of authority left on which to base a faith, they drifted here and there on the restless ocean of doubt, clinging to the broken remnants of truth, and unhappily parting with one fragment of revelation after another, until they scarcely knew what remained to them.

Would you know how this revolt found its way
to our England? The way was prepared for it by
those destructive civil wars waged for forty years by
our fathers in the rival conflicts for the crown. A
civil war of such a character, and so protracted, draws
into its desolating path the whole life, spirit, and
vigour of a nation. Then the arts of peace languish,
education descends to a low ebb, learning is left
uncultivated, the quick-spirited youth of the nation
abandon the Church for the sword, a general de-
moralisation takes place, and spiritual culture is
neglected for partisan warfare. The very women
throw themselves with passion into conflicts that
absorb all minds alike. Whatever else suffers, religion becomes the greatest sufferer. Fixed to one
line at last, the life and treasure expended on the
crown gave it a price in the mind of the nation to
which every other right was taught to yield. Then
arose the doctrine of the divine right of kings, with
a tendency to absorb within it the independent rights
of the Church. In the voluptuous, cruel, and rapa-
cious Henry VIII., the crown fell first. The new
nobles, put in place of the old barons who fell in the
wars, like the new men of new Italy, were eager to
exchange their faith for the freedom of the world,
and to grasp the monastic property to form their
estates, regardless of its being the patrimony of the
poor. And so, left without leaders, and deprived
after a time of their Catholic bishops, gradually and
sadly the people fell from the faith whose voice they
heard no more.

But a religion based on rejection of the voice of

the Church, and the denial of her authority, carries the spirit of negation in its womb. With time it will pass from revolt to revolt until it deny the fundamental truths of Christianity; until the ring of a single anathema, in place of the hundreds that protected the doctrines of the Trinity and of the Incarnation in the early Councils, sounds offensive and cruel to men's ears; until sects of educated men in England, in the name of science, proclaim that they know everything except God, but that God can never be known; that the world is their concern, not His; and that as they deem that He can never interfere with the course of this visible universe, it is useless to pray to Him to guide it to our welfare. "When a man cometh into the depths," says the Scripture, "he scorneth."

When revolt has taken a deep hold of the religious part of man, it will not stop there in its terrible path; after assailing the foundations of faith, it will assault the foundations of the social system. No longer upheld by the Church, because the Christian basis of society and law have been discarded as encumbrances, kings fall, states are overturned, revolution follows upon revolution, and the whole stability of human government is undermined. The fermentation of pride in human hearts melts down the principle of religious authority into the vagaries of individual opinion, and dissolves the principles of human government into a conflict of classes and a strife of rival parties. And to this pass has the world come in this last half of the nineteenth century of our redemption.

After all this revolt, where now is the Church of God? Where rests the authority of Christ? Can we doubt it, my Catholic brethren, after the Vatican Council? Can we doubt it, after hearing a thousand bishops proclaiming anew the foundations both of reason, of faith, and of authority? The more wonderful is that unity from the fraternal conflicts that, in the spirit of episcopal freedom, went before decision. The greater miracle of grace, and of the action of the Holy Ghost, is that unity, when we behold the minority to a man confess the voice of the Church in the Vicar of Christ supported by the decision of the vast majority. It is here that you have the admirable spectacle of Christian humility and authority united: united in the whole body of the episcopate, united in their clergy adhering to them, united in the faith of the flocks obeying the voice of their pastors, united in the closely welded adhesion of the chief pastors without exception to the apostolic chair of unity. And this unity of the Church, fruit of the prayer of Christ and of the unifying spirit of the Holy Ghost, is all the more conspicuous from the contrast with the few, the very few, diseased already with the conceit of their learning, and lifted up in the pride of their private judgment, who, at the sharp touch of truth, have fallen away, and have left the Church in better plight for the purification.

And so, my brethren, I come to the question for which I have been preparing you, What is a Catholic bishop in this nineteenth century? Ever a high priest after the pattern of the great High Priest

according to the order of Melchisedec, in his character and spiritual power he is always the same.
But as the world changes its front, and alters its
conduct towards the Church, each change in its mood
brings the action of the bishop out in some charac-
teristic attributes of his Divine Master, which in one
age becomes conspicuous, whilst in another it shews
less visibly.

In the early ages of the Church the bishop had
to be first in suffering and martyrdom. He represented our Lord to the world as priest and victim.

In the Middle Ages the bishop had to resist oppression of the poor from kings and nobles, and to
meet them therefore on equal terms. He represented
our Lord in His sovereignty.

The dangers of the present age are intellectual; it
is an age of false science and false theories respecting
God and the human soul. The age is striving to do
without God; in science, in government, in the education of the people, man is held up to himself as all-
sufficient for himself. The Church is bid to stand
aloof from the moral guidance of human affairs. It
has become a point of policy amidst nations nomi-
nally Christian to banish God Himself from the affairs
of men, and in His place to take possession of the
souls and consciences of men, that they may be managed according to the desires of nature, and as if no
better principles of guidance, no brighter light from
God, had ever been given.

And has God no witness left? Is there no prophet any more? There is. To this age of unbelief,
to this age of godless teaching, to this age of troubled

minds and distressed consciences, the bishop is the mouthpiece of God, and represents the prophetic character of Christ.

He preaches. To the world, which, like a wayward child, is impatient to be taught, he speaks as one having authority, devoid of human respect and indifferent to human criticism, even as St. Paul disregarded " the judgment of man's day;" as the appointed messenger of God he speaks with clear, decided, unhesitating tones. Holding possession of the whole body of revealed truth, in season and out of season he presses the advantage of truth against error in all its shapes and combinations, he plants those accurate definitions and those precise expositions which reveal to man the mind of God, and strike error to its centre.

He rules. By the moral law and the right of his authority, he binds the consciences of men and holds them to the law of God. Where might is in the ascendant in place of right, and the law of right is unacknowledged, as with the trumpet of the doom he makes the principles of right, truth, and virtue to be heard, and their necessity to the cause of God and the welfare of society.

He consecrates—securing God's portion in the world, His *acre*, His tabernacle, His altar, as the sources of grace to men, and of blessing to the earth. He will not hear the cry that God keep to His heavens and leave the earth to Cæsar, without rebuking it.

And never were the bishops of the Church placed in a better position for the exercise of their prophetic office. Stripped of earthly splendour, disencumbered of the world, set free from the odium that fell upon

them from alliance with the State, and standing on
no other ground than that of apostolic authority, the
bishop of the nineteenth century is all the stronger
for the change. No longer the servant of princes, he
is tenfold the servant of the people. He is tempted
to no compromises of policy between the cause of
God and that of the world. What was said by an
eminent orator to the Revolutionary Assembly of
France towards the close of last century is everywhere
exemplified in this :—" Drive the bishops from their
palaces, and they will find refuge in the poor man's
cottage ; snatch their jewelled crosiers from their
hands, and they will grasp a staff of wood."

If ever a Catholic bishop was strong, he is strong
in this hour of the world's history. He is strong
because he is free. He is strong because he lives a
simple and frugal life. He is strong because he is a
bishop and nothing but a bishop ; strong, therefore,
in the vivid consciousness of his high office. Strong
he is in the affections of his people, of a people who
hold the faith with loss of advantage in this world,
that makes the representative of that faith all the
dearer to their souls. Strong, and vigorously strong
is he, because more closely than ever united with the
apostolic chair. Such is the Catholic bishop of this
nineteenth century. The arduous difficulties that
beset his path but plume his courage. The heat and
pressure of the combat with ignorance and error bring
out his light to greater radiance. On so much has
he to think, against so many things has he to guard,
in so much must he endure in the patience of his soul,
so much has he to construct, so many affairs to set in

H

order, that every spark and atom of his sacramental energy is brought into life and action.

And if ever the essential qualities of the perfect bishop were required, they are demanded in our day and circumstances. His *learning* is called for to withstand and confound the intellectual follies, to detect the sophistries and fallacies of writers, who constitute themselves the guides of men both for this life and the next; and to know how to steer the bark of the Church amidst the tempests of life. His *virtue* must be as calm as it is firm and solid, as tender in compassion as unflinching in justice ; upholding the cross and bearing its reproaches with a martyr's spirit, a pattern to the flock in all the charity and patience of God. His *wisdom* must appreciate the circumstances of the times in a great spirit, among the blended elements of the new and old conditions of human life and society, discerning and holding to that in which the will and providence of God is made manifest.

Such, my brethren, is the bishop whom the Church demands and whom the world stands in need of in this latter part of the nineteenth century. And so let us all with one heart and voice pray to God that, through the grace of the Holy Ghost, such may be the Right Reverend Prelates who are this day consecrated to the saving of souls. What times are reserved for the devout and zealous bishop whom God has given to you, God alone knows. Armed with the spiritual strength of the episcopate, he is about to bless you for the first time. May he rise in pastoral vigour whilst our arms grow feeble! And may he be to you a burning and a shining light when our eyes grow dim, and our light is sinking from the world !

VI.

The Discourse

Delivered at the Opening Session of the Fourth
Provincial Synod of Westminster.

"Speak to the priests, the sons of Aaron, and say to them, They shall
be holy to their God, and they shall not profane His name : for
they offer the fire-offering of the Lord, and the bread of their God,
and therefore they shall be holy. . . . . Because they are consecrated to their God, and eat the bread of their God. Let them
therefore be holy, because I also am holy, the Lord, who sanctify
them."—LEVITICUS xxi.

MOST REVEREND, VERY REVEREND, AND
REVEREND BRETHREN,—In our first Provincial Synod we gave our local Church its canonical
organisation and the outlines of its discipline. In
our second, we provided the rules for the administration of its temporalities, and planted a guard against
their alienation. In our third and last Synod, our
deliberations were chiefly occupied with our mixed
colleges, with the spirit and scope of our higher
education, and with that question, more than once
urged upon us by the Holy See, of establishing
diocesan seminaries according to the provisions of
the Council of Trent. And judging from the draft of

subjects that now await our consideration, the work
of this fourth Synod will be of not less vital import-
ance than that of the three whose decrees are already
in operation ; for in so far as external legislation can
accomplish a thing so great, nothing less is contemplated than to place the crowning virtue of sanctity
upon the ecclesiastical edifice already constructed.
In other words, it is proposed, that from the Church's
traditional doctrine and law, we should draw up and
give synodical force to those precepts of sanctity,
whereby both bishops and priests advance in holiness,
and augment the sacred energy of their pastoral
labours.

What makes a small army to prevail against great
numbers ? Is it not its high spirit, its vigorous discipline, its keener weapons, and its more skilful direction ? And what gives the victory to God's servants
over the hosts of error and sin? Is it not the force and
elevation of their inward spirit ? Is it not that strong
discipline of the saints that gives steadfastness to
wear, and power to wield, the armour of God ? The
calendar of the Church and her whole history bear
witness that God's ministry is fruitful in proportion
to the sanctity of His ministers.

If I concentrate your attention upon the diocesan
as opposed to the regular clergy, it is because the
regular clergy have their own rules of sanctity
provided by their founders and enforced by their own
superiors ; and that being exempt in their internal
affairs from our synodal action, they look to their own
chapters for their spiritual government. Yet for the
very reason that they are so happily provided, ought

we to take care, that the diocesan clergy be not left
without precise definitions of that rule of sanctity,
which their Divine Founder, our Blessed Lord Himself, has attached to their order and profession. Nor,
in treating of the sanctification of the clergy, is it
possible to overlook those youthful aspirants to the
priestly office, upon whose holy training the future
of the Church depends. From the holy seminarist
comes the holy priest.

Having glanced at the chief subjects that await our
deliberations, I come, my brethren, to the text of my
discourse. The sacred Scripture tells us, that what
God demands before all things of His priests is holiness. He requires science, or He will reject them;
zeal to do their office, or they will be a useless
encumbrance. But the highest and most indispensable
attribute of God's priest is sanctity. What, then, is
sanctity? It must be considered in its two aspects,
as it looks to man and as it looks to God. As it
looks to man, sanctity consists in freedom from
whatever is unclean or spiritually impure, be it in
mind, in heart, or in body. As it looks towards God,
sanctity consists in devotion to His love and service,
and in the oblation of ourselves through His gifts to
Him. It is this union of purity with devotion which
generates that odour of sanctity of which the Holy
Spirit is the inspiring principle. But the perfection
of sanctity is measured by the degree of charity of
which the humble soul receives the vital flame. For
"never," says St. Thomas, "can human nature be
perfected unless it be united with God."* And as

* S. Thom. in 5 cap. ad Ephes.

holy things are for the holy, and the holiest mysteries of grace demand the holiest ministration, so the higher the order of sacred ministration given to man, the greater is the degree of sanctity demanded of him. Even to the Levites, who served the sons of Aaron in the sacrifice, it was said :—" Be ye clean, ye who carry the vessels of the Lord."

Of the priests, God demanded a threefold sanctity. The first was detachment from the common life and pursuits of men, and dependence on God. God was their inheritance and their lot, and they lived upon what was offered to God. They were to touch no unclean thing that the Lord had declared unclean, nothing that bore the shadow or resemblance of offence. They were not even to come near the dead bodies of their dearest relatives, because death is the likeness as it is the fruit of sin, and the death of Christ had not yet made it holy. Their first degree of holiness, then, was abstention from things unholy and profane ; lest, ministering in the holy place, and nigh unto God's communicated presence, they should bring spiritual uncleanness into proximity with God. " They shall be holy unto their God, and they shall not defile His name."

The fire-offering was the burning incense, the symbol of prayer, the image of a soul that in the fire of charity exhales herself unto God. The bread-offering of their God was daily placed on the golden table that stood before the Mercy Seat. It was the prophetic figure of the Eucharistic sacrifice and communion. And of the priests who made this offering and divided this bread, a second and a higher degree of holiness was

demanded. They were not only to be clean and con-
tinent in person, but devout in their oblation. "They
offer the fire-offering of the Lord, and the bread of
their God, and therefore shall they be holy." "*Holy
to the Lord.*" This was the inscription borne on the
brow of the high 'priest, a sign to all the priests, of
whom he was the summit, of their consecration to
God. "*Doctrine and Truth.*" These words he carried
engraven upon his breast, an admonition to them all,
that God's priests shall be taught of truth, and shall
walk in its light. "Because they are consecrated to
their God, and eat the bread of their God. Therefore
they shall be holy." God would have no one to
receive His unction, to stand at His altar, to touch
His sacrifice, to be so close to His communicated
presence, to shadow forth the Divine Priesthood of
the Son of God, who is not both pure, and devout,
and holy, with communicated sanctity. Wherefore
God commanded that His priests should have that
third, that imitative, that unitive degree of sanctity.
"Let them therefore be holy, because I am holy, the
Lord, who sanctify them."

But if the thrice holy God demanded a thrice holy
priesthood in the sons of Aaron, what purity, what
devotion, what sanctity does the same God ask of the
Christian priests, who continue the sacrifice of the God
Incarnate? They bore the image of Christ in outward
shadow ; and we His character engraven in our soul.
They offered earthly things ; and we the heavenly
mysteries. They could accomplish nothing for the
souls of men ; and we have received Christ's power
both to cleanse and to sanctify them. "Behold,"

says our Lord, "I make all things new." But amongst those new things, never did He contemplate His priests without His humility ; or their handling the fruit of His sufferings without His patience ; or their exercising His power without the sanctity that is the secret of that power. Let us, then, make all things new, my brethren, heart, voice, and work. And may His Holy Spirit clothe our minds with light to see, and our wills with strength to work out, the law of sacerdotal holiness, to the glory of His name.

I dwell upon this argument the more readily, my brethren, and you will listen to it the more devoutly, because there never was a time when the sacred prerogatives of the Catholic priesthood more required to be exalted. For, on the one hand, we have the miscellaneous hosts of daring unbelievers, who scoff at all priesthood as a worn-out fable and a human imposition ; whilst, on the other hand, we have increasing numbers of men, who daringly lay claim to the sacerdotal office that their fathers rejected, and that without title of descent, or colour of tradition, or power over the sacrifice, or that law of sacerdotal purity that devotes the priest to the virginal victim. And even within the sanctuary of the Church there are some to be found who measure the standard of sacerdotal sanctity with eyes that have but too secular a colour in them.

Very near should we be to the Holy Sacrifice, my brethren ; and very keenly should we feel what the souls of men have cost ; and what a thing it is to offer and dispense the life-giving blood of Christ, before we can realise the holiness demanded of the priest.

The Priesthood and the Incarnation of Christ form one sole and indivisible mystery. To divide them is to separate Christ from Himself. The stupendous union of God and man in one person, is the preparation of the Priest and the Victim in one person. Conceived of the Holy Ghost, born of the Virgin Mary, in her, as in His temple, was Christ clothed with a body, anointed as a priest, and consecrated a sacrifice for the sins of the world. " Wherefore, when He cometh into the world, He saith : Sacrifice and oblation Thou wouldst not : but a body Thou hast fitted to Me. Holocausts for sin did not please Thee. Then said I : Behold I come : in the head of the book it is written of Me : that I should do Thy will, O God." And as St. Paul again says : " Christ did not glorify Himself that He should be a High Priest, but He who said to Him : Thou art My Son, this day have I begotten Thee. As in another place He saith : Thou art a Priest for ever according to the order of Melchisedec." Not by His eternal generation from the Father is Christ a High Priest, but by His temporal generation in Mary of the Holy Ghost ; for His Priesthood is in His human nature, although united with the Divine personality. And yet He is a Priest for ever, because through the eternal predestination, and the prophetic declarations and sacrifices, He is in very truth " the Lamb that was slain from the beginning of the world." He took our nature in its mortal condition, that, except our sin, He might in all things suffer like unto us. He took

it from a pure source, most pure, that, united to the
Godhead in His sufferings, He might purify the
world. "Whom God the Father hath anointed with
the Holy Spirit and with power." For which reason
He was both Jesus and Christ: Jesus for our salvation; Christ for the unction of His priesthood.
"For in Him dwelleth the fulness of the Godhead
corporally."

That Godhead which in that human nature dwells
is the word of the Father, and the very God; through
whom all intelligent creatures were made, and by
whom their reason is illuminated.

Reflect on the wonderful mysteries that come together in the sacrifice.

The first, most high and unsearchable, is the
hypostatic union of the priest with the Eternal
Word.

The second, most awful and profound, is the
identity of the priest with the Victim.

The third, most dreadful and significant, is the
choice of the cruel and ignominious Cross for the altar
of sacrifice. Why was the Cross chosen for the altar
of sacrifice? The Cross was chosen that the malice
of sin might be revealed to its utmost depth. The
Cross was chosen that pride might be searched through
by humility, and sensuality by suffering. The Cross
was chosen, on which to offer the most consummate
expiation; and to show how exceeding was the
charity with which God has loved us. The Cross was
chosen, with all its load of shame and suffering, as
the counterpart to the tree of paradise; and that with
the Lord of life suspended on it, the Cross might be

the example, strength, and grace of all suffering souls, guilty or innocent, who, in the times to come, should cling to it for light and comfort.

The fourth great mystery in the sacrifice, most generous and consoling, is the oblation, through the Divine High Priest and Victim, of all humanity upon the Cross. The body was offered with the head, the Church with her suffering Pontiff. All whomsoever His blood shall ever touch were nailed with Him on the Cross, and St. Paul, who knew this secret well, has said : "If one died, then all have died." And again, "For ye are dead, and your life is hidden with Christ in God." And once more, "Knowing this, that our old man is crucified together with Him, that the body of sin may be destroyed." And summing up the truth in himself, the Apostle says, "With Christ I am nailed to the Cross." For the Cross is the altar of the whole world, and its virtue passes unto all who embrace it with belief, and who suffer in its spirit. Even the innocent and the humble are immolated upon its branches, and are perfected by the immolation. Wherefore St. Leo says :—"Our Lord Jesus Christ stood forth one and alone, in whom all die, all are buried, all rise again." And again :—" The Cross of Christ is the mystery of the true altar that was foretold, where through the saving Victim, the offering of human nature should be celebrated."* Wherefore as "all those who are Christ's have crucified the flesh with its vices and concupiscences," they can say with the Apostle : "I fill up the sufferings of Christ that are wanting in my flesh for His body, which is the

* S. Leo, Serm. iv. de Passione.

Church." The fourth mystery, then, is the oblation of the body of humanity together with the Head.

The fifth, of unspeakable condescension, is the creation of a human priesthood by the word of the Divine High Priest, to prolong the Sacrifice over earth and time, and to bring its fruits to all the children of men.

The sixth, most diffusive of life and charity, is the communion of Christ, through the action of that priesthood, with all souls that are drawn to Him in faith and love.

The seventh, embracing all these mysteries in one, is the unity and identity of the sacrifice offered by men on earth with the sacrifice that is offered by Christ in Heaven. So that, as St. Chrysostom says, the arm of Christ is extended into the oblation of the priest. This unity is expressed in that solemn prayer to which tradition attaches so profound a significance, where the priest says after the consecration :—"Suppliantly we entreat Thee, O Almighty God, command that these gifts be carried by the hands of Thy holy angel up to Thy sublime altar, unto the sight of Thy Divine Majesty ; that whosoever, from partaking of this altar, shall receive the all-sacred body and blood of Thy Son, may be filled with all grace and benediction, through the same Christ our Lord." He hath entered into the heavens with His blood, having found eternal redemption ; and there, both High Priest and Victim, He maketh perpetual intercession for us. And He has the ministers of His power and dispensers of His mysteries upon this earth ; and what by His creative word they do, He Himself

accomplishes, be it to cleanse the souls of sinners in
His blood, or to nourish the hearts that He has justified with His life. "For the cup of blessing which
we bless, is it not the communion of the blood of
Christ? And the bread that we break, is it not the
partaking of the body of the Lord?"

Wherefore St. John, in the Apocalypse, beheld in
the temple of heaven the Son of God as the Bishop
of souls, clad in the bright garments of the priesthood, offering at the golden altar that is before the
throne of God ; and, at the same time, standing upon
that altar, and pleading as the Victim, who is the
Lamb for ever slain. And the seven eyes of the
Lamb and the seven horns of His power, are His
seven spirits sent forth into all the earth. And the
four-and-twenty white-robed elders who there minister around the Divine Bishop and Shepherd of souls,
are the representatives of the entire priesthood of
Christ ; who sing this liturgical hymn : "Thou art
worthy, O Lord, to take the Book, and to open the
seals thereof : because Thou hast redeemed us in Thy
blood, out of every tribe, and tongue, and people, and
nation, and hast made us a kingdom, and priests, and
we shall reign upon the earth." Stupendous is the
mystery ! Wonderful beyond all reach of created
intellects is the extension of the sacrifice ! Inconceiv-
able to men without belief is the condescension to us
sinful creatures ! But God is charity. Love is His
very nature. And when the Almighty and Infinite
Charity puts forth, towards the fallen creatures He
would save, the supreme act of His love, however
closely veiled from corporal sight, that act, from the

very nature of it, must be an act of supreme condescension. The higher and more godlike the gift,
and the more unworthy the recipients of its power,
all the greater and more worthy of God is the condescension. What is all the condescension of God, of
which humility is the reflection, but the stooping
down to sinful men to save them? And He who
stooped His priesthood down to the Cross and to the
grave, can He not stoop it down again into the
breasts of us unworthy creatures? The same motive
works in the one case as in the other; He stoops to
save mankind. One, therefore, is the High Priest,
and through His exceeding love of human souls,
many are the priests who share His sacerdotal power.
The unction from the Divinity that fell unmeasured
upon the humanity of Jesus, has fallen with measure
upon us. Wherefore, my brethren, having such a
High Priest and Lord of our ministry, and such a
Victim delivered into our hands, " holy, innocent, undefiled, separated from sinners, and made higher than
the heavens ;" can there be less expected of us, than
that, according to our grace, we should be holy in
life, innocent with at least recovered innocence, and
undefiled from the world?

But the pure God would have the pure and all
purifying sacrifice to be handled purely. For which
reason, the old Greek liturgy, whose clergy in the
earlier period of the Church were equally bound to
celibacy with those of the West, puts this prayer, as
he approaches the moment of consecration, into the
secret breast of the priest : "For no one who is entangled in the desires of the flesh is worthy to

approach to Thee, O King of glory. For to minister
unto Thee is a great and fearful thing, even to the
very powers of heaven themselves. Nevertheless,
through Thy unspeakable and infinite love of mankind, without any change or alteration in Thyself,
Thou hast been made man, and Thou art called our
High Priest, and Thou, as the Lord of all things, hast
given to us the consecration of this solemn and un-
bloody sacrifice. . . . Thou art He that maketh the
offering and art offered, Thou dost receive and art
distributed, and to Thee we give the glory, together
with Thy Father, without beginning, and Thy all-
holy, and good, and life-giving Spirit."

The first demand upon the priest to be holy arises
from the purity, the sanctity, and excelling dignity
of the sacrifice. " They offer the fire-offering of the
Lord, and the bread of their God, and therefore
they shall be holy." The second demand upon their
personal holiness is in that they offer in the power
of Christ and in the name of the Church which is
His body. " They are consecrated to the Lord, and
eat the bread of their God, and therefore they shall
be holy." The third demand upon them to be holy
is, that they represent Christ to the people, and are
the channels to them of His light and grace, and have
received power as well over the mystical body of
Christ, which are the faithful, as over His very Body
and Blood. " Let them be holy, because I am holy,
the Lord, who sanctify them."

In the priests of the old law the sanctity was
legal; in the priests of the new law it is interior
and spiritual. Of that Sion on which the Holy Ghost

came down in fire was David inspired to sing: "Let
Thy priests be clothed with justice: and let Thy
saints rejoice." And God answered David's prayer:
"I will clothe My priests with salvation; and her
holy ones with exceeding joy. There will I bring
forth a horn to David: I have prepared a lamp for
My anointed." The horn of David's strength is
Christ. The lamp prepared for God's anointed is
the light of justice in the flame of charity. And so
of this Sion God says in Isaias: "I will not rest
until her just one come forth in brightness, and her
saviour be enkindled as a lamp." He clothes His
priests in justice, and then do the saints rejoice;
with salvation, and then they rejoice exceedingly.
Ah! my brethren, the truly holy priest causes many
holy ones to rejoice. He multiplies the holy ones.
Through him, the holiness of Christ shines to the
world anew. When we would weigh the worth of a
priest, we must take St. Augustine's standard. He
must not be measured, says the great father, by
what he holds in common with good and evil men,
because the sum of his value is in his sanctity.*

The question, then, arises, and asks for reply:
Apart from all incidental obligations, and considered
simply as a priest of the pastoral order, what is the
law and rule of sacerdotal sanctity? With what can
it be compared? And how shall we bring it out?
As I approach this vital question, I see three obstacles, in the shape of three preconceptions, that
stand in my way, and which it will be my first duty
to remove.

* S. August., De Civit. Dei, l. xx. c. 21.

The first is a misapprehension of the sense of the word *secular*, as applied to the diocesan or pastoral clergy.

The second is a misapplication of theological light.

The third is a misconception of the character of that sanctity which God calls for in the priestly order.

I do not say that these misconceptions are set up in formal theory; but that, owing to the want of precise examination, and of clear apprehension, a misty haze has been allowed to settle about these points, that exerts a retarding influence on but too many of the pastoral clergy.

In his Three Books in defence of the Monastical Life, St. John Chrysostom exalts its great holiness and security, and likens it to the life of angels. Yet, in the midst of his fervent eulogy, the Saint stops to lament that, through a custom brought in by men without warrant from the gospel, the Christian laity in the world should be distinguished from the monks by the name of seculars. He says that this designation is undoing the world; for that it causes the laity to think that diligence in aiming at a holy life belongs to monks, and that the laity may live carelessly. Not so, says the Saint, not so: but the same precepts and counsels of holiness are given by our Lord to all men. He addressed the Beatitudes to all without distinction ; and the command to love God with our whole heart, and mind, and strength, and the injunction to be perfect as our Heavenly Father is perfect, were addressed to all. When our Lord intended to make a limitation, He expressed that limit clearly ; as when He said on virginity :

I

"All do not take this word; let them who can take it, take it." As St. Paul likewise said: "Concerning virginity I have no command of the Lord, but I give counsel." Hence the golden-mouthed Saint concludes that all are called to a perfect life, although the monastical is the most secure.*

If I next quote a passage at length from St. Francis of Sales, it is because this most holy bishop and learned theologian has clearly summed up in it the doctrine of St. Bernard, of St. Thomas, and of St. Bonaventure, indeed of all the greatest and holiest divines; and that he addresses it to the laity. In his Introduction to a Devout Life, St. Francis says: "Charity alone puts us into the perfect life. The three great means for acquiring charity are obedience, chastity, and poverty. Obedience consecrates our heart, chastity our body, and poverty our means to the love and service of God. These are the three branches of the spiritual cross; but all three rest on the fourth, which is humility. On these three virtues, as they are solemnly vowed, I will say nothing; because this regards religious persons. Nor will I speak of these virtues as they are simply vowed. For although vows give much grace and merit to the virtues, yet it is not necessary to vow them to render us perfect, provided we practise them. When they are vowed, and especially when they are solemnly vowed, they put a man in the state of perfection. But to put us in perfection itself, it is enough that we practise them. For between the state of perfection and perfection itself there is a great difference.

* S. J. Chrysost., Contra Impugnatores Vitæ Monast. l. iii.

All bishops and religious are in the state of perfection, although it is but too visible that all are not perfect. Let us then endeavour to put these virtues well into practice, each after his vocation ; for although they may not put us into the state of perfection, they will not the less give us possession of the perfect life. And so we are all bound to practise these three virtues, although not all after the same manner."

St. Chrysostom lamented the spiritual result of calling the laity by the name of seculars, whereas St. Paul says to all : *Nolite conformari huic sæculo ;* "Be not conformed to this world." In the Middle Ages, after the sacerdotal order began to be systematically united with the religious state, and men under religious rule were called to a great mission in the Church, and even at times to the pastoral care, by way of distinguishing the one class of priests from the other, the term secular, which had heretofore been limited to the laity, became attached to the diocesan clergy. From custom the designation glided into the canons, and so this infelicitous term became consecrated by ecclesiastical usage. It is not for me to censure this use, but to guard against its abuse. And the misapprehension of which I speak springs from the vague and hazy notion that the secular clergy are not called to the holy, interior, and perfect life, but that they may walk more freely in the secular path than is allowed to religious men under like circumstances. Whereas the term secular refers simply to the sphere in which their ministry is exercised. They have their work in the world, but in no sense of spiritual laxity do they belong to the world. This our Lord expressly said : "Ye are not of the world, as I am not of the world." Theology places the bishops in the highest state of perfection, and yet they have a work to do in the world that is greater than that of their clergy. The less the clergy belong to the world, the stronger they are to convert the world. It is the unworldly saints and servants of God who, in the secular priesthood, have accomplished great things for the salvation of souls ; and our Lord put the true spirit of the missionary priest before us when He said to the seventy-two : " Go : behold I send you as lambs among wolves, carry neither purse, nor scrip, nor shoes ; and salute no one on the way."

It is much to be regretted that the instructions and prayers that we hear at our ordination are not more deeply meditated on in our after-life, for there we have the true sense of the Church upon the perfection demanded of ecclesiastics. The very initiation into the clerical life so closely resembles the initiation into religious life, that their language is almost identical. It emphatically inculcates the abandonment of the secular life for a life devoted to God. In giving the tonsure the bishop implores of God that to His servants, hastening for His love to cast the hair from their head, He would give His Holy Spirit "to keep always in them the habit of religion, and to protect them from worldly hindrances and from secular desires." Whilst the hair is being cut from the crown of their head, they declare that " the Lord is the portion of their inheritance, and their

cup." Before investing with the clerical habit, the
bishop prays for blessings on them who, in God's
name, "are going to have the sacred habit of religion
put upon them;" and whilst investing them he says,
"The Lord clothe thee with the new man, who is
created in justice and holiness of truth." And finally
he prays, that "they who have cast off the *ignominy*
of the secular habit, may be cleansed from all *ser-*
vility of the secular habit." Such, my brethren, is
the Church's true sense of the ecclesiastical spirit.
When St. Francis of Sales received the tonsure, and
some who were present, struck with his demeanour,
declared that he might have been receiving the
religious habit, the saint emphatically replied, "It
is the religious habit."

The second obstacle I find on my path is the misapplication of theological light. Moral theology has
two branches; the one regards the judgment of sin,
the other the cultivation of virtue. But the first is
much more cultivated in the schools as a science
than the second. It prepares the priest to be the
judge of consciences; and under the specific name of
moral theology it teaches the commandments of God
and the Church, and the obligations of life in all its
states. Applied to individual cases, it takes the
name of casuistry. It draws the line both fine and
close between what is of obligation and what is not
of obligation; between what is of sin and what is not
of sin. The other branch is that which is properly
called spiritual or ascetical science; it fits the priest
to guide souls in the more generous way towards
God, and to build them up in virtue and holiness, for

it supplies the motives and the means for advancing in the way of perfect life.

But whilst the first of these sciences is chiefly cultivated in the schools, and afterwards kept up in the conferences, the second is not systematically taught amongst us, but is left in great measure to take care of itself, and is only obtainable by private zeal and devotion. A certain amount of spiritual reading, with but little order or method, is most commonly the sum of attainment in this direction. But is it not obvious, my brethren, that what a man has learned scientifically he will hold to the most tenaciously ? He will hold it in clear principles, in lucid order, and as a habit of the mind. He has a promptness in putting it in exercise, and the ready application of his exceptional skill in that one direction will always be to him a singular gratification. But the whole tendency of judicial theology is to draw sharp the lines between the strict obligation of duty and the liberty of taking one's own way. Reduced to its ultimate principle, it is the science of discovering the least amount of obligation and the smallest claim of duty that is consistent with an easy conscience. And when we have to judge some poor soul who has fallen into sin, or into peril of sin, and to apply the means to bring that soul back into the way of duty, nothing can be more valuable and efficacious.

But here, my brethren, is the peril and the snare ; lest, vain of our juridical light in theology, and neglecting the higher light that leads up to God, we measure the calls of duty, the precepts of authority,

and our very vocation to sanctity, by the lower light
of legal obligation rather than by the higher light of
perfection. Lest we run our course by the ropes
beyond which there is palpable offence, and not by
the rule of sanctity. Lest we comfort ourselves with
the notion that perfection is an ivy that only grows
on monastic walls. If we pervert our theological
light in analysing the claims of duty, when God is
calling us to act in all generosity and charity, instead
of rising to the mark of our supernal vocation we
shall go down and down until we touch the common
level of human weakness. Our spirit will be languid;
our ministry will suffer loss; and moanings will be
heard in the hearts of the faithful, not loud but deep.
"What a great deal of good might be done were it
not for the priest ! " If the faithful are keen though
commonly silent judges of what becomes the priest,
it is because they carry the true type of sacerdotal
sanctity in the deposit of their faith. The man of
God is he who follows the inspirations of God, which
are always generous and noble. But if we attempt,
in our theological dexterity, to run ourselves upon
the line of obligation, we shall be frequent trespassers,
and shall damage ourselves in irrecoverable ways.
The divine way open to the priest is that of holiness
and generosity.

The third obstacle of which I spoke is the practical
misconception of the character of that sanctity which
God demands of the sacerdotal order. In some
degree this arises from misconstruction of the term
secular; in some greater degree, from the misapplication of judicial theology ; but the principal

cause of the misconception is the want of clear, cogent, and definite teaching of the sense in which the Church regards the character of the priest, and what her great divines have said upon the sanctity which that character demands.

In those earlier ages of the Church when, as a common rule, the monastical and sacerdotal states were separate, the priest was held up as a model to the monk, as belonging to the higher order of sanctity of the two. We have examples of this teaching in the Dyonisian Book on the Ecclesiastical Hierarchy, in the writings of St. Jerome, of St. John Chrysostom, of St. Isidore of Pelusiote, and of other fathers. The holiest saints of the monastic life shrank from accepting the priesthood with an unspeakable reverence and fear. They saw in it a dignity so divine and an office so holy, as to exceed the strength of men and of angels. They dared not think that they could reach a sanctity commensurate with its responsibility. "Think what those hands should be," says St. Chrysostom, "and what that tongue, to utter those words. What can be thought of more pure and holy than the soul that receives so great a spirit." * "Pure even from remote imaginings should his mind be who ministers in things so divine," says the writer of the Ecclesiastical Hierarchy. "The cleric is the professor of sanctity," says St. Augustine. "A priest is nothing if he be not holy," says St. Thomas of Villanuova. "The pastors of the new law," says the Catechism of the Council of Trent, "are nearer to God, and ought to be transformed

* S. J. Chrysost., de Sacerdotio, l. vi. c. 4.

from brightness to brightness, as from the spirit of
the Lord."

The interior virtues cannot be measured, nor can
we take the quantities of spiritual perfection. For
they are the steps of the soul's progress towards the
infinite good. And yet we have a principle by which
to test the perfect disposition ; a principle that St.
Bernard never tires of teaching, nor St. Bonaventure
after him. And it is this : that to aim at perfection
and to strive after it, is taken for perfection ; whilst
not to aim and to strive after it, is to be far from it.

You, my brethren of the religious life, to whom
these principles are so familiar, can have no wish to
hold them exclusively. Rather would you say with
the prophet : " Would that all might prophesy, and
all might have the spirit of God !"

To answer the question that I have raised, I must
invoke the great divines. And first let us hear the
theologian by eminence of the best Patristic times,
and he may be accepted as representative of his
brethren. In his Apology for his flight from ordination, St. Gregory Nazianzen says : " I dare not affirm
that he who is called to form souls to virtue is
adequately prepared by keeping himself as pure as
possible from the stain of sin, unless he be well
advanced in goodness. He must expunge all evil
impressions from his soul, and write better in their
place ; so that he may proportion his virtue to the
dignity of his ministry. Nor should he set any limit
to his progress in the perfect life, but make each step
a footing from which to step on higher. Let him
make no great thing of surpassing numbers in holiness

if he still fall short of the greatness of his calling.
To measure what he owes to God Almighty, the beginning and end of all things, by comparing himself
with other men, is a poor standard for one whose
virtue should be compared with God's rule in the
Divine law." *

St. Thomas has treated the question of clerical
sanctity with his wonted precision as well in his Trac-
tate on the Perfection of the Spiritual Life as in his
Sum of Theology. Perfection, he says, consists pri-
marily in the love of God as the Supreme Good ; and
secondarily, in the direction of that love to our neighbour, with whom God has associated us, and whom
we should help with loving service towards the same
divine beatitude. This twofold love, flowing from
one principle of charity, is the true perfection of life.
But a man is carried up in the love of God in proportion as he is free from the impediment of those
other affections that war in his concupiscence. And
when he makes the three great renunciations, and
makes them permanently by vow, his renunciations
are a lifelong worship and a lifelong sacrifice ; and
if he be faithful, they put him on a permanent way
towards the interior perfection of charity. This is
the *state* of religious men, a state that aims at perfection.

But there is a higher *state* of perfection than that
of the religious man, based as it is in permanency
upon a higher principle ; and this principle is the
perfect love of souls intrusted to us in the pastoral
care. This is the state of bishops, the most perfect

* S. Greg. Nazian., Orat. i.

of human states, not only aiming at perfection, but implying perfection. The religious state rests on the permanence of a threefold renunciation made to God, that removes the obstacles to perfect charity ; the state of bishops is based on the permanence of a three-fold love of souls, committed to their charity and care by the ordinance of God. This pastoral charity con-templates those souls as God's creatures, in God's image made, and capable of God. This pastoral charity loves and does good even to them who hate and persecute. The bishop whom it animates spends himself and is spent in toil and care and suffering for the good of souls. He is the good shepherd who lays down his life for his flock. And "greater love than this no man hath, that a man lay down his life for his friends."

The religious man brings himself to God : the bishop brings himself to God, and brings many others to God. The religious man is intent on his own per-fection: the bishop is intent on perfecting many souls. The cause cannot be less than the effect, and he who perfects others must himself be perfect. Not only, then, is the state of bishops the more perfect of the two states by reason of its higher principle, but like-wise by reason of the more intense, the nobler, and the wider scope of that charity towards God in many souls, to which he is bound by his office and calling.*
After this exposition, the angelic doctor points out that, notwithstanding their respective states of per-fection, unhappily there are both religious and bishops who are far from perfect ; whilst happily there are

* S. Thom., Opusc. xvii. de Perfect. Vitæ Spiritualis, per totum.

other souls that, although outside the states of perfection, are yet actually perfect through their grace and charity. So that charity is always the test of actual perfection.

Then the luminous doctor and saint evokes another principle out of the ecclesiastical state itself as calling for perfection of soul. A participated care of souls, exercised by a priest under a bishop, may not have that permanence that constitutes a *state;* but the sacred orders themselves have a permanent and unchangeable character. Their grace, their spiritual dignity, and the relations in which they constitute us towards Christ Himself in the Holy Sacrifice, and the divine administrations, form the basis of a demand upon us for high interior perfection. So writing on the Sentences St. Thomas says : " Whosoever are devoted to the divine mysteries should be perfect in virtue." *
Again, in the Supplement to the Sum, he says : " For the rightful execution of orders common goodness will not suffice, but an excelling goodness is required." †

In his Sum of Theology, the angelic doctor thus concludes: " If a religious man be not in orders, it is clear that the dignity of the cleric surpasses that of the religious, because his order exalts him to those nobler ministrations in which Christ Himself is served at the altar ; for which a greater interior sanctity is required than the religious state requires. For which reason Dionysius says in the Ecclesiastical Hierarchy, that " the monastical order should follow the sacerdotal orders, and by imitating them ascend

* S. Thom., In Senten. d. xxiv. 9, 3.   † In Supp. 9, 35.

to divine things." Wherefore, all things else being
equal, if he who is in sacred orders does anything
against sanctity, he sins more grievously than a
religious who is not in sacred orders, even although
the religious be bound to regular observance, to which
he who is in sacred orders is not bound." * Then he
observes that priests who have care of souls in the
second place, and in dependence on their bishop,
come nearer to bishops than to religious in respect
to care of souls ; although they are less like to bishops
than religious are with respect to that perpetual obligation which a *state* of perfection requires.† Yet it is
not to be overlooked that a certain character of permanence is given to the English missionary priest, by
reason of his oath to serve the mission for life, an
obligation in bonum Ecclesiæ, from which the Holy
See can alone absolve him. ‡

The next divine whom I quote is one whose authority stands very high on spiritual questions. In his
tract on the Hierarchical States of Life, the celebrated
John Gerson says : " The state of priests having care
of souls is not merely a state of perfection to be gained,
but a state of perfection to be exercised ; forasmuch
as it not only involves the duty of bringing souls
back to God, but of purifying, illuminating, and
perfecting them by hierarchical acts. For which
reason this state is superior in the hierarchical order
of the Church to the state of simple religious."§ I

* S. Thom., 2. 2, Q. clxxxiv. a. 8.   † Ibid., ad. 5.
‡ Vide Constitut. of Alexander VII., Cum circa juramenti ; also
the Decree of Propaganda, 27th of April 1871.
§ Gerson, de Statu Curatorum.

come next to the great authority of Suarez. After
carefully investigating the question in his Treatise on
the Religious State, he concludes, that "in a certain
way the secular clergy are placed in the inchoate
state of perfection, because they have a ministry that
greatly excels, by reason of which they are obliged
to great virtue." * And treating professedly of the
state of priests with cure of souls, which he calls the
status pastoralis, he says: "In theory it may be
conceded that the pastoral state is more perfect than
the simple religious state." But he significantly adds,
that "practically that condition is rarely fulfilled." †
The Council of Trent points to the same conclusion
in saying, that " small offences in others become most
grievous in the clergy." ‡

To this teaching we may add the words of St.
Charles Borromeo, addressed to his clergy in his fourth
Council : "If," he says, "there be great sanctity
required in the other institutions of Christian piety,
assuredly ought that sanctity to be greater in you,
who are the ministers of God's mysteries and the
dispensers of His grace." Nor ought we to forget
the piercing words of that almost divine book, the
"Following of Christ:" "If thou hadst the purity of
an angel, and the sanctity of John the Baptist, thou
wouldst not be worthy to receive and handle this
sacrament. . . Behold! thou art made a priest. . .
Thou hast not lightened thy burden, but art now
bound with a stricter bond of discipline, and art
obliged to a greater perfection of sanctity."

---

* Suarez, de Statu Relig. c. 14. † Ibid., c. 21.
‡ Con. Trid. Sess. 22, c. i. de Reformat.

The conclusions I have quoted from those great
divines are not to be looked upon as mere theological
speculations. They are quoted for the guidance of
the clergy in such practical books as the "Selva" for
Clerical Retreats of St. Alphonsus ; in the "Parocho
Istruito," a book for clerical guidance esteemed at
Rome and throughout Italy ; and in the Manual of
Ecclesiastical Life drawn up for the use of the pontifical seminary of Pius IX. But let us pass to yet
higher authority.

In her sacred rites of ordination the Church has
expressed the sanctity that becomes her priests with
a most clear and constant voice. What are the seven
orders by which we slowly ascend to the sacred priesthood but so many new departures from the world,
and so many new ascents into the sanctuary, each
calling for a greater degree of sanctity, until we reach
the holy of holies. The engagement to chastity is
the equivalent of a vow. The promise of obedience
makes the canons our religious rule, and the voice of
the bishop as the voice of Christ, whose place he
holds. And St. Ambrose says, that "the form of all
justice" in the priest* includes the contempt of
money. The Church says to the priest at his ordination : "The Lord chose the seventy-two, and sent
them two and two to preach ; that in word and act
He might teach the ministers of His Church that
they ought to be perfect, founded, that is, in the
power of the twofold love of God and of our neighbour. . . . Wherefore in your conduct hold fast to
the integrity of a chaste and holy life. Understand

* S. Ambros., de Officiis.

what it is that you do. Imitate that which in your hands you hold ; so that, celebrating the mystery of the Lord's death, you may come even to the mortifying of your own members from all vices and concupiscences. Let your teaching be the healing medicine of God's people. Let the odour of your life delight the Church of Christ, that by word and by example you may build up the house which is the family of God."

In the preface the bishop prays, "that the form of all justice may shine forth in them." After investing them with the chasuble, he asks that "they may be established in those rules of discipline that Paul delivered to Timothy and Titus ;" and that with inviolable charity, full of the Holy Ghost, "they may rise up into the perfect man, unto the measure of the age of the fulness of Christ, in the day of God's just and eternal judgment." And as their ordination nears its accomplishment, they hear those tender and trusting words of their Lord : "I will no longer call you servants, but My friends ; because you have known all things that I have wrought in the midst of you."

Such, my brethren, is that type of sanctity which the Church looks for in her priests. And the more worldly the atmosphere in which their work is cast, the more they stand in need of that self-discipline which gives spiritual strength, to enable them to resist the world's influence. They need interior perfection to compensate them for what outwardly they sacrifice; they need it as a power with which to bring other souls to perfection of life. But perfection of life comes of desire, of effort, of combat, and of patient growth. We are not called without receiving the graces of our calling. God never fails us. When we fail Him, it is through departing from our interior, where light and the divine operation are left behind, and we wander abroad in extroversion of soul.

Exceedingly great is the responsibility of training our young aspirants to the sanctuary. What is planted in the root will grow up in the tree. Whilst youth is open, susceptive, and responsive, whilst habits are yet in process of formation, whilst the graces of vocation are fresh to the spiritual sense, and penetrate sharply, and wound the heart with love and wonder; let some holy man full of the sacerdotal spirit mould the young cleric to the virtues of his state, and draw up into the light the germs of sanctity which the Holy Spirit has planted in his soul. Never should the culture of his spirit be postponed to the culture of his mind. Light and holiness come from one Divine Source, and it is our duty to keep them united. What is light without force? But spiritual force lies in accumulated graces, from which comes forth the virtue to heal souls, and to enkindle in them the flame of charity. But the capacity for charity is founded in the depth of humility. And spiritual fertility is so far apart from earthly fertility, that it depends for its force on holy purity.

" The flame of the pastor is the light of the flock," says St. Gregory, "and so holy should be the life and conduct of the priest, that in him, as in a mirror, his people may see both what to follow and what to

K

shun." * Study gives knowledge, but holiness gives wisdom. Knowledge is *not* power, but the light that guides power to its aim. And what attraction is to the material world that charity is to the spiritual world ; it is the divine force that draws souls freely to God as to their centre and place of rest. One priest who works in the spirit of the God of charity will do more for His glory in saving souls than a hundred who work in their own spirit.

The "form of all justice," which the Church asks for us at our ordination, is most certainly that charity which is the bond of perfection. Coming in sweetest flame from God, it attracts us to ascend from virtue to virtue until we reach its very fountain. "This charity," says St. Augustine, "is the truest, fullest, and most perfect justice ;"† and to that justice of charity is the pastoral priest more fully bound than other Christians, forasmuch as our Lord has based the pastoral care in love of Himself ; and the dignity of the sacred ministry and the character of the priesthood in a nearer reflection of His own eternal office. The priest who loves perfectly will do great things and count them little ; will do many things and count them few ; will work a long time and count it short ; for to him, as to Jacob, the days will seem few by reason of the greatness of his love.

May charity sign our decrees ; and the Holy Spirit seal them with His wisdom ! May the unction of Jesus bring them into the hearts to which they are directed, and His blood make them fruitful !

* S. Greg., Mag. in Registro.
† S. Aug., L. de Nat. et Gratia, c. 42.

VII.

Science and Wisdom,

A First Discourse to the Clerics of St. Bernard's Seminary.

"By wisdom shall the house be built, and by prudence it shall be strengthened. By instruction shall the store-rooms be filled with precious and most beautiful wealth."—PROVERBS xxiv. 3.

VERY ancient, my brethren, is that form of speech by which the house is taken for the family. Before the days of Solomon the word house was used to express the family of Abraham, and, long before his time, to express the family of Noah. To this day, men who have an ancestry speak of their house when they mean their family. What the life is to the body, that the family is to the house, and it is of the family that Solomon speaks when he tells us, that the house is built up by wisdom, and strengthened by prudence, and, to put the Hebrew and Syriac texts together, through doctrine and science is filled with beautiful and precious wealth. In this inspired description you have set before you some noble Hebrew family, whose sons are slowly built up like the gradual rising of a mansion in the wisdom of the Scriptures and the expositions of the doctors.

Every text of the Old Testament opens to us a diviner sense through the light of the New Testament, and it can scarcely fail to strike your minds that this description offers a portrait of the spirit that should distinguish the ecclesiastical seminary. The seminary is the bishop's family, and its members are his spiritual sons; to whom he may well say with Solomon : " My sons, study wisdom, and make my heart joyful, that you may give an answer to him who reproacheth me." To you, looking onwards to the sanctuary, come the words of the prophet : " The lips of the priest shall keep knowledge, and they shall seek the law from his mouth; because he is the messenger of the Lord of Hosts." To you is the divine admonition directed : " If thou reject knowledge, I will reject thee, that thou perform not the priesthood unto Me." Wherefore, my sons : " Understand the fear of the Lord, and find out the knowledge of God : because the Lord giveth wisdom : and out of His mouth cometh prudence and knowledge. He guardeth the salvation of the righteous, and protecteth them who walk in simplicity, keeping the paths of justice, and guarding the ways of the saints."

This seminary is the seed plot from which should spring into the diocese ecclesiastical life and vigour. Whosoever are called to co-operate in its foundation, whether founders or contributors, whether superiors, professors or students, are doing a work for the future enlightenment of the diocese, of which only those who come after us will be able to estimate the value. Thus far it is but a seminal principle, one of those small and humble beginnings that carry hope rather than performance in its bosom. But God's designs are eternal, and we are of a day; and what He destines for long growth and large expansion, He sets down in small beginnings. Out of the humblest elements, He creates the greatest things. Haste has in it a violence that belongs to human weakness, and what springs up in haste runs rapidly to decay. God's works are founded in secret, they grow up in secret, and they show their strength with time. Planting the germ in silent obscurity, and surrounding it with nourishment, He sends down His silent influence upon it, and leaves the rest to patience and the years. But this we can with certainty predict, that unless the seed be good, neither the growth nor the fruit will be satisfactory.

Of this seminary you are the first plants, planted by our Heavenly Father, who provides it with truth for light, with charity for an atmosphere, and with the fountains of science for its irrigation. Open your minds to know, and your hearts to feel; that your mental and moral growth depends for the rest on your own good will. The provisions for your cultivation are bountiful, but everything must still depend on your own generosity. If you heartily respond to the rules of discipline, to the exertions of your teachers, and the paternal authority of your superior, then is the future of this seminary secured. For need I remind you that as the Church in its beginning was virtually contained in the twelve apostles, the future of this seminary is virtually contained in you. Whoever come later will graft themselves on your spirit, and will take their tone from the habits

and traditions they find already prevailing. Cherish-
ing the consciousness of your vocation, its light and
its grace, keep steadily in mind what is expected of
you. By your docility and discipline be the good
foundation of this house, that, by wisdom it may be
built, by prudence strengthened, and by instruction
the store-rooms of your minds may be filled with
spiritual wealth.

When I called the seminary the episcopal family,
I used the language of the Church, and spoke her
sense. The rector represents the episcopal authority,
and the professors the episcopal teaching ; and when
the clerics respond to that authority with reverence,
and to that teaching with docility, they bend themselves to the paternal authority of their bishop, and
in bending to him with reverential docility, which is
another name for clerical humility, they hear and
obey the Church of Christ. For the old maxim of the
Fathers is always fresh and new, that "the Church is
in the bishop and the bishop in the Church," and
that "where is the bishop, there is the Church."
For this reason the apostolic bishop and martyr St.
Ignatius says : "Let nothing be done without the
bishop ; " and again : " As the cords are fitted to the
harp, so are the priests and deacons fitted to the
bishop, that they may accord together in harmony."

You have been studying that mental and moral
philosophy which prepare the way to theology. That
science has taught you to understand your own mental
and moral faculties, their objects, their order, their
operations, the corporal powers which serve or obstruct
them, and the laws of their right and accurate use.

But you will take a very defective measure of the value of this science, if you look upon it as no more than an instrument to train you to the skilful use of your faculties. When rightly pursued and properly applied, the chief value of philosophy is the knowledge it gives us of ourselves and of the objects most worthy to be sought. The very word philosophy— the love of wisdom—expresses these two aims. And the whole scope of the ancient pagan philosophy was expressed in these two maxims: " Know thyself: " " Seek the Supreme Good." Philosophy, pursued in the light of nature, leads on to the desire of more light, and of clearer knowledge both of the Supreme Good and of ourselves ; and this can come only of God's revelation. Hence Plato's advice, that we must wait for some Divine One to teach us. For after all its searchings and investigations, the eye of our natural understanding finds itself bounded by a horizon beyond which it has not power to penetrate ; whilst from what we know already, as well as from the yearnings within us for greater knowledge, we gain the intimate conviction that beyond that horizon, due to the limitation of our natural powers, those greater truths are to be found which bear upon our life and make known to us our good, but which we cannot reach without greater mental strength, more abundant light, and a divine revelation. The true philosopher, the real searcher after wisdom, divines this want of a revelation from the very nature of the truth that he already sees, from the unsatisfied capacity of his mind, from the instincts, wants, and aspirations of his moral nature, from the view he has already obtained of a First Cause and a Supreme Good, and from the unsatisfying and disappointing character of everything that falls short of a Supreme Cause to satisfy the intellect, and of a Supreme Good to content the heart. And when he examines the traditions of the human race, he finds his conclusions confirmed by the universal voice of his fellow-men, proclaiming that God has from time to time revealed the knowledge of Himself to mankind. Let me dwell for a moment on the testimony which the natural reason finds in the attributes of that truth which comes within its sphere. The several truths that reason beholds are found to be universal and unlimited in their character, unchangeable in their forms, and spiritual in their nature; yet having a wonderful tendency to unite, and to ascend from lower into loftier generalisations; so that if, in philosophic contemplation, we ascend from truth to truth, we find the higher truth including the lower truth, and ever as it ascends into higher generalisation, truth becomes more simple, pure, universal and absolute, containing the inferior truths, as light contains the colours. This sublime ascent of truth leads us up in search of the First Cause; and as our moral instinct tells us that truth is a radiation from good, it leads us in search of the Supreme Good.

From this high aim the ancient philosophy never descended, nor the philosophy of the Christian schools. It remained for the moderns to degrade the name of philosophy by applying that name to the pursuit of the material and physical sciences. Aristotle tells us that the end and aim of philosophy is

the Supreme Good. Varro told the whole history
of philosophy, when he classified its systems to
his time by their difference of view with respect to
the Supreme Good. And Seneca asserted that it is
the nature of philosophy to seek the Supreme Good.
The older Italian philosophy of Pythagoras joined a
severe moral discipline to its mental efforts with a
view to the same end. The Oriental philosophies
did not differ in this respect from the Greek. Wilder
they might be, and from the predominance of imagination over the light of intellectual distinction, more
inclined to pantheistic conclusions; but their pro-
fessed aim was to seek after wisdom, and to seek the
crown of wisdom in the Supreme Good.

Finding the scope of its vision so limited in comparison with the signs of infinite truth that lie beyond
its reach, so limited in comparison with the aspirations and unsated wants of the soul, true philosophy
ever culminates in the desire of a revelation. It ends
in the cry for more light, more truth, more good.
And as reason has reached its extreme horizon
where doubt contends with certainty, the true philosopher, after reaching the summits of his natural
light, longs to hear the God of nature speak, and to
listen to Him as the Supreme Master of truth. He
is conscious that where human reason begins to fail,
it is the most reasonable of all things to accept the
divine reason on its own authority. When once,
however, the voice of divine reason is heard through
revelation, and with grateful and submissive faith
accepted, it is wonderful how that revelation of the
divine reason expands and exalts the natural reason

of man, and to what an extent it explains the source and character of his reason.

How many of the illustrious Fathers of the Church were drawn by their study of philosophy to the Christian faith! In Christ they found all, and far more than all, that to which in their philosophic investigations they had aspired. Embracing the humility of Christ, towards which fidelity to their natural light had disposed them, to their rapt wonder and amazement they found open to them a light and a science so far beyond the anticipations of reason, yet to their reason so consonant, of their reason such a nourishment and confirmation, whilst it explained to them the whole mystery both of this life and the life to come. Far, however, were the converted Fathers from relinquishing philosophy when they took to theology. By the light of God's revealed reason they purified their natural reason, corrected its former errors where the subjective frailty of the man had misled them, and devoted that reason, increased in light and strength, to the service of religion. This process gives a singular charm to the earlier writings of St. Augustine and to the works of Clement of Alexandria. It was the combination of philosophic with religious science that gave the Fathers skill and power to combat the errors of their time, whether pagan theories or heresies dissolving the principle of faith.

On the other hand, we see men in almost every age importing false philosophies into the Church, and, by applying them to the interpretation of the mysteries of revelation, generating the most revolting

errors, and the most desolating heresies; and it
would be difficult to point to any great heresy that
has not some false philosophy at the root of it. To
find that false philosophic principle is to obtain the
key to the heresy.

Examine whatever false theories you will affecting
the nature of God, or the relations between God and
His creatures, and on examination you will find that
the author of each, whoever he may have been, first
erred in his pride as to the just respects of human
reason towards God's revelation, and as to the becoming posture of the human mind towards the divine
authority. You have an awful example of this in
Abelard, who, although he prefaces his system with
the principles of intellectual humility, casts them at
once aside, and proceeds to measure God's eternal
mysteries upon the scale of his human intelligence.
The abuse of philosophy leads to the abuse of theology: and hence the Church has watched with as
much solicitude over the philosophy as over the
theology taught in her schools.

If St. Augustine commends the philosophy of
Plato, he commends the good side of it that led
him to search for revelation. If St. John Chrysostom
inveighs with vehemence against that philosophy, he
condemns the bad side of it, which gave occasion to
errors so numerous and fatal. Carried away by his
vivid imagination, Plato ventured on speculations
that reason could neither confirm nor follow, whilst
bereft of that revelation for which he longed, he had
not the light of divine reason with which to correct
his aberrations. Hence the schools adopted his

great disciple Aristotle as the sounder and more sober expositor of human reason, whose philosophy, Christianised, so to speak, by St. Thomas, became a valuable servant to the Church.

There are three reasons why a priest should possess himself of that sound philosophy which the great thinkers of the Church have matured. The first is his own enlightenment, that he may develop his mental and moral powers, and gain skill in the use of his light. And here I pause to express a surprise that has held me for so many years, and will never, I think, abandon me. It is wonderful how few clerics in comparison with their numbers, ever enter into the delight of this science, or return to it after their course of study is over. So true, as a rule, is it, that the last thing a man is inclined to is to reflect upon his own nature, and the last thing he cares to know is himself. I know that there are minds, and not a few of them, so constituted, that they have but little natural inclination to this kind of study. Their power of intuition is feeble, their light for generalisation is low, they live much in sense and little in mind, their turn is for the concrete, for the sensible world and its particular facts. These are the men who, unless they have great piety, have but small interior resources, or none. With the helps extended to them they might rise higher in thought, but they will seldom take the pains or give the labour. And yet he who can understand the elements of theology, or even the first chapter of the catechism, ought surely to be able to comprehend the elements of philosophy, provided he be attentive and patient in taking the first mental steps. The difference between a philosophic and an unphilosophic mind is this, that the one thinks by principles and the other loads itself with undigested details. A principle well gained and well applied is like a fixed star in the mind that illuminates many things. And the secret of scientific study is to get at the principle of the subject, to examine the details by the light of that principle, and thus the whole subject becomes orderly, luminous, and a clear mental possession.

The second reason why a priest should cultivate a sound knowledge of philosophy is this, that theology is based as well on the knowledge of man as on the knowledge of God. Moreover, theology proceeds upon philosophic methods, and employs philosophic language; so that without accurate knowledge of this science the student of theology must be frequently at fault. What is the main conflict of the Church in this epoch? Is it not the conflict with false philosophies? Have we not a flood of writers and talkers who sap the foundations both of revelation and of reason until infidelity has become a social fashion and a boast? And how will you get at the foundations of all this false science except through the knowledge and skill of true science? I have only to point to the first dogmatic constitution of the Vatican Council to shew how the Church feels that in this age her first contention is with the abuse of reason; and that, as in the days of her contest with paganism, philosophy must become the assiduous servant of theology.

The third reason, and the most important is this,

that, as a director of souls, the priest ought to be intimately conversant with the interior powers of man, with the nature of their operations, with their mutual dependencies, and the action and re-action upon each other of the spiritual and sensual forces. He who best understands the complicated elements that move in man will best guide him on the spiritual path ; and supposing him to be a spiritual man, will the most ably guide him through his difficulties. If St. Thomas borrowed so much light from philosophy to illustrate theology, St. John of the Cross and St. Francis of Sales are almost as deeply indebted to that science for the explanation of God's interior ways in the soul. And who that knows the history of St. Teresa, does not remember that interesting moment of her life, when at last she got the key to the understanding of herself from a devout scientific director, who explained to her that the imagination comes not of the intellect but of the corporal senses? Who does not remember her frequent declaration that from her own experience she knew that the safe directors were the men of science? For a priest to neglect the science of the human faculties and powers appears to me as senseless as for a medical man to throw aside the study of anatomy and physiology. And this leads me to observe that the latter science is not without great value in direction, for many a trouble of the soul takes its rise from physical causes that are mistaken for spiritual ones; and when they are well understood, and properly managed for what they are, they no longer disturb the peace of the conscience.

When science puffs up and fills the heart with conceit, it is because that science is not ruled by wisdom.
Wisdom is the balsam that keeps science from corruption. But for wisdom we must go to God. That
man is still a barbarian in science who does not
understand the source of the mental light with which
he works. Ignorance of the fontal source of our intellectual light, and the absence of due reflection upon
it, are the causes of all that mental egotism, and of
those desolating errors that have usurped the name
of philosophy. Yet the wiser pagan philosophers,
Socrates, and Plato, and Aristotle, had discovered
the truth that man is not the author but the recipient
of his mental light. When this is once discovered,
the understanding begins to comprehend herself, and
her dependence, and the modesty that truth demands
of her. This is the beginning of wisdom, to know
what we are, and to know what we receive, and from
what or from whom we receive it. This was the
divine philosophy of the Hebrews, as clearly expressed
in the Psalms as in the sapiential books, and still
more explicitly put forth in the Gospel of St. John.
There can be but little doubt that the wiser Greeks
had come into some kind of contact with this divine
philosophy of the Hebrews, and we know that they
sought wisdom from the Oriental nations.

God has given us a magnificent illustration of our
mental light in the material light through which we
see the visible world. How is it that with an organ
so small as the eye in our head, an organ not half-an-
inch in breadth, we are able to take into our mind
the vast expanse of this visible creation, with all that

it contains? How is it that from the eye the vision
passes to the brain, and so to the mind, by a nerve
that is an almost invisible thread? It is by the gift
of light. Light is the middle term between us and
every visible thing. Light reflects to us each object
in nature, and brings the knowledge of its presence
to the mind. Light not only exhibits the presence of
things, but their distinctions, their divisions, their dis-
tributions, and their relations with each other. Light
is the great revealer, the interpreter, the beautifier
and the harmoniser of the creation. Light is the
unitive principle that brings what is remote, what is
distant, what is intermediate, and what is near us
into one ; yet always through the co-operation of the
mind that views them. The element of light through
its colours reflects to us the various qualities of things.
Light, in short, is the messenger to the mind from
all the facts that exist in the material world ; not that
it brings to us the facts themselves, but the truthful
forms of the facts, giving us full security for their
existence, however rightly or wrongly we may put
our own interpretations upon them.

Where is the source of light? It is not in us, it
is not in the earthly things that it reflects. Its source
and fountain is placed in the heavens, at an unimaginable distance from us. One sun is the illuminator of
all men, and reflects to the mind of each the vision
of the whole creation around him. The curtain of
clouds cast up from the earth may conceal the sun
from our sight, but his more temperate rays illuminate
us still. Even the orb that glimmers in the night but
reflects to us in more feeble light the rays of the

departed sun. An image of the state of man when, deprived of the direct light of revelation which directly reveals the Divine Author of truth, he is left to the reflected light of his reason, waxing and waning amidst the shadows and obscurations of nature.

What is, and whence comes, our artificial light, as we call it? It is the light imbibed from the sun in forests, flowers, rocks, and animal life. You will remember Stephenson's conversation with his friend on the line. "What," he asked, "is carrying us so fast along?" "One of your engines," was the reply. "And what moves the engine?" "Oh, I suppose the steam." "No," he said, "it is the sun"—the power of the sun stored up in the coal. Whether directly given from the sun, or reflected from the moon, or stored up from the solar rays in the crypts and cells of nature for our use, the sun is the original source of material light to man. Such is the word of science : and such is God's care of His creatures.

The sun is the poet of the creation, beautifying and giving splendour to the things of this earth—a truth the ancients felt when they personified him in the graceful and eloquent Apollo. His light interprets the works of God to our intelligence, and is the chief provider of imagery to our mind. Light, again, is the unitive principle : with the human mind to co-operate, it brings the several objects of the landscape into fellowship and harmony. But this is not all. As, to use the words of St. Paul, "from things invisible all things visible were made," the visible universe is full of signs and traces of the Supreme Intelligence who gave it existence; and the visible

L

forms of things brought to our eyes by the light, and purified in our mind, become the figures and illustrations of spiritual things, and as such are employed in our spiritual thinking, and in our modes of expressing the things that belong to our intellectual perceptions.

We may now turn from the exterior to the interior world, from sense to mind, and from the material to the intellectual light. Yet ought we to carry along with us what has been said of the material light, because it is the outward and visible image of the intellectual light.

However enormous the disproportion may be between the eye and its range of vision, it is explained by the intervention of light. And however amazing the disproportion between the mental sight of the individual man and the universal truth, it is explained by the presence of a spiritual light, analogous to our material light, but in its nature far more wonderful. The very thought of our dependence on this light brings man down to his littleness and divests him of his conceit. For as the eye neither creates the light nor the landscape, the mental eye neither creates the truth nor the light by which the truth is illuminated. As without material light the eye would be in darkness, so without mental light the mind would be in darkness. Can that which is limited produce what is unlimited? Can that which is changeable produce what is unchangeable? Can what is particular produce that which is universal? Yet in every general truth we contemplate something that is fixed, certain, universal, unlimited, unchangeable, and eternal, one and the same to every mind that sees it clearly. And

what we thus affirm of every truth, we equally affirm
of the relations between truth and truth. Let us
ask then with holy Job, "Where is the way where
light dwelleth? And where is the place of darkness?
That thou mayest bring everything to its bounds,
and understand the way of its dwelling." *

The wisest sages of antiquity divined the source
of this light. The Scriptures of the Old and New
Covenant reveal it. The Fathers of the Church
expound it. The Catholic philosophers and divines
have reduced it to a system. And, to use the words
of the Church, the Council of the Vatican, after
speaking of the light of revelation as "the light of
most pure faith," declares, that "the same God who
revealeth mysteries and infuseth faith, hath put the
light of reason into the human mind." † From which
it concludes that, as God cannot contradict Himself,
faith and reason cannot contradict each other; but
that where there is contradiction, either the faith has
not been rightly understood, or opinion has been
mistaken for reason. We have thus a guiding star
by whose light we may proceed in safety. To speak
with the Fathers, there is one sun of all intelligences,
one primal source of all intellectual light. If it were
not so, how could truth be one? Why do we always
reason on the one incontrovertible principle that truth
is intolerant of contradiction? And why do men,
to close every question as to their veracity, exclaim
by an instinct of nature that—It is God's truth?

As we are illustrating reason from theology, let

* Job xxxviii. 29, 30.
† Constit. De Fide Cathol. cap. 4, De Fide et Ratione.

us first look to the Divine Fountain of intellectual light. "God is light," says St. John, "and in Him there is no darkness." And the consubstantial Word of the Father is "the Light of light." We will pass over that wonderful chapter in the Book of Wisdom, which describes the illumination of man as the work of Divine and Eternal Wisdom, and come to the beginning of the Gospel of St. John. "In the beginning was the Word, and the Word was with God, and the Word was God. . . . All things were made by Him, and without Him was made nothing that was made. In Him was life, and the life was the light of men ; and the light shineth in darkness, and the darkness did not comprehend it. . . . That was the true light, which enlighteneth every man coming into this world." Not only the Christian man, by the light of faith, but every man coming into the world, by the light of reason, does the Eternal Word illuminate. But with the natural man "the light shineth in darkness, and the darkness doth not comprehend it." The natural man does not comprehend that he would be darkness, did not the Creative Word give him light. And, again, he does not comprehend who it is that gives him light. There are two lights given to man from one primal cause, the light of reason and the light of faith ; but each of these lights has its own principle, its own object, and its own way of coming to the soul.

Let us first consider the natural light of reason. St. Augustine had constantly to reproach the Manicheans that they could not distinguish between the light which is God, and the light which God creates. The intellectual light which God puts into the mind at its creation, and which constitutes his reason, is a light created by the Uncreated Word, an image and a reflection, limited in its nature, of the Uncreated Light. Shining in our darkness, it makes us in the image of God. To use the expressions of St. Augustine and St. Thomas, this light of reason contains the primary or seminal principles of truth and justice. And Leibnitz has made the profound remark, that, when we say there is nothing in the intellect that was not first in the senses, we must except the intellect itself. An effect cannot be greater than its cause. How, then, can universals be extracted from particulars? Sense gives us the principle of individualisation, as St. Thomas observes; universalisation must come from another cause, and that cause is in the rational light. The function of sensible facts is to awaken the intellect, to bring it into action, and to furnish those images and forms which are illuminated and rendered universal by the principles contained in the mental light. The mode of contact between the forms of particular things and universals is one of the greatest mysteries of science. What we can say with certainty is this, that particulars come of the senses and universals of the light of reason. But remembering that colours presented from individual objects to the eye are limitations of the pure light, and yet are light, so, it may be, that specific forms brought into contact with the intellectual light are so informed by that light as to partake of its universality. St. Thomas says, " The forms abstracted from sense have the principle of their intelligibility in the light of the active intellect."

The light of reason is not a direct but a reflected light, as light is reflected on the earth when the sun is hidden in the clouds ; or, to use the illustration of St. Basil and St. Gregory Nazianzen, as the sun is reflected in the waters. The difference between the reflected light of reason, and the direct, though obscure light of faith, is well expressed by St. Augustine, comparing his mental state before and after his conversion. " I read," he says, " whatever books I could obtain on the liberal arts, and I understood them without help, and enjoyed them, yet I knew not whence the truth came, and the certainty that I found in them. Because my back was to the light, and my face was directed only to the things illuminated." * " But," he continues further on, " my rational mind, as it then was, knew not that it stood in need of another light to make it partaker of the truth. For Thou wilt light my lamp, O Lord God; Thou wilt enlighten my darkness; and of Thy fulness have we all received." †

The opinion that in this mortal life we see the truth in God Himself, whether in the natural or revealed light, is a dangerous illusion, fraught with the most fanatical enthusiasm, and the Church has in her wisdom condemned it. Against this error you will nowhere find more forcible arguments than in St. John Chrysostom's series of discourses against the Anomœans. The light which is God is His Divine Substance, which no man hath seen at any

* S. Aug. Confess., L. 4, c. 15.   † Ibid., L. 4, c. 25.

time. "Reason is the light of my mind," says the most accurate St. Gregory Nazianzen.* Implanted in the soul at its creation, the light of reason slumbers in the child until it is awakened to action, first by the objects of sense, then by the voice of instruction, afterwards by its own free energy. Recalling what we have said of its analogy with sensible light, in explaining the distinction between the potential and the active intellect, between the *intellectus possibilis* and the *intellectus agens*, St. Thomas thus illustrates the one from the other.

The eye of man has a capacity for light, and for beholding, in that light, the colours and forms reflected from objects. This is the *sensus possibilis*, the potency or capacity of a sense not yet brought into action. When the eye is filled with light, the images of things in that light awaken attention; the will sets the eye on observation; it becomes active; it compares one object present in the light with another, puts them in their order and dependence, and stores them in the memory. This is the *sensus agens*, the active sense, or vision. In like manner is the mind potential as to all knowable truth; this is the *intellectus possibilis*, capacity not yet brought into action, or not brought into action with respect to this or that truth. But when the mental eye is awakened by its proper light, and in that light the forms or ideas of truth are presented, the mind becomes attentive, compares truth with truth, and stores the contemplated truths in the memory. This is the *intellectus agens*, bringing the

* S. Greg. Naz. Iambic, 15.

potential intellect into activity, and making it receptive of the intelligible forms of truth. And as the images presented to the eye in colours require a certain amount of light in which they appear, so the forms abstracted from sense and raised in the mind, have the principle of their intelligibility in the light of the active intellect. "Hence," concludes St. Thomas, "there is nothing to prevent our ascribing the action of the active intellect to the very light of our soul, especially as Aristotle compares the active intellect to light."

As all eyes have not the same powers of vision, it is the office of the active intellect to proportion light to capacity. Weak eyes see best in a feebler light, and strong eyes in a brighter light. The eagle sees far and near in the open sunlight, the owl can but see things near at hand, and that in the obscure night, amidst the shadows of the earth. And we must remember that God can always give greater strength to the sight to see in a greater light, whether natural or supernatural, as He does when He gives us internal strength to see in the light of revelation. But St. Thomas concludes that the little light which is connatural to man, the light of reason put into the human mind at its creation, is sufficient to make him intelligent. This light, he observes, is not external to his mind, nor in another subtance ; it is *in* the mind and *of* the mind, yet the active intellect cannot exceed the measure of its light.*

When St. Thomas ascends from reason to revelation, he leaves all hesitation behind, and plainly tells

* St. Thomas, Summa Contra Gent., L. 2, c. 76–78.

us that "the light which appertains to the mind is
nothing other than a certain manifestation of the
truth," and quotes St. Paul, who says, "All that
is manifest is light."* And St. Augustine constantly affirms that there is nothing between the
manifestation of truth and the mind that beholds
it. And now, under guidance of the Angelic
Doctor, may we ascend anew to the First Cause of
all our knowledge, and learn the sense in which the
Scripture teaches that "the Lord is the God of
sciences."

The teacher moves the mind of the scholar; but,
as the Psalmist sings, "it is God who teaches man
knowledge." God therefore moves the human intelligence. As in every order of things secondary
causes depend on the first cause, the Divine Being
who gives the mind its potency to know, and
imprints on that mind the similitude of things
knowable, is the First Cause of our knowledge. He
who creates all things existing creates them after
the forms that have always pre-existed in His own
mind, and from Him they are derived into other
minds, so that they may be understood, being
received into created minds, that after their manner
they may subsist in them. God therefore moves the
human intelligence in so far as He gives it natural
or supernatural force to understand, and in so far as
He imprints on it the intelligible forms of truth, and
sustains and preserves them in existence. We must
therefore conclude, that although the operations of
the mind are from the mind itself as their second

* Sum. p. 1, q. 106, a. 1.

cause, they are from God as their First Cause. And so, to finish this exposition in the exact words of St. Thomas, " the intellectual light with the similitude of things is the sufficient principle of knowledge ; yet this is the secondary principle dependent on the First Principle. But the similitudes of things as imprinted by God on the created intelligence are not adequate to make God known to us in His essence. God moves the created intelligence without making Himself visible to that intelligence." *

My object in putting this exposition before you is not to teach you the science of the mind,—that you learn from your own professors. My object is to show you how you may obtain the greatest help and advantage from applying the science of the mind to the regulation of the mind, and to the formation of its habits. Coming, therefore, to the practical, in connection with the exposition already given, I will say something on the principle of study, on the spirit of study, on the method of study, and on the fruit of study.

The principle of study is expressed in the definition of knowledge. Knowledge is defined by St. Thomas to be the equalising of the mind with the truth. But desultory knowledge does not equalise the mind with the truth ; it gives the mind at best but the broken lights and fragments of truth. The mind is equalised with the truth when it possesses the order of truth, and sees the details of truth in the light of their principle. The order of truth is its great intrinsic evidence. For order is to truth

* Sum. p. I, q. 105, a. 3.

what justice is to law, and what harmony is to beauty. It is the primary law of truth. To know this or that truth is a great gain; but sometimes it is a great trial, from not being able to reconcile this detached truth with that, as not having the light common to both in which they find their accord. But to know truth in its order is to equalise the mind with the truth, because then we see the subordinate details as they are harmonised and accorded in their principle. This is scientific knowledge. It is to know truth in its principles, correlations, and dependencies. Science is the knowledge of truth in that order, juxtaposition, and sequence in which the objective truth exists in itself, and in which it is presented to our mind for investigation.

The mind is the recipient of truth, but it is the living, intelligent, and co-operative recipient, and therefore so much depends on the moral conduct of the mind in its pursuit and use of truth. As truth itself is most pure, most calm, and perfect in order, it demands that the faculties to which it is addressed be purified, calmed, and regulated. Order alone can reflect order. But to regulate our faculties well we must understand them, and know what they are, what they can do, and what they cannot do, what God does for them, and what, if we seek His help, He may enable us to do. What a light is thrown on the principle of study after you have realised to yourself habitually that God is the first cause of knowledge and man the second cause ; that God gives to the mental vision its force, and its light, and in the light the truth, whilst the effectual co-operation of the mind depends on its calmness and purity, and upon the attention, concentration, motion, penetration, patience, and perseverance with which the will energises the mind. To the elucidation of this principle we shall devote our second discourse.

Habitual realisation of the principle of study will inspire the true spirit of study. To equalise the mind with the truth demands the subjection of the understanding to the light of truth. For truth is from above, and the understanding is beneath it as its subject. The potential intellect or understanding has to be brought face to face with the active intellect, in which is the intellectual light, placed in and made of the mind, in which its Divine Author presents the truth for our contemplation. But truth is the master and we are the subject; truth the giver, we the receiver; truth the illuminator, our understanding the darkness illuminated; and veiled behind the truth, yet manifested in the truth, is the Divine Author of truth, who presents it in a created form to our understanding. How admirably does our English word *understanding* express its own function, for to understand is to stand under, to be subject, submissive, and obedient to the truth. Wherefore the true spirit of study is intellectual humility. Our Lord expressed this when He said, "Be ye children of the light." This humbleness of spirit cleanses the mental eye from egotistical films, and from the images of conceit, and opens it to the light. It frees the soul from the vapours steaming up through the imagination from the senses, and purges the mental vision from the cloud of prejudgments, so that like an unprejudiced

child we may come unfettered into the serene and
majestic presence of truth. And when this humility
possesses the heart as well as the mind, the whole
man is placed in his rightful posture towards the
Divine Giver of our light. St. Dorotheus has expressed what we would say in the profound maxim,
that "humility opens, but pride shuts up the soul."

No one who has not put it to practical experience
can understand how the mind advances in the light
of truth when prayer is mingled with study, and when
the understanding makes frequent ascents to God as
the Author of light and truth, and the First Cause of
knowledge. For "with Thee is the fountain of life,"
says the Psalmist, "and in Thy light shall we see
light." This is expressed in the two maxims—" Seek
truth from God," and, "Think in the presence of
God." When we think in God, we are on the side of
truth ; thought itself becomes a kind of prayer, and
God increases our light. But the habit of subjecting
our mind to God depends on the control of the will,
as the will itself depends for its strength and steadfastness on the energising grace which prayer obtains.
It is this dependence of the mind on the will in its
voluntary operations that makes us morally respon-
sible for the relations of our mind towards truth and
error.

As the object of our mental appetite, God has given
to His truth a certain delight, of which the more we
taste the more the desire of it grows ; so that the
possession of it comes to be loved by them who earnestly seek it, both because in itself it is beautiful and
magnificent, and because it beautifies, amplifies, and

frees the mind, and reflects that good of which our heart is in search, and leads us towards that Supreme Good of which every truth gives us some sign or reflection, greater or less according to its character. But of this we shall treat in our third discourse.

From the spirit of study we are led to the method of study. And here we must remember that the understanding has to deal with its own subjective agents and elements, which, if not kept in control, are often antagonists to the truth, as well as with her objective light. It has to deal with what both the external and internal senses present, not unfrequently with troublesome importunity, with what the imagination presents, with what books present, with what voices other than its own present, and also with what memory presents from its wonderful storehouse. All subjects thus presented the understanding must bring under the light of truth for its judgment and decision. This is reflection. It is the act of comparing whatever enters the mind with the light of universal truth. If that light affirms the subject, it is just or true. If that light contradicts it, it is unjust or untrue, or both. "Thy judgments go forth as the light," says the Prophet Osee. And our Lord says, "He that doeth truth cometh to the light, that his works may be made manifest, of what sort they are."

But the successful examination of any subject depends on three things. First, on the amount of our light with respect to that subject. Secondly, on the degree of attention that we give to it ; and this implies the calm, patient, and steadfast concentration of the understanding on the subject brought under your light.

Thirdly, on the due order of proceeding from truth to truth, passing from what is known to what is less known, and so to what is unknown. When you have mastered the principle comprised in the definition, which is the method of the schools, you will find it become like a fixed star to your mind, illuminating all the details as they arise in succession, whilst the details will illustrate the principle. This is the method *à priori* employed where science rests on known and unchangeable principles. But where subjects or questions are yet uninvestigated or unlocated, then the method *à posteriori* will have to be adopted, ascending from point to point in the way of search until the principle is found that gives light to the question, and determines what truth, or what degree or order of truth, there may be in that question. When you are able to see your subject in its distinctions, details, and dependencies by the light of its principles, you are in the intellectual possession of that subject. Yet you will be far from having a comprehensive view of that subject, unless you know the relations it holds with cognate subjects, and what dependence its principle may have on higher principles.

What makes a mind high and noble is the habit of thinking by principles and of acting on principles. What makes a mind large and fertile is not analysis, but the synthesis that should follow analysis. In the ordinary methods of teaching this second process is too much neglected. The process of analysis is generally followed in class, that of synthesis in lectures. Analysis gives detailed and accurate knowledge; synthesis gives large and comprehensive knowledge. The one is minute; the other elevated and constructive. Acute men are analytic; eloquent men, and men of genius, are synthetic and constructive. When a subject has been examined in its parts, so that each joint and division of it has received its proper light, the next process is to reconstruct the whole, so that from its central light or principle the subject may be illuminated throughout; after which should come that more ample synthesis in which the higher principles and broader relations are brought to converge upon the subject for its greater illustration.

To give an easy exemplification of the two processes, take a watch. You know its exterior, and its use, and have some vague notions about its construction. Under the guidance of a skilful watchmaker, examine the watch in all its parts and dependencies from the spring to the pointers; examine each part of the interesting machine separately, and the relation of that part with every other part, and with the whole. Having thus brought each part under the material light, and so under your mental light, construct the watch anew, and henceforth it will be full of light to you. The light, however, is not in the watch, but in your mind. Its beautifully-regulated movements have the spring for their principle and prime mover; but if you would reach a higher synthesis, you must study the nature of steel and the laws that regulate its elasticity, and will then reach the principle that the elasticity of steel is the motive-power of the watch, whilst the correlative know-

ledge will embrace the arts concerned in the production of the other elements that enter into the
composition of the watch.

Take an abstruse subject, the subject of divine
grace, for example. It forms a most important
section of theology. You begin with its definition,
the distinction into its various kinds, and the proofs
of them. You next consider the divers heresies
opposed to grace, and their refutations; after which
come the internal controversies on the more abstruse
and obscure questions that have arisen, and which
bear upon its nature, its modes of operation, its relations to free-will and to human co-operation. This
is the analytic process. But when, after this analysis,
we resume the sacred subject synthetically, we find
that it embraces all the supernatural operations of
God in human souls, in the angels and in the spirits
beatified. It pervades the whole sphere of theology, in one relation or another, whether dogmatical,
moral, ascetical or pastoral. On the side of God
grace leads us into the whole mystery of human redemption, and so to the mystery of the Incarnation,
and so to the adorable mystery of the Trinity.

On the side of man, either in a positive or negative
sense, it embraces the whole history and science of
human nature. The creation of man, his mere
nature apart from grace, his original grace, his fall,
the condition of man after the fall, the promise of
redemption, and the return of grace upon that promise, the institution of sacrifice in faith of redemption
to come, and the dispensations under the primitive, the
patriarchal, the Mosaical and the Christian law, are

M

all subjects most intimately connected with the divine dispensation of grace. The history of the Church, from the promise of redemption given in Paradise to the present hour, is the history of the combat of grace with fallen nature. The history of saints and holy persons is the history of the triumph of grace.

We turn to the Church as the divinely-constituted minister of grace; we hear the divine promises on which she is founded, behold the institution of the sacraments, those wonderful fruits of the Cross, and assured channels of grace; we look upon the awful and most tremendous sacrifice of the God-man; the descent of the Holy Ghost; the uprising of the Church in her divine authority, and its centralisation, divinely ordained, in one person; the preaching of the word of truth, the ministering of the Sacrifice and sacraments, the succession of the episcopate and priesthood; the spread of the Church in its order and unity through the world. And what do we find the Church to be, but an organised authority divinely instituted, and directed by the Holy Spirit, for the ministration of truth and grace to men.

When we follow the gifts of divine grace in the souls of men, we may see why St. John Chrysostom loved to give to Christianity the name of philosophy. For it inspires the soul with the love of Eternal Wisdom, leads the mind to the First Cause and the heart to the Supreme Good, and that in a way so direct and above the powers of nature, that when the natural man sees all things human sacrificed to a Wisdom so far above his comprehension, he stands perplexed and astonished at the spectacle. We follow the workings of divine grace in its internal combats against pride and sensuality, in its immolation of the pomps and vanities of this life to the Cross, in its patience under suffering and persecution, in its re-joicings of hope, in its radiance of charity, in the production of all the Christian virtues, in its out-ward combats against the world and the devil. We see the wonderful conversions which grace operates, the great sacrifices cheerfully made for the sake of it, the commerce of many souls with God through its influence, the intimate union of other souls with God whom grace in its abundance has purified, and all the Christian sanctities and edification which exhibit the fruits of grace. We see the earth covered with sanctuaries, religious houses, and institutions for every work of charity and mercy both spiritual and corporal, and whether monuments of the past or institutions of the present, they all tell the history of grace, inspiring and moving souls to works of re-ligion, mercy, and charity. We see that the first in-tention of their founders and conductors has ever been, whether through corporal, mental, or spiritual charity, to bring souls to the knowledge and the grace of God. But to witness the consummation of grace, we must assist at the departure of those souls whom it animates, and mark the peace and confidence with which, having the sure hope of life within them, they quit this corrupting earth and their own corruptible body. And even then shall we never understand the wondrous power of grace, until, through the merciful deliverance of God, we see the whole assembled sanctities of heaven crowned with the divine beatitude for the works of grace wrought upon this earth.

Thus on whatever side we turn to survey the wonder-work of divine grace, from whatever true source we build up the synthesis of grace, we gain some comprehensive perception of its marvellous power, of its rich fecundity, and of its unbounded fruitfulness, wherever it is received by grateful and responsive souls. And the history of divine grace rises into a sublime and magnificent demonstration of the love and munificence of God to man. But when we consider what a prodigious, what an incalculable amount of this most precious grace, obtained for us at infinite cost, is given to souls whose obstinate indocility makes it fruitless, the proof of God's patience and long endurance with His creature rises to a sublimity so awful as to overwhelm the soul with terror.

In thus extending our synthesis of truth, the mind enlarges its vision, ascends to a higher position from which to contemplate the truth presented to our consideration, and becomes far-sighted, fertile, and eloquent from the delight of truth.

The fruits of humble Christian study are so admirably expressed in the words of St. Paul, that I shall add nothing to them—" The fruit of the light is in all goodness, and justice, and truth." I will only, then, remind you that the true end of study is to equalise your understanding with your light, in so far as you are capable of accomplishing it.

What made a St. Augustine, a St. Bernard, a St. Thomas, a St. Bonaventure, and all those holy and luminous Doctors of the Church? They were men of like nature and passions with ourselves, but they were faithful to their light, kept their spirits pure and calm, and by constant ascending to the First Cause and Supreme Good with open heart and subject mind, sought light and truth from God who is the light and the truth. They prayed almost as much as they thought, and their thinking was a kind of prayer, because they thought in God "the Father of lights," and in "the Word of Truth," under the movement of "the Spirit of the living God" helping their infirmity. This habit shines forth in their writings as in their lives; and their maxims, even when transplanted from their minds into ours, have in them a grace and profundity of inexhaustible truth that illuminates so many things. What a miracle of light is the pure and serene soul of St. Thomas, a soul truly angelic, because absorbed in the contemplation of objective truth to the absolute forgetfulness of self. Through all his voluminous writings, embracing the entire circle of mental and sacred science, the author never once appears. You look in vain for an *ego* or a first person singular; it is always a *videtur* or a *probatur*. The objective truth is brought to you without the intervention of a finger or a shadow of the subjective man.

Such, then, is the mystery of knowledge. The process is obscure, and especially so to the natural man, but the result is luminous, and that in proportion to the soul's purity, humility, and nearness to God. To you, who have learnt something of what I may call the mechanism of the mind, of its light and its operations, I hope the mystery is growing less obscure. Stand under your light with the reverence of a disciple, and under the Master of your light; for He says, "I am the light of the world; he who followeth me walketh not in darkness." And again He says, "Be ye children of the light." Not only the light of faith but the light of reason will increase to you through piety and culture, as the Vatican Council teaches in the admirable words with which I conclude—"When reason, illuminated by faith, seeks in a sober and devout spirit to have some knowledge of divine mysteries, that is most fruitfully obtained, as well from the analogy of those mysteries with what is naturally known, as from their connection with each other and with the ultimate end of man. But reason is never made competent to see those very truths as they are objectively constituted; because those mysteries by their very nature exceed the human intelligence, so long as we are exiled from the Lord; so that even when given through revelation and received through faith, they still remain covered with that veil of faith, and are invested with a certain darksome obscurity. For we walk by faith and not by sight." *

* Con. Vat. Const. De Fide Cathol., c. 4.

VIII.

Science and Wisdom,

A Second Discourse to the Clerics of St. Bernard's Seminary.

" By wisdom shall the house be built, and by prudence it shall be strengthened. By instruction shall the store-rooms be filled with precious and most beautiful wealth."—PROVERBS xxiv. 3.

IN our first discourse we saw how the store-room of the mind is filled with the precious and beautiful wealth of science. We have now to see what the office of instruction is in the building up of science. What we have already learnt in the first discourse will have prepared our minds for this second examination. There we saw how God is the first cause of our knowledge, and the mind itself the second cause ; that God presents to us the truth in the light that He gives to the mind, strengthens the eye of the understanding to apprehend the truth, and energises the will to move the understanding in the investigation of truth, to adhere to the truth when found, and to rejoice in it. As the truth already found is but the foreground to the vast regions of truth beyond, of which what is already known gives intimation, but to which the mental eye has not yet reached, the charm of truth invites us to go further in its quest, to seek its beautiful order, to ascend to the light of its principles, and, helped from that greater light, to descend anew to its conclusions.

In coming to the functions of the teacher, I assume, as a matter of course, that he is duly qualified, duly authorised, and in possession of that science which he is set to teach. And, although my observations are applicable to all teaching, I shall keep especially in view those sciences of philosophy and theology on which you are engaged.

I ask you, then, to reflect, whilst I help you to think, on these two questions. In what does the teacher of science help the student ? In what must the student of science help himself ? The answer to these questions will take us once more into mental science, and far into it, and in such a way as greatly to enhance its practical value. As the will plays so great and important a part in the acquiring of knowledge, it must likewise take us into the practical science of morals. Coming also to that revealed truth which brings such a flood of light upon our natural reason, we must pass into the supernatural region of theology. I might bring to my aid many great Fathers of the Church, both Greek and Latin ; but, considering the limits of time and patience, I shall be mainly guided in my exposition by St. Augustine.

Language is both the instrument of thought and the instrument of teaching. And however variously it has been developed by man, in its origin it is the gift of God. You will nowhere find more cogent or

copious proof of this truth than in the great work of
the Count de Bonald. Had we been created in the
condition of spirits without bodies, we should have
had purely spiritual methods of thought and of
communicating thought, as St. John Chrysostom
observes, and have had no need for speech or writing.
But, constituted as we are, our very thinking partakes
in its way of our compound nature. Thought is
awakened by imagery, and is invested with imaginary
forms, and, as the soul uses the body, so thought uses
language as its instrument. Words are not truths,
but arbitrary ciphers or conventional signs of truths.
If words were truths, or transparent vehicles of truths,
or if there were some natural, objective and essential
connection between words and the truths they are
employed to express, then all men would in all
their words speak the truth. There would, in that
case, be but one universal language common to all
men. If words were anything more intimately connected with ideas than as mere arbitrary signs, to
which those alone who have been taught to unite
them have got the key, we should have no languages foreign to our understanding, or striking
our ears with sounds that do not reach our sense.
But words are sounds, and truths are sights, presented
not to the mortal but the mental eye. Words, therefore, can only be the signs and symbols of ideas. As
St. Anastasias says, "Speech is the messenger of a
mind having knowledge sent to another mind. But
the messenger knows not the message; that is only
understood by the mind that receives it." Truths are
not in words but in minds.

The object of scientific teaching is truth and the order of truth. But where is that truth? You will say it is in the mind of the teacher, and thus far you speak correctly. But where does the disciple find the truth that the master teaches? Not in the mind of the master, for that is closed to his vision. Not in the words that he utters, because words are not truths but indicators. They are like so many flying fingers pointing at truths. Where, then, is the truth to which they point? In your own mind, yet, perhaps, until it was pointed out to you, you did not see it, or see it in that order.

You come from your text book with the substance of your lesson in your mind, before the teacher has opened his lips. How came that knowledge into your mind? Not from the book, for truth belongs to some living mind, and the book is dead ink and paper. The letters printed there are but the material symbols of spoken words, as spoken words themselves are but sounds ; and these sounds are but the audible signs of truths beheld in the mind. Printed words, mere signs of signs, are at a second, rather at a third, remove from his views of the truth who wrote them for the printer. First, you have to translate the printed letters into words ; secondly, you have to pass from the words to their accepted meaning ; thirdly, from their whole context you have to gather that particular sense which the author has attached to them.

I stop here a moment, that from this analysis I may point out the superiority of spoken over written instruction. Spoken instruction, as you will have observed, is nearer the fountain of the teacher's mind ;

it calls but for one translation instead of two ; it partakes more vividly of the teacher's mental life. The
vibrations of the living and accentuated voice, coming
warm from the mind's vision and the heart's conviction, awaken attention, enkindle sympathy, and stir
the disciple's mind to corresponding activity. "The
words of the wise are as goads," says Ecclesiastes,
"and as nails driven in." For the same reasons, the
living voice plants a far deeper impression on the
memory than the dead letters of a book, yet a book
has this advantage, that although it demands a greater
spontaneous exertion, and leaves a feebler impression,
it gives us more leisure to turn back upon its contents,
and to dwell upon such parts of it as are the most
suggestive to our lights.

Words, as we have said, are indicators or pointers,
by help of which the teacher points to the truth,
to its divisions, relations and unions, as they are
visible to his own mind ; that you, being stimulated
and armed with signs directing you to that truth, may
look for it in the light of your own mind ; where,
although it may have been present, you may not have
hitherto observed it, or not have observed it with the
same clearness. I am at this moment speaking of
those principles or truths that are visible in the light of
reason or in the light of faith, which form the interior
elements of philosophy and theology. Of the facts
from the exterior world, from the teaching Church,
or from history, I shall speak later on. It will be
sufficient to remind you at present, that when external facts are presented by the teacher, they are
presented in imaginary forms, figured in his speech ;

and by the help of analogous images in your own memory or imagination, you are able to form them anew after your own manner. But these forms of facts are illuminated and rendered intelligible, if they be natural facts, by the light of your reason ; if they be supernatural or revealed facts, by the supernatural light which, to them who believe, is infused with faith, and perfected by charity. With respect to these supernatural facts, nothing can be more reasonable than to believe the voice of that Infinite reason which created all human reason, and is the Author of its light.

From the visible world I will now draw some illustration of what passes between the teacher and the disciple in the process of teaching what to the mind alone is visible. With my finger I point to that picture on the wall, and by this sign draw your attention towards it. If instead of using my finger, I say with sounding words, "Look at that picture," by that sign I equally call the attention of your mind to it. But the picture is neither in my finger nor in my words. The light intervenes between the picture and my vision ; it equally intervenes between the picture and your vision. Before I called your attention to it, the picture was of course before my mind ; and now that I awaken and direct your attention to it, the same picture is before your mind. By a mysterious process, which St. Thomas ascribes to the soul being the form of the body, the image of that picture which the light has brought to your corporal eyes, has become an image of your mind, illuminated by another light, by the interior light of your intelligence, so that you are able to reason upon it. So much has it become your mental possession, that if you turn your mind from the external picture, its form is still before the interior eye of your understanding.

Again with verbal signs I direct your attention to that painting. For, although.you have obtained a knowledge of its general character and contents, there may still be much in it that, however present to your mind, is not yet present to your understanding, has not yet become knowledge. My words direct attention to the graces of form and the beauties of colour, to the harmonies and contrasts of light and shade, and to the expression of sentiment in the features and action of the figures. I then ascend to a higher point of view, I show how the contention between the sun and the atmosphere gives a subtle quickening, a certain vibration as of a gentle life to the landscape ; and how this tender vibration of nature seems to be reflected in the sentiments of the group in the picture who contemplate the scene.

From the picture you have passed into the mind of the artist. To your own mind it has become a possession, first by analysis, then by synthesis. Yet that picture with its contents was present to you from the first, and the instructor has simply directed the attention of your understanding to what was already unconsciously present in your mind. St. Augustine has used the similitude of two persons looking at the same wall, to explain how the teacher and his disciple look each with his individual mind at the same truth. Bossuet for the same purpose has used the analogy of the picture.

Let us take an illustration that comes nearer to pure mental operations. You have a geometrical figure drawn on paper, but with its demonstration you are yet unacquainted. The lines of that triangle, like the words of a syllogism, are but signs. The true triangle, its pure lines and angles, are in your own mind. The notions of space and quantity are already in your mind, and the teacher appeals to certain first principles (and postulates respecting them) which are likewise present in your mental light; then, using the lines and angles drawn on the paper and his own words as indicators, he enables you to accomplish the demonstration through the light in your own mind. Plato has said that God is the great geometrician. But Job had amplified this truth a thousand years before his time. And the Book of Wisdom says, "Thou hast ordered all things in measure, and in number, and in weight." This science is alone perfect in the Divine and Eternal Reason, and God has put a certain reflection of it in the light of our human reason. Hence there have been men who have drawn out the elements of the science from their own minds, before receiving any help from books, or teachers, or scientific language ; the youthful Pascal, for example, and Fergusson, whilst yet an untutored boy.

Let me take a final illustration from objects of sense that you have never seen. Take a wall map of some country of which you know little or nothing. You look at it, and it gives you a general impression that is vague and void to your understanding of its significant contents. It is nothing but lines, streaks,

and scattered words, the sounds of which you may
have never heard. The map has become an image
in your imagination, and next a form in your mind,
which the light of your mind has made intelligible.
It is a mental map suspended, so to speak, in your
intellectual light. But there is very much in that
map that your understanding does not see or cannot
translate. With wand to point out the contents of
the external map, and words as indicators to the
mental map, I trace the mountain ranges, the rivers
rising from them, their tributaries, and their course
to their exit in the ocean, and as fast as I trace upon
the mental map present to my own mind, you follow
the traces on the mental map present in your mind,
and your understanding of the map begins to grow
clear. I show how the mountains fertilise the plains
with their crumbling soil as well as with their streams,
and how, therefore, the richest and most beautiful
districts must necessarily be where the mountains
join the plains. I point to the sites of stored-up
minerals, and to the richer soils produced by primæval
forests. I am then able to deduce the reasons why
ports are here ; why cities are there ; why a great
labouring population will be in this district; and why
a resort of pleasure-seekers should be there. Whilst
this process is going on, image after image is called
up of like things from your memory, and become
associated in new forms of application with that
mental map, and are transferred by analogy to the
region of which the map is a symbolic representation.
You gain by degrees a certain scientific knowledge, in
a general way, of a region that you have never seen.

So it is in every region of science. The master appeals to certain principles, and imaged forms in the pupil's mind, and defines, distinguishes, calls up analogous subjects from the memory, compares, infers; and the student looks for the truth of what is affirmed or denied in his own mind; whether those truths be reflected in the reason, in the light of faith, from the authority of a revealing voice, or reflected from facts addressed to our senses. Having prepared your mind by these illustrations, we may now listen to the conclusions drawn by St. Augustine; and, although he has expressed the same principles in many parts of his voluminous writings, for convenience of reference I shall here limit myself to his earlier work, " De Magistro."

After a long dialogue with his two disciples on the use of words as signs and indicators, the great doctor observes that, although we believe whatever we truly understand, yet many things we believe that we do not understand, accepting them on adequate authority, such as things distant from us, and facts of history. "But," he says, "to understand universal truths, we consult not the mind of the teacher who is addressing us, but the truth presiding in our own mind, of which the teacher admonishes us by his words." Then ascending to the region of theology, he continues— " He who teaches us as we look to Him, is Christ dwelling in the interior man, that is, the power and eternal wisdom of the unchangeable God, whom every rational soul consults; yet His truth is open to each one only in accordance with the good or evil will that renders him capable or not capable of understanding. And as when we are deceived about external objects, the fault is not in the light, so when we fall into error, the fault is not in the truth."

The great anatomist of our mental operations next points out that, all our perceptions being of things sensible or of things intelligible, it is the mind itself that perceives the corporal elements of the world, through the senses acting as their interpreters. Having the images impressed on our memory, we carry them within us, as sure and certain documents. "But," he observes, "these are our own documents, and if he who listens to my instruction has known the presence of the things I speak of, and has felt them, it is not from my words that he learns, but from the images, from those things that he carries in him. If he has not the same images, he believes my words rather than understands the things that I say.

"But where there is question of things seen with our mind, that is, with the intellect and reason, we then speak of the things we behold as present in that interior light by which the inward man is illuminated, and of which he enjoys the fructification. And if, with simple internal sight my eye sees what I say, it is not in my words, but in his own contemplation, that he comprehends what I am saying. Wherefore I am uttering the truth to one who beholds that truth, which is not obtained from my words but from the truth itself, which is so far manifested in him as God opens the truth to him. So much is this the case that if, before being instructed, he had been questioned, he could himself have expressed that truth. What can be so absurd as to suppose that he

N

gets that truth from me, when, even before I have spoken, if properly interrogated, he could himself express that truth. It not unfrequently happens that, when he is first questioned, the disciple will deny that which on being further questioned he will admit; but this comes of his limited power of perception, which will not enable him to consult that light in his mind on the whole of the question. Yet, after he is advised to take it part by part, and is questioned on each part, he recognises that truth which, when taken altogether, he could not at first apprehend."

In concluding, St. Augustine ascends once more from the natural to the supernatural light, and from reason to theology. He says: "Let us believe and even begin to understand, how truly it is written by divine authority, that we call no one master on earth, because all have one Master in heaven. What He is Himself in heaven He will Himself teach us; but meanwhile He teaches us through men by signs, that, by turning internally to Him, we may be instructed : and learn that to know and love Him is that blessed life which all men seek, but which few rejoice in having truly found." *

Often in his other writings St. Augustine repeats that the one Master and the true Teacher is within us; that His chair is in heaven and His school on earth; and that the place where He teaches is the human breast. And, long before him, Clement of Alexandria had explained the doctrine of the one Master. He says in one place : "If the Scripture

* S. Aug. De Magistro, c. 11, 12, 13. ¦

tells us that one is our Master in heaven, it is obvious that all men on the earth are His disciples: for so Truth hath affirmed."* And, in another place, he says: "He who is teaching learns more than he knew before ; and in the act of teaching he becomes himself a hearer with them that listen to him. For one is the Master of the teacher and of them who are taught, the Master who invigorates both the mind and the reason."†

If in your own minds you have seen and comprehended what has thus far been pointed out, you have obtained the means of knowing how far the student must help himself. It has become clear and obvious that the work of study must be accomplished within your own mind, by the exertion of your own understanding, and with the help of your own light. He who wants more light, must go, as the saints went, to the Divine Fountain of light. He whose mental sight is weak, must ask of God to give it strength, and to give to his will a generous appetite for truth.

Next to these internal gifts, we can have no greater blessing than a wise and enlightened teacher. Were we as God's angels, we should have the manifestation of truth, without veils or words ; but in our constitution of soul and body informed by soul, God has ordained our enlightenment on the twofold principle of outward teaching and inward light ; on the exterior and interior word brought together in conjunction. And, as St. Augustine observes, in the order of instruction authority goes first and reason follows. And in the supernatural order, where man

* Clemens, Alex. Pedag., L. 1, c. 5. † Stromat, L. 1, c. 1.

is so feeble and liable to error and delusion, and where consequences are so tremendous, God has invested the teaching voice that represents Him with divine authority, to speak in His name, and to judge the lights and the spirits whether they be of God ; as He has also given into the hands of His ministers sacraments which bring down light to the mind.

Notwithstanding all that has been said respecting the use of words, when winged from a pure, luminous, and fervent soul, they gain a power of awakening the understanding to truth and the heart to justice, which flows from the grace of the teacher. Solomon says in Ecclesiastes : " The words of the mouth of a wise man are grace." And again : "The words of the wise are as goads, and as nails deeply fastened in, which by the counsel of masters are given by one shepherd." We feel this force in the sentences of Holy Scripture, enfeebled more or less though they may be by translation into other than their original language. Yet even here there is a divine provision; for one of the wonders of Holy Scripture is that, God has not merely expressed His divine truths, which are so far above us, in our human words, but He has expressed them in a constant succession of imagery drawn from human life and the world we live in. This succession of certain analogies, nearer or remoter, with the eternal mind of their Creator, becomes a language to express His truth in a way more vivid and home-coming than words. Thus God speaks His divine truths to us in a double language ; in the language of sensible nature as well as the language of words.

How we feel the gentle, searching power of our Lord's words, especially when we realise their coming from His Sacred Heart! And when He also speaks internally, imparting light and grace, His words enkindle light, and fire, and strength. All this He tells us where He says : " The words that I have spoken to you are spirit and life." Yet not to all ; for on one occasion He said : " All do not take these words, but those to whom it is given by my Father." The mind must be opened, and the truth interiorly presented to it ; or the seed of the Word falls on barren ground. The words of holy men share this awakening power, because the spirit of Christ is in them. All power awakening minds comes in the first instance from the one Fountain of Truth.

From all that has been said, this peremptory con- clusion is inevitable, that the student of science, whether human or divine, can do nothing unless he open out his understanding, and put his mind into exertion ; and unless, as St. Augustine warns him, with patient progress he take, part by part, that which is too much to be comprehended at once in its totality.

The same rule holds good in the study of literature as of science, if we are to penetrate below its surface. For literature is the expression of human nature in its diversities ; and the key to the study of human nature is in ourselves. All the elements of human nature are to be found in their germs and principles in the individual man. The words of the poet which have been a maxim of human life for so many ages, express this truth : " I am a man, and nothing that befalls man is strange to me." When Louis XIV. asked the great preacher Massillon, how he, in his retired life, knew so much of the weaknesses of men in spheres so different from his own, the preacher replied to the king—"I learnt them from the study of my own heart."

Let me now give you a few brief maxims from the Fathers as rules for the conduct of the mind.

St. Augustine notes, that "The soul grows larger by what it learns, and becomes smaller by suffering its learning to perish." *

He also says: "The teachable man is he who is gentle and mild in the patience of learning." †

Again he says: "Nature holds this order in whatever we learn; authority comes first and reason follows. Reason is first in the order of truth, but authority in the order of time." ‡

St. Ambrose says: "Whosoever teaches himself, has many to learn from, if he have the virtues for his masters; for the one thing he needs is self-discipline." §

St. Basil says: "What is learnt impetuously is not likely to abide with us: but what is taken up with a pleasant ease and content will rest durably in the mind." ‖

St. John Chrysostom says: "It is the spirit of a child to fancy you see all at the beginning; and to pride yourself on the first contact with truth as if you had reached the end of it." ¶

---

* S. Aug. D. Quan. Animæ, c. 18.   † De Baptismo, L. 5, c. 26.
‡ De Moribus Eccles., c. 2.   § S. Ambros. De Virgin., L. 2.
‖ S. Basil Super Psalm, 1.   ¶ S. Chrys. Hom. 29 Sup. Genes.

St. Gregory the Great says: "Nothing is so easy to learn as truth." * And again: "We cannot presume that a science is taught unless it has been learnt by attentive meditation." †

St. Bonaventure says : "No one is a good student who listens not with reverence to the words of his teacher, who does not often revolve what he has heard in his mind, and who does not test his thinking by observation." ‡

Peter of Blois says: "Once raise in yourself the love of learning, and it will not be easily lost; for passing into desire it will perpetuate itself." §

In these maxims I present you with a cluster of lights that, severally well reflected on, may pass into your mental habits, and help you much in the discipline of your understanding.

Truth in itself is one, simple and universal; yet by reason of the limits, lowness, and want of purity in the vision, of creatures so frail, fallen and far removed from God as we are, we receive it dividedly, and consequently in many forms, and with many limitations. But the more our minds become abstracted from the corporal senses, and the more we enter into the contemplation of the truth, the more does the truth manifest itself to be, of its own nature, one, simple and universal. Truth willingly accepts union with the soul that seeks it with pure intention, expanding her growth with its light, refining her from

* S. Greg. M. Pastoral, p. 3, c. 1.
† Ibid., p. 1, c. 1.
‡ S. Bonavent. Serm. 2, De Uno Doctore.
§ Peter Blessen, Epist. 81.

her grossness, and raising her hope to the good of which truth is the bright harbinger.

Truth is chaste and tranquil, just and in equitable order, serene and royal, most beautiful and profound. It commands us, and cannot by us be commanded or constrained; because it is eternal and unchangeable. The apostle tells us: "We can do nothing against the truth, but for the truth." Godlike is truth, yet the proper food of spirits and souls. For "not in bread alone does man live, but in every word that proceedeth from the mouth of God."

We have only to consider the attributes of truth, and to understand from whom it comes, to know the conditions it demands of the soul. Before truth can freely unite with a soul, it demands that that soul be just and pure, loyal and a lover of the God of truth, reverential, submissive and grateful. To love truth is to win truth; and lower truth leads to higher truth, making the luminous path of the mind from earth to heaven, where is the God who is light, the God who is truth. If then with David you say: "I have chosen the way of truth," remember what Wisdom tells you: "They who trust in the Lord shall find truth." And the prayer of them who trust in God for the truth, our Lord has clasped in His own prayer, opening the way for that prayer and giving it effect from His own, where He speaks to the Father: "Sanctify them in truth, Thy word is truth."

Their own experience inspired the Fathers to speak magnificently of the purity required for the reception and entertainment of divine truth. And if from their number I select St. John Climacus, it is because with a lucid brevity he has summed up their whole doctrine. These are his words :—

" The increase of the fear of God is the beginning of charity. But perfect chastity is the foundation of theology. He who through this virtue has his faculties united with God, is taught by God through His word in a secret and mysterious way. But what makes chastity perfect is the implanted word of the Father, by His presence inflicting death on death, so that when death is extinct, the disciple of theology becomes illuminated. The word of the Lord, sent forth from the Lord, is holy and abideth for ever. The man who knows not God speaks of divine things in conjectures and probabilities. But the chaste disciple of theology enters with his mind into the doctrine of the Most Holy Trinity, three persons in one God." *   In another place the same holy contemplative says : " Vast and profound is the depth of the divine dogmas, and as a man who is entangled in his garments swims at his peril, so cannot that man lay hold of the secrets and mysteries of theology who insults them by his vices." †

This chastity implies a double purity, one for each of the two elements in man ; purity of sense, heart, and imagination from corporal defilements, and purity of mind and will from spiritual defilements— from that pride, vanity, and irreverence, which make the spirit wanton. Our Lord sets forth the beautiful yet terrible law of pure things for the pure, when He says : " He that doth evil cometh not to the light. . .

---

* S. Joan. Climac. Scala Perfec., Grad. 30.
† Ibid., Grad. 27.

But he that doth good cometh to the light;" and when He said : " Blessed are the clean of heart, for they shall see God." This is the crowning of purity, that after seeing God's truth with pure eyes, we may at last see the God of truth and purity.

IX.

Science and Wisdom.

A Third Discourse to the Clerics of St. Bernard's Seminary.

"By wisdom the house shall be built, and by prudence it shall be strengthened. By instruction the store-rooms shall be filled with all precious and most beautiful wealth."—PROVERBS xxiv. 3.

WE considered the mental sources of science in our first discourse. In our second, we saw what the teacher contributes, and what the disciple himself must contribute, towards filling the store-room of the mind with instruction. In this concluding discourse it remains for us to consider how wisdom builds up and prudence strengthens the whole interior man.

Wisdom is so far above knowledge that it directs science to its end, and presides over its course as a watchful guardian. The pagan philosophers sought after wisdom as the end of their speculations, although in the night of reason they did not reach those summits of wisdom that are revealed in the open day of revelation. Yet it must be confessed that, having the Supreme Good for the aim and end of their re-

searches, the best of them had far more exalted
notions of its character than many laborious moderns
have, who abuse the name of philosophy. With
them, as with the Church, philosophy implied the
love or pursuit of wisdom. And by wisdom they
understood, as we understand, the knowledge of high
things in their noblest principles, and highest causes ;
causes that we know to be spiritual, unchangeable,
and eternal. They did not so abuse the term philosophy as to apply it to systematised observations,
classifications, and deductions limited to irrational
and material nature, and abstracted from all consideration of their First Cause and their final end. Though
not strangers to the inferior sciences, if detached
from the consideration of their higher causes, they
would not give to them the name of philosophy, not
discerning in them the search for wisdom. Such
sciences, so pursued, they would call physical or
mathematical, but not philosophical. It would amaze
them to hear men professing the love of a wisdom
that looks no higher than the earth, or than irrational
natures.

There is a lower and a higher wisdom. There is a
natural wisdom that goes not beyond the scope of
human reason, and a divine wisdom that is imparted
to man through faith and by God's revelation
Again, there is a wisdom which is little more than a
higher order of intelligence, and a wisdom, highest of
all, which is conversant with the Supreme Good.
Intellectual wisdom is either particular or universal.
It is particular when it ascends to the first cause or
principle, in each particular department of know-

ledge; it is universal, when it ascends to the First
Cause of all knowledge. Let us explain and exem-
plify. Each science may be considered as a pyramid,
of which the many concrete facts form the wide basis,
above which rise the nearest, lowest, and most limited
generalisations, illuminating the facts beneath; these
ascend into higher and fewer generalisations, giving
light to those that are lower; and these again ascend
into others yet fewer and more simple; until at the
summit of the science, we find some one most simple
and luminous principle, that crowns the pyramid,
comprises in its light the essence of the subordinate
principles, and holds in its dependence all the subordinate truths of which it is the prime illuminator.
Whosoever holds this first and highest principle, in
clear intelligence, and can promptly bring it to bear
upon the minor principles and particular truths that
are subordinate to its light, possesses the wisdom of
that science. The new facts that come under that
science may or may not modify its subordinate
principles, but they receive light from its first principle.

Take the science of logic, which regulates the mind
in searching for truth; it depends on the principle
of contradiction. Take the science of law, which
regulates human rights; its first principle is justice.
Take the science of physics, which is concerned with
material things; its first principle is force. Take the
science of metaphysics, which concerns the spiritual
world and its operations; its ultimate principle is the
First Cause. Take the science of morals, which
embraces human motives and the conduct of the

will; its ultimate principle is the Supreme Good. These last two sciences, ascending to the First Cause and the Final Cause, constitute the philosophy and wisdom of the ancients. The knowledge of each of these sciences in its first principles constitutes the particular mental wisdom of that science.

Universal wisdom, intellectually considered, embraces all knowledge in its due and perfect order. From the First Principle of all things it beholds all intermediate and subordinate principles, descending by cause and effect, or by principle and consequence; embracing all sciences and all things in their coordination and sequence; forming one universal pyramid of knowledge, which, from God as the First Cause and Final End of all, is illuminated all through from its spiritual summit to its material basis with descending and ever-decreasing light. And hence to obtain greater light upon what is inferior, we must ascend with it to principles that are higher. For, as St. Thomas says, we can judge nothing thoroughly except through its principle. Wherefore theology, as the wisdom of God revealed to man, throws light on all the sciences, as the heavens enlighten the earth. Wisdom, as it is universal, is one, whilst the sciences are many. If the Book of Wisdom teaches us that wisdom is manifold, it likewise declares that it is one and simple. It is one and simple in its own nature, but manifold in its communication. To use the illustration of St. Ambrose, it is in many forms communicated to man like the numerous impressions made from one seal. Wisdom is at the head of the intellectual virtues, as remarked by Aristotle, because it is concerned with the First Cause, which is God.

Thus far I speak of intellectual wisdom exclusively. Limited to the mind, however high its light may reach, it is but a dry light, and is therefore but a limited and imperfect kind of wisdom. True wisdom is a moral as well as an intellectual virtue; it passes from the mind to the heart, from the understanding to the spiritual sense, and pervades the interior man. For wisdom is especially concerned with the good of which truth is the resplendent reflection.

We gain a clearer apprehension of the virtue of wisdom when we have noted, with St. Thomas, that it is not only perceptive but judicial. Upon this he thus enlarges : " Science is subject to the mind as a higher principle, and the mind is subject to wisdom as the highest principle. Thus both science and the mind are subject to wisdom, which judges both the operations of the mind, and the conclusions of science, and its principles."* Again he observes that "wisdom exercises a twofold direction over man; over his intellect and over his affections." †

Wisdom, then, is of the heart as well as of the mind. It is the *mens cordis*, and *cor sapiens intelligere* of the Holy Scriptures ; ,the wise or understanding heart, which the holy men of God prayed that they might receive. The wise heart is the interior, spiritual sense ; as it is touched with a sense and consciousness of the Infinite Good, or with movements towards

---

* S. Thom. Sum. 1, 2, q. 57, a. 2, ad 2.
† Ibid., q. 68, a. 4, ad 5.

the Supreme Good, by which we are able to estimate
and judge whatsoever is presented to the mind in its
relation to the Supreme Good. Wisdom, therefore,
is the highest spiritual sense, judging, as we have
heard St. Thomas say, both the operations of the
mind and the conclusions of science. Who is there
who has never felt an admonition from the depth of
his interior sense, that something has gone wrong in
the working of his thought, which must be either
rectified or given up? How often does our sense of
better things correct the unwise thoughts of our
mind? We see them at last, and allow them to be
unwise; that is to say, they are not conformable to
our sense of good.

However inapplicable in other languages, St.
Isidore's etymology of the Latin word for wisdom
presents us with a true definition of it. *Sapientia*
is *sapida scientia*, the light of truth in the sweetness of good. David prayed for wisdom when he
begged of God to illuminate his heart. And he
exhorts us to wisdom, when he sings to us: "Taste
and see that the Lord is sweet." Solomon asked of
God to give him a teachable heart, and God gave to
him "a wise and understanding heart." All through
the Sacred Scriptures the heart is spoken of as the
seat of wisdom, or, when devoid of wisdom, as the
seat of foolishness. . St. Paul prays for the Ephesians
that the eye of their heart may be enlightened to
know the great things of God; and our Lord explained the internal condition of them who rejected
Him in unbelief in the words of Isaias: " He hath

blinded their eyes, and hardened their heart, that they should not see with their eyes, nor understand with their heart."

When the prelates of the Church enter upon their synodal or other grave deliberations, they ask the Holy Spirit of wisdom that He would deign to glide into their hearts and be their teacher.

"Wisdom," writes St. Bonaventure, "is twofold. There is a wisdom that is *from* the Eternal Word, and there is a wisdom that is *in* the Eternal Word. But the wisdom that is *in* the Eternal Word is the fruit of piety; because no one comes to the vision of the Eternal Word except through piety." * Not that the vision of the Eternal Word is in this life an open vision ; but through piety it is begun through gaining the sense of Christ ; as St. Paul says : " We have the sense of Christ, if so be that we feel after Him."

In God, the Supreme Truth and the Supreme Good are one and the same. But to us who live more in mind than in heart, and very much in our corporal senses, often does the truth beam with tepid rays into our mind, because we are tepid before our heart is touched with the sense of that goodness which the truth reflects. We loiter with the herald truth instead of hastening to the King whom truth proclaims, and in whom is every excellence that our heart can desire. For this reason, and from their own wide observation and experience, the great spiritual writers have declared with lamentation, that a large number of those who study

* St. Bonavent. in Sentent. L. 1, d. 3, p. 2, d. 2.

O

divine things, study with zeal, but not with wisdom. They use their mind without their heart ; they gaze into the field of science with the mental eye, ranging with toiling brain from point to point ; yet, because their heart is not upon the God of the sciences, they lose the sweets and delights of study, and its solid fruits. They send not the heart after the mind to feel the good of which truth is the messenger, and the sense of which would ease and comfort all their mental toils. They rarely know how to throw their soul into their pursuit ; and so they know but little of the consolations of study. Yet, as St. Augustine tells us : "No one is happy without wisdom, because no one is happy without the Supreme Good, which we both discern and hold to in that truth which we call wisdom." * And still to speak with St. Augustine : "Unless wisdom be sought with all the powers of the soul, it can in nowise be found. Yet when worthily sought for, wisdom cannot be concealed from its lovers, For with love it is sought and by love it is found." †

When the spiritual sense is imbued with wisdom, we easily conquer the animal senses. The inward sweetness that comes of the divine gift of wisdom is so pure as to cause a loathing for the defiling emotions of the corporal senses, and so it leaves us free to ascend to the Fountain of truth.

When, again, we have the root of wisdom, not only the high but the low things of God's creation become rich to us in lessons of wisdom. With God's

* S. Aug. De Lib. Abitr., L. 2, c. 9.
† Id. De Morib, Eccles. Cath., L. 1, c. 31.

wisdom in the soul, we see reflections of His wisdom
upon all His creatures, even to the lowest of them.
All were created in wisdom, and each bears some
trace or image of His wisdom or goodness. The fly,
the ant, the leaf, the flower, the grain of mustard-seed,
the sand on the shore, the worm that crawls on the
ground, when considered in wisdom are all wonderful. And from each of them has the Holy Spirit
drawn some vigorous similitude in the Scriptures of
that which God asks from man, or has sent on His
behests. The ant is called up to teach the slothful
man. The green leaf refreshed from the waters is
the figure of the just man drawing his life from God.
The lily is the emblem of God's beautiful work as
compared with the work of man. The grain of
mustard-seed is the figure of the Church's marvellous expansion from its small beginning. The worm
is the awful figure of the God Man in His humiliation. The fly was the terrible punishment of Egypt.
In creating these little things, God already designed
them for man's instruction. And, what comes most
home to our needs, He humbles us by their teaching. They are all formed from types in the mind
of Eternal Wisdom, and of each God has a loving
thought and care.

Pre-occupied through the senses, youth is thought-
less of many things. But meditative age is like
wondering childhood, in that it sees the world full
of mysteries. Who that reflects can despise an atom
of earth, a drop of water, a grain of wheat, or a
breath of air? Of these our body is composed, and
by these it is nourished. Into these small things,

as we incorporate them, life enters, and the soul informs them. Who can say how life takes hold of them? or how after a time it lets go of them? Calculate the number and quantity of this world's elements that have constituted or fed the living organs of human souls. Estimate the stores from which these elements have been supplied. Number, if you can, the provisions that God has prepared for the life, instruction, convenience, comfort, pleasure, probation, and trial of the human race. Return them anew to their original atoms and their original chaos, that you may comprehend the multitudinous ordering of them, and the inexhaustible exercise of Divine Wisdom in adapting elements so weak to the service of the human soul. So true is it that God has poured out His wisdom upon all His works.

But when we enter the human soul thus served by the whole visible creation; when we there find the light and truth that in luminous forms shadows forth to her things infinite, unchangeable, and eternal; when we there find a want, a sense, a desire that nothing short of the Supreme Good can content or satisfy; we are brought to the irresistible conclusion, that if the world is made for man, man himself is made for God.

Science presents the spectral images of life. Wisdom is full of life. It is the principle uniting truth with goodness. It is sense as well as sight, and often surpassing the reach of sight, it gladdens as well as illuminates the spirit, having the fragrance, the fruit, and the ripe relish of good that builds up the interior man. It is like the warm radiance of

the sun in comparison with the cold reflection of
the moon. As St. Bonaventure says, it comes less
through reason than through prayer. It is the
science of the saints, to whom knowledge is but the
way to the God whom wisdom finds. The love of
God is wisdom in its perfect action, drawing the
stream of wisdom from its Eternal Source. You
have a most beautiful, I may say a typical illustration of the way in which the love of God sheds the
light of wisdom on all inferior things in the humble
St. Francis, whose tender love for all God's little
creatures enabled him to realise their being in God,
and their kindred with man. Yet, as St. Gregory
the Great observes—" To be wise is not always to
understand, for many persons have a wise sense of
eternal things that they in nowise understand." *
Just so have the blind a sense of things they do not
see, but hope one day to know. Just so, too, we
feel many things in our own nature that we do not
understand.

One wise man is more precious to the world than
a hundred learned men who have not wisdom. To
that one we fly for counsel in our doubts. In him
we trust in the hour of difficulty. From him we
seek for safe and sound direction. He it is who
rescues his fellow-men in the day of peril. Yet he
willingly leaves to them the credit of the acts that
have been directed by his wisdom. "A little city,"
says Ecclesiastes, "and few men in it: there came
against it a great king, and invested it and built
bulwarks around it, and the siege was perfect. Now

* S. Greg. M. Moral, L. 1, c. 16.

there was found in it a man poor and wise, and he delivered the city by his wisdom, and no man afterwards remembered the poor man. And I said that wisdom is better than strength. . . . The words of the wise are heard in silence, more than the cry of a prince among fools."

The wise understand life's trials and sufferings, and look to them for deep instruction. Having seen the Eternal Wisdom humbled in the earth and crucified, they comprehend that there is a mysterious power in suffering and humiliation to loosen us, as Christ loosened Lazarus, from the bonds of death. The Cross is God's wisdom to the wise, and to them who stand in need of wisdom. Submission follows love, and proves that love is genuine. From His obedience to humiliation and suffering, Christ taught us the profound and practical truth, that through humiliation the eyes that pride had closed are opened, and through suffering the soul is rescued from the oppression of the animal senses, and detached from the body of sin ; that she may listen to the claims of wisdom ; and that obedience may break the bonds of egotism. "Let no one," says St. Augustine, " expect such a prosperity as to be able to reach high wisdom without humble obedience." * As the inspired proverb teaches, "where is humility, there is wisdom." This St. Jerome illustrates in the following words— "When a man searches for a concealed treasure he digs deep into the ground, throws out the encumbering earth, and will not relax his efforts until he finds the gold he seeks for. And when the treasure

* S. Aug. Serm. 22 in Palm, 118.

a man seeks for is wisdom, he has to clear out what is earthly in him, and to make in himself a deep trench of humility, never resting until he finds the treasure that he wants."*

St. Chrysostom has put the whole wisdom of the Cross in the crystal casket of one brief sentence—a sentence worthy to be kept in everlasting remembrance. He says—"To be crucified in doing good is divine."

Depend upon it, whatever trials you suffer, whatever combats you undergo, are so many essays in the school of wisdom. They form a course of spiritual theology of the utmost practical value. From what you learn of that which passes within you, between your heart and God, you learn what passes in the hearts of other men, and so you win the secret of conducting other souls through the trials that bring them to their sanctification.

Prudence is a virtue in close alliance with wisdom. What, then, is the office of ¡prudence? St. Thomas will tell us. The difference between wisdom and prudence is this, that prudence is chiefly concerned with human things, and wisdom with divine things. Prudence selects, ordains, and regulates the means that conduct to our Supreme Good, and to our happiness; whilst wisdom contemplates that Supreme Good and happiness. Prudence, therefore, and whatever things are concerned with prudence, are subject to the dominion of wisdom.

We have been gradually advancing the steps of our instruction from human wisdom to that divine

* S. Hieron. in Proverb, L. 1, c. 2.

wisdom which is the chief of the seven gifts of the
Holy Spirit. This is that fourth and last degree of
wisdom, as St. Bonaventure teaches, which embraces
religion, which seeks piety, which makes life a worship. "We begin with the gift of fear," observes St.
Augustine, and advance step by step through the
intermediate gifts, until we reach their consummation
in the gift of wisdom. This is the final gift because
it tranquillises the soul, and makes her peaceful,
fruitful, and joyous." * "The Holy Spirit accumu-
lates this gift upon His other gifts," observes St.
Anselm of Canterbury, "when He breathes wisdom
into the soul, enabling what is correctly understood
in the gift of understanding to be sweetly relished
in the gift of wisdom, in virtue of which gift we pursue what is worthy to be pursued from the pure love
of rectitude. Dwelling in this edifice of His gifts, the
Holy Spirit rules the whole family of the soul's
interior senses, and so disposes them to His service,
that they ascend to God and descend to our neighbour, and the soul is able to say with the Psalmist:
'The Lord ruleth me, and I shall want for nothing.
He hath set me in a place of pasture.' "†

Hugh of St. Victor has expressed the relation of
the gift of wisdom to that of understanding in these
accurate terms: "The knowledge of truth will not
make a man perfect unless it be followed by sweet
experience, because experience is the mistress of
understanding." ‡ The divine gift of wisdom radiates

* S. Aug. De Doctrina Christ., c. 7.
† S. Anselm, L. de Similitud., c. 131.
‡ Hugo de S. Victore, Super 7m., Angel. Hierarch.

the soul, making her sense conformable to the sense
of God. It illuminates the intellectual powers to
make them beautiful, warms the affective powers to
make them pleasantly responsive, and energises the
active powers to make them robust and vigorous.
Hence the gift of wisdom has been always looked
upon as the most complete and noble of God's
gifts, and the crown of all His gifts to man.
If science knows God reflectively, through the
creation, wisdom knows Him directly, through experience: if science knows God by illumination,
through the Holy Scriptures, wisdom knows Him
directly, through inspiration : if science knows God
in the light of intelligence, wisdom knows Him in the
sensible movements of sweetness; and what intelligence provides, as St. Gregory observes, that wisdom
matures.

St. Thomas tells us that this supernatural wisdom
is a certain created participation of the Holy Spirit.
And St. Bonaventure, in his Treatise on the gift,
points out to us, that "the wisdom descending from
above, that wisdom which is both the splendour of
truth and the delightful sense of good, has God for
its principal object, not precisely as God is the truth,
but as God is the true good, the good that attracts
our will and draws us to love Him and delight in
Him. Wherefore," he concludes, "the gift of wisdom
is a supernatural habit infused into the soul by the
Holy Spirit, to know God and to love Him with
delight." *   And the seraphic doctor teaches, what
all saints and holy souls have experienced, that

* S. Bonavent. De Dono Sapientiæ, c. 1.

wisdom is chiefly cultivated in contemplation. St. Laurence Justinian will tell us further, that "wisdom is a certain gust and relish of divine things, moving in the soul to perfect faith, strengthen hope, and infuse vigour."* Then St. Theophilus of Alexandria will teach us how the soul is prepared for the gift. He says—"God's wisdom works His good in us after we have offered Him the hospitality of a chaste heart, and have transformed our thoughts into works."†

St. John the Evangelist has three times used the word unction to express the nature and operation of wisdom; thus intimating that wisdom is like an oil infused into the heart, and penetrating the spiritual sense. "Little children," he says to his disciples, "you have the unction from the Holy One, and know all things." And he says again—"His unction teacheth you all things." St. Augustine comments on these words in the following terms—"One is your master, Christ. When no one speaks to you outwardly He speaks to you inwardly. Yet, if any one is teaching you outwardly, let Christ be in your heart; let His unction be in your heart, lest, having no inward fountain to refresh you, your heart should thirst in loneliness. The interior Master teaches, Christ teaches, His inspiration teaches. Where His inspiration, where His teaching is not, in vain does the outward teacher fill your ears with sounding words."‡ Where Christ inwardly teaches, the Holy

* S. Laurent. Justin. De Divino Connub., L. 1, c. 12.
† S. Theoph. Alex. Ep. Pasch., 3.
‡ S. Aug. in Ep. Joan. ad Parth. Tract. 3, n. 12, 13.

Spirit inwardly touches the soul with love of the truth. On this subject let us hear the words of a great divine who is commenting on the words of St. John—"Christ is truth, but He is also charity. Christ the Word is the truth, but the Holy Spirit is the Spirit of Christ and the Spirit of truth. There is no Spirit given without Christ, and no Christ without His Holy Spirit. Whoever sees the Truth without loving it, cannot be said to have seen the truth. Whoever understands the Sovereign Beauty without loving it, cannot be said to have understood the Sovereign Beauty."*

The light created from the Uncreated Light and the love created from the Uncreated Love unite in the gift of wisdom. Hence charity is so luminous in wisdom. Hence St. Paul tells us that "the spiritual man judgeth all things, even the deep things of God." If light is penetrating, if unction is penetrating, far more deeply penetrating is that sweet and gentle fire that glides from the Holy Spirit into the spiritual substance of the soul.

The Wise Man had experience of this light, this unction, this gentle fire, when he wrote in the Holy Scriptures—"I wished, and understanding was given to me : and I called upon God, and the spirit of wisdom came to me. And I preferred her to kingdoms and thrones, and esteemed riches as nothing in comparison of her. . . . I loved her above health and beauty, and chose to have her instead of light : for her light cannot be put out. . . . She is an infinite treasure to men ; which they that use become the

* Thomassini, Dogmata, Tom. 5, Prolog. c. 9, n. 10.

friends of God, being commended for the gifts of
doctrine. . . . For in her is the spirit of understanding, holy, one, manifold, subtile, eloquent; active,
sure, sweet, loving that which is good." Then the
contemplation of wisdom inspires the desire of being
united with her, and the Wise Man continues—" Her
have I loved, and I have sought her from my youth,
and have desired to take her for my spouse : and I
became a lover of her beauty. . . . I proposed therefore to take her to live with me ; knowing that she
will communicate to me of her good things, and will
be a comfort in my cares and grief. . . . Moreover
by means of her I shall have immortality."

Then the Holy Spirit moves the Wise Man to pray
that wisdom may descend to him from heaven, and
become his bride—" Give me that wisdom that
sitteth on Thy throne. Send her out from Thy holy
heaven, and from the throne of Thy Majesty, that she
may be with me and may labour with me, that I may
know what is acceptable to Thee. . . . And who
shall know Thy thought except Thou give wisdom,
and send Thy Holy Spirit from above : and so the
ways of them who are on the earth may be corrected,
and men may learn the things that please Thee."

The whole language of Scripture indicates that
whilst truth is addressed to the mind, wisdom is
given to the interior sense. To add wisdom to knowledge is to add love to light ; and the love of good, as
tasted by the soul, passes to the understanding, and
gives a light to the intelligence that comes not merely
of truth but of reality. This is the secret of wisdom.
It keeps the soul pure and reverential ; and, being a

certain sense of the Supreme Good in the very core
of the heart, by that spiritual and interior sense we
are able to judge the value of whatever we see, hear,
read, or know. It is not a mere barren contemplation, it includes a movement towards greater good
and higher life. By its instinct and light we are able
to distinguish the false from the true, the right from
the wrong, the wise from the unwise, and the holy
from the unholy. Moreover, as wisdom comes of the
touch of the Holy Spirit through the created veil, it is
a reader of thoughts, a discerner of spirits, a compre-
hender of the inward condition of souls, and of their
spiritual needs. This is the science of the saints.

The signs of the presence of the gift of wisdom are
its fruits, and these are enumerated by the Apostle
St. James, who teaches that "the wisdom that is
from above, first indeed is chaste, then peaceable,
modest, easy to be persuaded, consenting to the
good, full of mercy and good fruits, without judging,
without dissimulation. And the fruit of justice is sown
in peace to them that make peace." And the same
Apostle teaches how this wisdom may be gained:
"If any of you want wisdom, let him ask of God,
who giveth to all men abundantly, and upbraideth
not; and it shall be given him." And when through
prayer and contemplation, the gift descends in light
upon light, and in flame upon the interior sense, and
the mind and heart have entered into possession of
the gift, it makes the open day of the soul, and
invites her to the festal banquet in which the twelve
fruits of the Holy Spirit are displayed.

The Wise Man calls wisdom "the spirit of understanding." It puts into the understanding a spirit to exercise its functions wisely, wisely to choose the subjects presented to the mind, wisely to distinguish what is true from what is false, and wisely to use the knowledge obtained. Remembering that wisdom gives the spirit of understanding, let us turn back for a few moments to science, that we may consider it in the light of wisdom. St. Paul distinguishes two kinds of science—science truly so called and science falsely so called. True science rests on objective principles and on truths that exist independently of the individual mind ; it is exercised on the conclusions that necessarily flow from them. Where doubt begins, science ends ; although there is a scientific method of dealing with doubts. Opinion can never constitute a science, because opinion is persuasion without certain knowledge ; it consists of subjective notions apart from the perception of objective truth. Opinion is a persuasion liable to change. The sciences that involve human conduct and responsibility, those of government, of legislation, of political economy, of philosophy in its true sense, of morals, and of theology, have fallen outside the Church into utter confusion. Nor is the cause of this confusion far to seek. Modern society floats uneasily about on the crumbling sands of opinion, egotism, and self-interest. But neither opinion, which is always shifting, nor egotism, which is a malady of the soul, nor self-interest, can ever form a science. For science is a system of truths illuminated by fixed and constant principles, and commanding the assent of all minds that know them. Egotism and self-interest can only generate personal opinions. The science of political economy, for example, has been reduced by what are called great thinkers to personal interests; which, whatever else becomes of it, destroys the notion of a science. And thus it is with other so-called sciences affecting human responsibility: outside the Church they have lost their fixed foundations; they are constantly invented anew to be as constantly destroyed ; they are but bundles of personal views and sentiments devoid of all authority, and succeeding each other like the fashions.

Truth comes from God and error from man. Truth must be antecedent to error in the very nature of things, because error is the abuse or denial of truth. The greater and nobler the truth is, the greater and more numerous will be the errors raised in the course of time against it; because truth is imperative of submission to its authority, whilst the pride of the human heart is insubordinate, and reluctant to bend itself under the dominion of truth. The proud man prefers changeable opinion to certain truth, because over opinion he can assert his dominion, whilst unchangeable truth asserts its dominion over him. And the man who is intractable to truth will aim at revolutionising with his free and changeable opinions both truth and government, be it religious or political. This is the freethinking that generates liberalism, the greatest adversary of liberty.

It is in the nature of error to overlay the truth, and in presenting its counterfeit to affect the presentation of what is true. The sovereign Lord of truth presents to us the genuine coin bearing His image and superscription, and fraudful man substitutes the baser metals of the earth, on which he forges the counterfeit image and superscription. God presents us with the luminous portrait of things as in truth they are, and conceited man daubs the lustrous portrait over with a feeble imitation from the soiled colours of his own imagination.

The secret of false philosophies is to be found in the obtruding of what belongs to the subjective man into the place of objective truth. It is a fundamental maxim of sound philosophy that the pure intellect in presence of the pure truth is never deceived. When a wise man sees the truth he recognises it ; and whatever his foregone prejudice or conception of his interest may have been, he casts them aside and submits to the truth as to a master who holds possession of his true interest and consolation.

Pride has self for its object. Sensualism is another kind of pride, the grosser egotism prompted by the senses. But when pride, generated by self-love, takes the place of that wisdom which is generated by the love of God, and when the outward senses, instead of the interior sense, become the chief prompters of the soul, they work upon the imagination, and fill it with subjective forms or notions spiritually or sensually more or less impure, that cloud the mind and eclipse the view of pure, objective truth. It is in the nature of all such egotistical thinking to turn the mind inwardly upon its actual contents and operations, and to accept them as the representations of truth. And when the egotistical passion, proud in the consciousness of a certain energy, is enhanced by a love of mental exertion, a love of singularity, a love of distinction ; a love, despite the common sense of mankind, of seeming to hold dominion over truth ; or, most dismal of all, a love of taking the position of a creator ; then there comes a blinding of the intellect, and a predominance of imagination, enormously exaggerated by means of the rational light remaining in the mind, that leads to the confounding of the subjective imagination of the man with the objective truth of God.

The rational light is still there, however clouded and obscured, and from it is obtained the power of generalisation. But as the broken light remaining is mingled with the images of the imagination, it gives to them a subtlety, a capacity of fusion into each other, and consequently a semblance of universality far more than belongs to them. For, when the pure intellect is obscured, it is marvellous how much is lost of the light of distinction. And as wisdom is excluded by egotism, its light is not there to discern what is true from what is imaginative illusion. Semblances are mistaken for truths just as we sometimes mistake clouds in the horizon for mountains, or sands in the desert through the shimmer of light upon them for refreshing waters. Yet the ardour of creation goes on ; the rational light is humbled down to subserve the imagination ; the universe is constructed anew ; the puny creature with audacious impiety reduces God Himself to an element in His own creation ; and the final result is a pantheistic system in which its author deifies himself.

P

All false philosophies having a subjective basis end in pantheism. In them the light of reason which reflects God's truth is perverted to the service of the subjective phenomena that pervade the imagination. Wisdom is not there to warn and correct the errors of the mind, common sense is discarded, egotism is predominant, and their authors justly incur the terrible denunciation of the Almighty— "Thou hast caused me to serve in thy sins." Intellectual crimes are among the greatest, for they put out light, pervert the whole man, and through him lead to the perversion of many others. Pantheism is the Satanic crime, the greatest perversion of the gift of intelligence, the greatest abuse of God's light. In the saddest experience it enables us to comprehend how Lucifer, that bright spirit, sealed with the resemblance of God, through his attempt to equal the Most High God, fell into ruin. It enables us to understand how he delights to have followers of his otherwise unimaginable audacity.

I have recently examined an elaborate exposition of the last and most flagrant system of German pantheism, written by an earnest English disciple. It professes to reveal the secret of Hegel.* Hegel himself declared that one man alone understood him, and yet that that man did not understand him. An English lecturer on philosophy, of some note, has called Hegel's system an impenetrable adamant, and his commentators say that his depths are beyond the reach of other minds. But is this the character of truth? Is not truth self-luminous? As far as

* Stirling's Secret of Hegel.

natural truth is concerned, when discovered by one mind, is it not open to every mind that is clear and acute ? Is there no sense in St. Gregory's remark, that nothing is so easy to learn as truth ? Are the mysteries of some one eccentric mind to overthrow the common sense of mankind at large ? Is such a one to be allowed to blot out the conscience by which men have always lived, and to which they have always trusted ? Are these unintelligible speculations to be suffered to destroy the hope of the future life that makes the present tolerable ?

I look into this system. It is but a remodelling of the old Hindoo system pushed in many of its conclusions to greater extravagance. A universe is offered to us of which the external and visible manifestation is unsubstantial delusion, and of which the internal substance is thought ; nothing better than human thought ; thought constantly rising and falling, thought incessantly appearing and disappearing to give place to its successor. What further proof need we to show that the author of this universe never got beyond the sphere of his own subjective thoughts, from which he has woven his new universe ? This universe formed of human thought has necessitated a new logic, a new morality, a new religion without a personal God, but with the State for its deity ; new laws of nature, and new laws for mankind ; a new philosophy, and an absolutely new encyclopedia. When we look into these novel sciences, what do we find ? We find imagination in place of truth, the subjective confounded with the objective, and a course of reasoning travelling upon double middle terms, and splitting the major premises from the conclusions. Yet even this mode of progress can scarcely be inconsistent with a logic having for its basis the denial that there can be contradiction, and that propositions which contradict each other, when seen in a higher light, are absolutely identical. The radical absurdity of the theory is obvious at a glance, since, by the very nature of thought, its author is compelled to employ the principle of contradiction for the purpose of maintaining its non-existence.

The expositor of Hegel's secret considers the proposition *ex nihilo nihil fit* to be decisive against all controversy as opposed to Hegel. As if this proposition were applicable to divine as well as to human creations. As if it were not absolutely decisive against Hegel's system, whose basis is this, that *nothing* is always in the state of becoming *something*.

The forming of some new world from the excited fantasy of the individual, with its author for its deity, is a well-known mental malady, of which examples may be found in our lunatic asylums.

Folly stands opposed to wisdom, and as opposites belong to the same science, it is for wisdom to consider the ways of folly. There has been a folly put forth of late by men claiming the sanction of philosophy, that comes not short of the extremest examples denounced in the Holy Scriptures. It is comprised in this formulary, " God and the supernatural are unthinkable, therefore inaccessible, and to be dismissed from the mind with reverence as unknowable." This is a new phase of the old Epicureanism, exiling God from His own creation. In an age of luxury and incessant dissipation, of waste of the mind in endless literature as well as of the senses in pleasure, a formulated folly of this character is sure to have followers and to become a dreary fashion. The conceit is far too low and miserable to be argued with; it comes of a pride of so un-intellectual a description that to be cured it must be humbled. A man without a communicative God is a man without a conscience ; and a man without a conscience has fallen from the attributes of humanity, and become a monster. Yet this we are told is progress. Progress undoubtedly it is, a progress of descent from all that is noble and elevating in man to the lowest gulf of barbarism. Must we say that the sun is unthinkable because the imagination can never compass what science tells us of its vastness ? Must we say that that beneficent luminary, on which our mortal life depends, must be dismissed from the mind as being inaccessible to thought because we have never seen it ; because at the enormous distance at which we are placed from it, all that reaches us is the final vibration of a small number of the sun's countless rays, lessened in their vigour by their refraction through the atmosphere? For man to isolate himself from God is to blot out of himself the source of wisdom as well as of philo-sophy. Except in profane intention, no man can free himself from God ; this would effect his own annihilation.

There are men who bore their eyes into matter until they can no longer see spirit, and who crowd their imagination with material forms until they blot from sight both God and the soul. But materialism can never form a science, much less a philosophy ; it is utterly incapable of an intellectual principle. Material atoms, however arranged, can never be the recipient of truth, or the generator of thought. Behind such theories, there is a sensualism and a pride at work which take a strange content in that kind of imaginary self-exaltation that feeds itself on the lowering of all men. It is the natural result of pride, whether spiritual or sensual, to seek in its degree the exaltation of self in the degradation of humanity; but it culminates in tyrants and materialists. Justly do the Scriptures, justly does the common sense of mankind, stamp the note of folly on men who use the powers of the soul to deny the existence of the soul, and the light of God to deny the existence of God. The words of the archangel Raphael come home to them with a terrible truth—Those who shut out God from themselves and from their mind, over them the devil hath power.

Many years ago I saw a painting by Rubens at Cologne, the contemplation of which opened one of those intuitions that become a light to the mind for life. The subject of the picture, treated with extraordinary power, was the stigmatisation of St. Francis, a subject at which fools mock, and on which wise men deeply ponder. The crucified Seraph fills the air above with a light that reveals the mystery by which man is won to wisdom through suffering and love. Beneath the wooded rocks of Alverno kneels the humble and loving saint, absorbed in contempla-

tion of the Eternal Wisdom crucified, and by His
crucifixion re-opening the way of man to his Supreme
Good. The wounds of the love-burning Seraph dart
their fiery rays into the feet, hands, and side of God's
servant, and in the triumph of the tranquil ecstasy
over excruciating pain and sorrow, we see how nature
must suffer in having its narrow limits expanded by
the sudden receiving of a great enlargement through
the fire of divine love. Yet is the strain of suffering
lost to sense in the ecstatic joy of that celestial
communion with the Eternal Good. A wonderful
knowledge has come with the wonderful gift, not by
the cold way of science and ideas, but by the way of
wisdom, in which the light comes forth to the mind
from the good implanted in the heart.

Beneath this realisation of God's divine communication to His humble servant, the artist, with a profound
instinct, has symbolised the mockery with which
puny minds, inflated with conceit, greet the great
mysteries of God. Beneath a broken fragment,
fallen from the towering rocks, squats an inflated
toad, peering up with its keen eyes to a white butterfly
that hovers above the stone with expanded wings,
and is exerting some rayless, magical influence upon
the unpleasant creature that peers up with inflated
conceit from below. Placed elsewhere this incident
would only raise a smile ; but in its obvious relation
with the mystery of divine communication above,
it rises in significance to the awful and the terrible.
You think of Satan aping the angel of light, and of his
victim aping illumination. You see the sophist with
his butterfly light working out his travesty of the works

of God's eternal wisdom, yet reaching no higher than the images of his brain, or the small things that come within the scope of his senses. And one is reminded of the saying of a profound mystic, that "the wisdom of God is the scourge of fools."

How much of sophistical speculation owes its origin to the moral unsoundness of the spirit in which it is conducted! In the owl-light, when the earth is between the eyes and the sun, all objects are blended with indefinite shadows. The shadows are nothing save the absence of light, yet they are easily confounded with realities. The old Persians had a proverb that, " Pride is like the night, in which you cannot distinguish the beetle from the ground." . He who would create the universe anew, had better first understand the universe into which he has so recently come in the character of a poor and helpless stranger. But to do that he must wait for the sunlight. Pride lives in the owl-light, and wisdom in the sunlight.

The Divine Wisdom is an ocean without shores or soundings, that in its simplicity beholds all things at once and everlastingly, beholds them in one, yet in all their diversities. The human wisdom participated from that Divine Wisdom through the gift of the Holy Spirit, is not like that of the ancient philosophers, but is divine. It comes not of the speculation of science, but from the union of the heart with God. Charity and wisdom come together to the soul, and increase together, and by them our thoughts and our works are tempered. Wisdom acts neither from excitement nor from compulsion; but is grave, serious, and guarded against the subtle impulses of nature. For nature moves from impulse, and is led by sensible impressions; but wisdom moves from grace, and is guided by the highest principles.

The learning of the schools gives knowledge, but God gives wisdom. The holy Fathers and saintly Doctors obtained this wisdom, not from their studies as exercises of the mind, but through their prayer and their contemplation, which, united to their studies, brought the infused knowledge from God. It was their humility and charity that opened their hearts to this divine gift of wisdom. Where wisdom is, it finds a singular relish in the words and the works of men who are holy and wise. Keeping the soul that it rules free from passions and commotions, wisdom shines from the soul's operations as from calm and placid waters. Wisdom is more in work than in speech. It is the property of wise men to do many things, and to say little about them. Wisdom grows by experience, and by listening to the wisdom of others; because God rewards our docility to them by giving us of their wisdom. It is a great part of wisdom to refer all things to God, and to weigh them in the profound balance of His judgments, according to the proverb—"Weight and balance are the judgments of the Lord, and His work all the weights of the world." Everything savours of what it is. The elated man savours of his pride, the animal man of his sensuality, and the wise man of the Divine Wisdom. Yet though the wise man discerns the spirit of the proud and the sensual, they cannot understand what is in the spirit of the wise man. They may reverence him, or stand in fear of him; but only the wise can understand the wise. It is the attribute of wisdom to be full of reverence.

The man who is most truly man is he who has been reformed by the supernatural gift of wisdom; he has become what God in His divine plan intended that man should be. And by virtue of this gift, and through its exercise, he is raised to a state superior to that of all mere natural men. It makes him simple in life and thought, sweet and efficacious in influence, comprehensive and clear in his views, and vivid in persuasion; and forasmuch as the forces of his heart are held in unity, there is nothing in him excited, affected, or coerced by self-interest or human respect. Then the wise man judges all things, not according to their outward magnitude or appearance, but according to their intrinsic value, and to their degree of goodness and sanctity; and he regards their relations to the Supreme Good as the standard and measure of their value.*

Not without reason, my brethren, has this seminary been placed under the patronage of St. Bernard. His writings put forth the sweetest and highest wisdom in most lucid order. And what he wrote, that he was—a saint who was strong in the science and wisdom of God. No other Father has given so complete an exposition of the true motives of study, and with a brief statement of his doctrine on this subject I conclude.

Of many things may we be allowed to be ignorant, says the mellifluous doctor, but not of God or of one's

* For the substance of the last three paragraphs, see Theoremata Venerab. Fr. Joannis a Sancto Samsone, cap. De Sapientia Divina.

self. Far be it from me to reprove the learned, or to discourage the study of literature. I know how studious men serve the Church, refute her adversaries, and instruct the more simple-minded. Yet the Apostle tells us—" Be not more wise than it behoveth to be wise, but be wise unto sobriety." What is it to be wise unto sobriety? It is to watchfully consider what we ought first and most to know. All science that rests on truth is good ; but time is short ; and in the course of that time we have got to work out our salvation with fear and trembling. Be careful, then, to know first and most what is nearest to your salvation. The nourishing foods that God has created are all of them good ; but if you take them out of due season, order, or proportion, they are not good for you. And so it is with the sciences.

St. Paul tells us again, that "knowledge puffeth up, but charity buildeth up." He is not so anxious for much knowledge as for the right method of knowing. What is this right method? It is to understand in what order, in what spirit, and to what end we pursue knowledge. In what order? That you first pursue what is nearest to salvation. In what spirit? That you most ardently pursue that which most enkindles love. To what end? Not for the sake of curiosity or vanity, but to build up yourself, and to build up your neighbour. Some seek to know for the sake of knowing, and this is vain curiosity. Some seek to know for the sake of making themselves known, and this is offensive vanity. These men escape not the sting of the satirist, who sings in their ears—" Thy knowledge is nothing to thee unless

others know that this thou knowest." Some desire
to know that they may sell their knowledge, and this
is filthy lucre. But there are some who wish to know,
that with their knowledge they may build up other
men, and this is charity : and, again, they wish to
know that they may build up themselves, and this
is prudence. Of all these motives the last two alone
are free from abuse, for those who use them "seek to
understand that they may do good."

Forasmuch as knowledge puffeth up, the soul
should first seek to know herself. This is the true
order, and the most useful method. It is the true
order, because what first concerns us is to know what
we really are. It is the most useful, because self-
knowledge does not puff us up; self-knowledge will
not let us be conceited ; self-knowledge humbles us
down, and gives us safe ground to build upon. And
without the foundation of self-knowledge the spiritual
building will not stand. But when we place our self
before our eyes, we find that we are in a region of
unlikeness, and are led to God, crying with the
prophet—"In Thy truth Thou hast humbled me."
Then God begins to deliver us; and we begin to
honour Him ; and so, the knowledge of our self leads
us to the knowledge of God. His image becomes renewed in us ; and, looking with the open face of confidence upon His grace, we are transformed unto His
likeness ; from brightness to brightness, as from the
Spirit of the Lord.*

S. Bernard, in Cantic. Serm. 36, 37.

X.

On Counsel.

The Discourse delivered at the Opening of the First Provincial Chapter of the Dominican Sisters of the English Congregation of St. Catherine of Sienna.

"Where there is no governor the people shall fall ; but where there is much counsel there is safety."—PROVERBS xi. 14.

I HAVE chosen this proverb of an inspired king, my sisters, as a basis on which to build your instruction, before entering on your first provincial chapter, because in its simple strength it embodies the great principle that has called us together, and because the saints have encircled it with beautiful radiations of light.

"Where there is no governor the people shall fall." A community cannot stand erect and hold together without a ruler to govern it, and the government is not safe without much counsel. Or, to put the whole sense of the Hebrew text with the help of a little amplification : Those who are embarked together, and are not steered by a well-advised pilot, shall fall as the leaves, and there is safety in much counsel. So the Fathers of the desert explain the text of the

Septuagint, as reported by Cassian in his Second Con-
ference, which is on discretion. "Those," said Abbot
Moses, "who are left without government, and who
are therefore without counsel and discretion, shall
fall as the leaves."

A well-governed congregation of religious is like a
flourishing tree. The stem of authority is in one
person whose strength grows out of the root of the
order. From the one stem grow the chief branches,
whose vigour comes forth of the strength of the stem,
and these are the local authorities. On the greater
branches live the lesser branches ; and these are the
subordinate superiors and auxiliaries. On all the
branches flourish the leaves, drawing their life and
freshness through the branches from the stem, and
through the stem from the nourishing root. The
leaves are the numbers who crown and glorify the
tree. But when the sap of life quits the branches,
and from the dying stem sinks back into the ground,
then fade and fall the leaves. "Where there is no
government the people shall fall."

To take the other image of the original text, a
religious congregation is like a ship in which many
persons are embarked on a common venture, and you
know how St. Catherine loved to use this similitude.
The pilot to whom the ship of souls is intrusted
must steer the vessel along the invisible track over
many waves, through many waters. He must watch
the compass, take observation of the celestial orbs,
note the signs in the clear as well as in the clouded
skies, keep careful calculations, and consult with
those who have an experienced understanding of the

way. He considers the times and the seasons, shapes
the trim of the ship to the varying winds; is one
in the calm, another in the storm; consents with
patience to delay when the elements are adverse;
advances with expanded wings when they turn anew
to favour his course. He keeps steadily in mental
view the land to be sighted, the port to be reached,
the safe landing of the freight of souls. But to avoid
the open dangers and the secret perils, to keep all on
board in safe order and good spirits, the conductor of
the vessel needs to be well counselled and on many
sides advised. So must it be with one who has to
guide and advance a religious society, which is in
character so manifold, in temperament so various,
and in its individual natures so diversely inclined. It
is no easy task to conduct a host of souls, having each
her own springs of action within her, by one compass
to one end of life. Multiply the members by the
changeable inclinations that move their natures severally, and then reflect what it is to draw these inclinations into one and the same spirit of duty, this duty
into love, and this love unto God; and so shall you
estimate how great is the task of guiding a religious
congregation in the path of the rule.

Of all the duties of religious government, there is
none that demands more consideration and discretion than that of putting the right persons in the right
places, and the wrong persons where they can do
least harm to the congregation or themselves. Abilities alone will not give the right persons, there must
be a keen eye to the right spirit. The spirit of the
right persons is simple, and their intention pure.

This spirit puts order into their faculties, and clearness into their judgment. The wrong persons are they whose motives are mixed with vanity, and who, consequently, when they have to look to others, carry themselves in their eyes. Such persons have scattered minds and a crook in their vision. For this reason humbler abilities are often more available than greater ones ; and for the same reason it is that true humility is so great a power. Discretion in ruling is far-sighted, and scents danger afar off, feels its breath when it comes nearer at hand, and wards off the pestilential influence before others become conscious of its presence. It sees the germs of future evils where others may see but some innocent occasion for amusement or distraction. Much counsel therefore does the superior need, who has to guide so many and such various characters into one rule of life and one law of discipline, that search to the very spirit and motive of actions ; and to adapt that rule and discipline to change of conditions without injury to its fixed and authentic interpretation.

St. Gregory Nazianzen felt all this difficulty when he wrote the *Apologia* of his episcopal government. A commonwealth of human beings, he says, is like a monster compounded of many natures, whose various habits incline them to take different and opposite ways. They have not the same voice or the same appetites. What one likes another dislikes. What pleases one is disagreeable to another. Whosoever has the care of a creature so variously constituted must have a wisdom that is large and variously accomplished. Nor is the difference so great between a creature so compounded of unequal dispositions and a community of Christians, concludes the great theologian and saint, but that the superior who manages it has need to be at once both simple and various;—simple in practising one and the same integrity towards all, and various in promoting the good-will of each one.

"And in much counsel there is safety." Observe, my sisters, that it is not said that in a multitude of counsellors there is safety. This is a frequent perversion of the text. But it is said that in much counsel there is safety. Magnitude is applied not to the number who give counsel, but to the weight and value of the counsel given. The number of truly wise advisers in every community of human beings is small, as small likewise is the number of them who can wisely govern. This is admirably looked to in the Constitutions of the Dominican Order, where in a provincial or even general chapter, although the number of delegates is considerable, yet they in their turn elect a small number of definitors on whom rests the decision of all important affairs.

Counsel is the deliberation that goes before judgment. It is the careful examination of the facts, and the just and accurate weighing of the reasons that influence decision. It is the subtle investigation and determination of the causes that should determinate what ought to be regulated or concluded. "Counsel," says St. Bonaventure, "is the eye and caution of the future." And "the helm that should steer counsel," observes St. Cyprian, "is the wisdom of the Divine law."

Q

But wisdom is a gift that is rare and precious, nor is it found in the land of them who live in delights. And so rare and precious is the wisdom that governs well, that with the exception of the Church, which the Eternal Wisdom guides, everything—society in this world, even religious communities, even great orders—come sooner or later to decay for the want of it. Hence St. Paul placed governments among the special gifts of the Holy Ghost, and in the same category with miracles and speaking with tongues.

"Be at peace with many," says the Scripture, "but let one of a thousand be thy counsellor." No one is fit to give counsel in the affairs of religious life, who cannot look at the case from God's side of it ; who is not humble enough to put self out of consideration ; who is not magnanimous above all human respect ; who is not open to receive as well as to give advice ; who is not ready to change her judgment with change of light ; who looks not more to God's reason in the question than to her own. For "with God is wisdom and strength ; He hath counsel and understanding." The affairs of religious life belong more to God's guidance than to ours, and in supremely guiding them to their issues, it is upon no personal reason of ours, but upon His own Divine reason, that God acts. Hence the wisdom of the religious is to seek and to follow the reason of God.

On the other hand, we hear the Prophet Isaias saying to Babylon, "Thou hast failed in the multitude of thy counsels." And we have the authority of Solomon to back our own experience, that the number of the unwise is unlimited. Or if you prefer the exact sense of Solomon—"The crooked is with difficulty brought straight, because the number of them who fail in sense is countless." The wise man speaks of the wilful as well as the unconscious failing of sense, of moral as well as of natural deficiency, of the unwisdom of the heart that leads to so much unwisdom in the mind. You know that the Vulgate and our own version use much stronger words. Yet they go not beyond the mind of Solomon, who estimates every one a fool who turns from God's presence in the world and from God's light in the conscience. No one is wise or fit for counsel who seeks not wisdom from God.

This truth calls for sturdy utterance in our day; yet whoever utters it aloud will need the martyr's spirit. Not here, my sisters, where humility puts delusions to flight, but in the two worlds outside— the secular world, and what is called the Christian world. For in both of them it has come to be thought that wisdom to advise, to make laws, and to govern, is not so much the gift of God, a gift granted to the few and faithful found, but to the forces of human nature diffused through the multitudes. But although so many persons declaim on this modern law of wisdom, and not a few persons half think it true, I do not say that those who are experienced in the government of the multitude believe it. For whatever becomes of the theory, the unbending law of human nature asserts itself, and practically, and for the time, it is always one who governs in every society of human beings, one whose real advisers are but a small number.

Let us listen to one of the wise, to a great and
learned Pope instructing a crafty king—to Pius II.
explaining the text on which we are engaged to Louis
XI. The Pope says : " When the Scripture declares
that 'where there is much counsel there is safety,'
it does not ask for a multitude of counsellors, but
for a mature and well digested counsel; and this
is more easily obtained from a small number than
from many. For a multitude is swayed by contrary
inclinations and by a diversity of affection, that do
not lift us up to the most just and elevated conduct,
but pull us down in the direction of confusion. The
counsel of numbers is hasty. Yet matters are never
well advised unless we attach more value to the
weight of the arguments that point to the conclusion
than to the numbers who vote for it. For it often happens that the greater part defeats the sounder part."*

Ponderanda non numeranda suffragia—weigh the
wisdom and weight of reason in them who give
counsel, rather than the numbers who stand to one
opinion—is the wise old law of deliberation. And in
the old canon law it was provided that the sounder
part should be followed in chapter deliberations; but
where a chapter exercises not a mere deliberative
but a decisive voice, then the sounder part is necessarily defined to be the major part. But the identity
of the majority with the sounder part rests on the
presumption that the majority will be wise enough,
after due discussion, to adopt the soundest views
put forth. When, however, a superior assembles a
purely deliberative council, that superior wisely

* Pius II. 1 Epist. 387, Apud Cornel. à Lapide in Textum.

follows the soundest advice that commends itself
to her judgment, in preference, at times, to the
sense of the majority.

One sister is wiser on one subject, another is
sounder on another. And on one and the same
question, one will see it best from one side, and
another from a different point of view. One from
her position will tell us more of the facts of the case,
another with her experience will penetrate further
into their bearing and significance, a third will look
at the question more keenly as it affects the spirit
and life of the community, a fourth will take it into a
higher light, where perhaps God's will is made manifest as to what should or should not be done in view
of the future sanctity of the congregation. One sees
the use, another the probable abuse. And, as a rule,
it is the numbers who supply the facts to be considered, the experience, and the general sense of the
congregation respecting them; whilst it is the few,
and mostly those who have been practised in governing and the wakeful discretion that comes of responsibility, who can best discern the significance of those
facts, of that experience, of the ultimate tendency
of what is commonly thought; and who best can
measure on the scale of discipline what in regulation
will best contribute to secure both efficiency and
harmony in the true spirit of the order. Yet sometimes the contrary will be true, especially in correcting
past errors; just as those who look on see more than
those who play the game. Again, it will happen
that one who has less than others of wisdom in
general, will have a particular light on some one

subject, to which perhaps she has given long and assiduous attention.

Commenting on the text, Cornelius à Lapide observes that the safety of a community rests on two things, both of which the Scripture insinuates—on the enlightened wisdom of those who govern, and on the faithful obedience of them who are governed. For in vain do superiors obtain the best counsel, in vain do they make the wisest regulations, unless they are taken up by obedience, and by an obedience whose humility so tempers zeal with discretion, as to secure its perseverance through all changes.

Shrewdly has this part of the text been explained by St. Dorotheus. "It warns us," he says, "not to be our own advisers, not to become our own disciples, not to persuade ourselves that we are fit to govern ourselves. Weak and soon vanquished are those religious who will have no guides, no helpers on their way to God. For He saith—' They who have no governor shall fall as the leaves.' When the leaf springs it is green, growing, and delightful ; but after a time it fades and withers, falls and is trodden on. Such is a religious who is governed by no one. At first she is fresh and fervid in fasting, in watching, in peace of soul, in obedience, in all good things. After awhile this fervour slackens, and if she look to no one to govern her, to no one to uphold her in the hour of trial, to no one to stir up and rekindle the sunken flame of fervour, she withers and falls to the ground, and in her state of lonely destitution is caught by her enemies, who work their will upon her."

And now, my sisters, let me give your minds a

little repose, and that upon a Phrygian tapestry of embroidered needlework. For by this name St. Cyril of Thessalonica calls his Moral Apologues. I speak of that St. Cyril who, with St. Methodius, converted the Bulgarians to the Church in the ninth century, who translated the whole Scriptures into their language, whose body was brought to Rome with great pomp, and entombed in the ancient church of St. Clement's, and whose portrait, together with the pictures of that magnificent ceremonial, painted on the walls of that long-buried church, have been brought to light in our day. You have the photographs of them, which I brought to you from Rome. Listen, then, to a piece of St. Cyril's word-embroidery.

"Where there is much counsel there is wisdom." An ant was going on its industrious way, when she met a little fox who was picking up materials with which to make a lair above the ground. After politely saying, " Good-day to you," the ant asked the little fox what she was doing. And the little fox said, "So far of my life I have lived in a dark hole ; but for the time to come I mean to live in the daylight, and have my nest there, for everybody finds it so pleasant." But the ant said, " Did you ever find anybody molesting you where you lived before?" "Oh no!" replied the little fox, " I was always so safe and so quiet. But I should like to enjoy the daylight." Then the ant said gravely, " However, sister, though I am not big enough to be counsellor to such a prudent person as you are, yet I venture to remind you—and depend upon it, whatever you may think of your new scheme, it is quite true—that you are no favourite with either the farmers or the skinners. The farmers don't like your zeal for their chickens, and the skinners care less for your life than for your coat. Before beginning a new affair like this, had you not best consult the old foxes? For 'counsel will keep thee, and prudence will save thee.'" To this good advice the young fox gave no very wise answer; for she said, "This does not very much concern me, sister, for I really think that I don't stand much in need of your advice." Upon which the ant gave this prudent reply, "All things in their beginning are very small to sight, but very great in power. From a little seed the great palm tree grows. Wherefore the greatest counsel should be taken over the first small beginnings. For a little error in the beginning becomes a great one in the end. A slight disease in the root when first planted, will work its way through the whole growth of the tree; for the character of the entire tree is contained in the beginning of it. Then add to this, that 'he who contemneth small things shall fall by little and little into greater things.' For which reason Solomon hath said in the Proverbs— 'Hearken unto counsel, and receive instruction, that thou mayest be wise in the latter end.'"

Half vanquished by the reasoning of the ant, the little fox said, "I grant that I ought to take counsel on this new undertaking, but nature has given me the shrewdest adviser at home." To which the ant gave this wise reply, "It is written, 'Be not wise in thine own conceit, and lean not on thine own prudence.' For 'calling themselves wise, they be-

came fools.' Do not four eyes see more than two ?
And when more rays of light come together, is there
not more light to see with ? Is not the ship safer
that is the better manned ? Of whom is counsel ? Is
it not of Wisdom ? And what Wisdom hides from
one she reveals to another ; being a lover of humility,
she gives commonly the counsel of right action for one
person through the voice of another. If you have
rightly judged the matter yourself, take another to
bear witness to it, and to confirm it, and you will
then be more certain, and will act on your judgment
with greater confidence. The more persons agree in
counsel, the more healthy will that counsel be. For
'where there is much counsel, there is safety.' So
that 'a wise man shall hear and be wiser ; and he
that understandeth shall know how to govern.'"
Then said the little fox to the ant, "I know that thou
art provident. Teach me, I pray thee, to whose
counsel I ought to listen." Upon which the ant
said, "To the counsel of the friend who is faithful,
who is large-minded, and who fears God." And
after saying this, the provident little creature bid
the cunning animal farewell, and went on her way.

Of counsel, what less can be said than that it
opens the minds of them who govern ; that it purges
the scales of delusion from their sight ; that it
broadens the field of light in which they behold the
scope of their duty ; that it lightens responsibility,
fortifies judgment, and strengthens confidence ; that
it augments the trust of subjects in superiors, and
will not suffer them who rule to be deceived.

Of counsel let us declare the generation and the

consummation. Counsel is of wisdom, and wisdom
is of God. In the Adorable Trinity is the Word, the
Wisdom, through whom the Father made all things,
and the Spirit of Counsel in whom He governs all
things. He hath placed His intelligent creatures in
societies, that being governed by reason and by
counsel, they may be a shadow of His own Divine
society. If in civil society men dwell together in
peace under one ruler, it is the remoter image ; but a
religious society is the nearer resemblance, because
there is the unity that comes of Divine authority, of
Divine wisdom, and of Divine love ; because there are
the gifts of the Holy Spirit, and among them are
understanding, wisdom, and counsel.

The law of the gift of wisdom is its distribution ;
the law of the gift of counsel is to unite together what
wisdom has distributed. By counsel the wisdom
divided to several becomes the possession of one
who rules. The law of distribution is taught by the
Holy Spirit of Wisdom in the book of Ecclesiasticus :
" All wisdom is from the Lord God, and hath been
always with Him, and is before all time. . . . He
created her in the Holy Ghost, and saw, and numbered her, and measured her. And He poured her out
upon all His works, and upon all flesh, according to
His gift, and hath given her to them who love Him.
. . . The fear of the Lord is the beginning of wisdom,
and it is created with the faithful in the womb ; it
walketh with chosen women, and is known with the
just and faithful. . . . Wisdom shall distribute knowledge and understanding of prudence ; and she ex-
alteth the glory of them that hold her fast."

The gift of wisdom is created in the Holy Spirit, is limited by number and measure, is traced upon each of God's works, is poured in separate gifts upon mankind, is given more abundantly to them who love the giver, is distributed in knowledge and understanding of prudence. Thus from all God's creatures may the wisdom of God be gathered ; from its vestiges in the creation, from the reason of man, from the sacred Scriptures, from the sense of the Church, from the hearts of saints, from the ways of God in the history of humanity, from all the uses of all creatures, from the graces and inspirations of God to individual souls. Wisdom is also gathered from all trials and sufferings and from the exercise of all virtues. God has so far and widely distributed the rays of wisdom, and has given the gift of wisdom to them who seek it, in which by counsel these rays may be gathered, that no one may say that wisdom is his own, and that the sense of its limitation in ourselves may promote the humility to which it is given.

Such is wisdom's law of distribution. But counsel is also a gift of the same Holy Spirit, and by counsel that is united into one which has been first distributed unto many. The Holy Scriptures say that "wisdom dwelleth with counsel." And hence our Divine Lord, to whom the prophet gave the title of "the Counsellor" as well as that of "the Mighty God," has said, " Where two or three are gathered together in My name, there am I in the midst of them." Yet when in His human presence He instructed us, to teach us humility He ascribed not His wisdom to Himself but to His Father. And He promised that after His departure the Holy Spirit should keep us in all truth. It is one of the most instructive truths of the Old Testament with respect to the distribution of wisdom, that the great prophet and lawgiver himself was taught the value of counsel by one who was not even of the chosen race ; and the Sanhedrim, the great council of the Hebrews, was instituted by Moses through the inspiration of Jethro. In the dark hour of Israel, the cry of Isaias was this : " Take counsel, gather a council : make thy shadow as the night in the mid-day."

When the Church was formed, by our Lord's direction the Apostles were united together in prayer, and the Holy Ghost descended in a flame that was parted in distribution to each one of them. When special difficulties arose in their apostolate, the disciples met together, and from their plenary illumination in council the decision came forth ; and it was headed : " It hath seemed good to the Holy Ghost and to us." So has the Church always acted, both as a whole and in her several parts ; in councils general, in councils provincial, and in the chapters of her religious orders, both general and local. Counsel is everywhere in the Church the provider of order, strength, and discipline. Being in the midst " it produces peace and perfect health."

From contemplating the principles of counsel and their general application, let us turn, my sisters, to the work before us. What is a provincial chapter ? The chapter, *capitulum*, is the head that enlightens and directs the whole body. As the head holds the sense of the whole man, so the chapter sums the sense of the congregation. As the heading of a chapter in a book sums up its contents, so the chapter of an order sums up the wisdom of the order, and of a province what wisdom the province contains. It is the congregation sitting in the council of its heads and representatives. It carries with it the organization, the mind, and the experience of the whole body. It is the sum of its aspirations and judgments. It is the whole body virtually present, thinking and deciding through its head. The work of the chapter is to examine, to correct, to provide, and to regulate.

The office of a chapter is well expressed in the Benedictine Constitutions of the congregation of Mount Cassino. " The work of the chapter," they say, " is to follow in the steps of the fathers, and so to lean on their authority, that the vigour of regular discipline, fraternal charity, peace, and lasting concord may be upheld with constancy of purpose in the service of Christ." The spirit in which a chapter should be held is most happily expressed by St. Charles Borromeo, in the Fourth Council of Milan, where he says, " Whenever chapters are to be held, prayers and invocations must first be prescribed. And when the members come to the reckoning of their responsibilities, they should begin with devout prayer that what is well begun may have a good and happy conclusion. By their gravity and uprightness, by their piety and devotion should the members of the chapter so apply themselves to the work in hand, that they may not only uphold all sound administration and discipline, but may, through God's help, raise the work to a higher perfection, and give it greater progress and expansion."

Congregations of religious women are comparatively new and recent in the Church, at least in their canonical form. Yet in earlier ages, in our Saxon kingdoms for example, where female saints founded a number of houses under a common rule, they must have had some common council for their common government, and of this there are traces in history. Great abbesses are even found sitting in the ecclesiastical synods. But this was an anomaly arising from their being in those times the representatives of large temporal and ecclesiastical, as well as religious, interests; and the instances were departures from the ordinary track of woman's religious life.

With the Sisters of St. Vincent of Paul began the congregational life of unenclosed women devoted to works of charity. And congregational life, with its priceless advantages as compared with isolated communities, has necessitated congregational government. But in its method of election congregational government cannot be squared upon that of an isolated convent, where all concerned live within the same walls and are all thoroughly known to each other. The great problem of this chapter will be the final settlement of the best method of electing the local superiors, that it may be submitted to the highest authority of the Church. You have in this the advantage of the far-seeing wisdom of your venerable foundress, the test of experience, and the knowledge of what has succeeded or failed in other Dominican congregations.

Everywhere is the old Dominican Order taking the new shape of congregations in its Tertiary form. In so many provinces of the Church have these congregations arisen, without concert, yet almost simultaneously, and that with full approval both of the superiors of the Order and the Sovereign Pontiff, that it is impossible to doubt that God has manifested His will and has some special design in their establishment. Yet the Constitutions of the Order have not provided, and could not by anticipation have provided, for this new state of things. The provinces of the first order of men differ in so many respects from congregations of the third order of women, that the governmental provisions for the one cannot in all primary points be applied to the other. This your late mother and foundress felt from the beginning; this your late general failed not to see and admit; this the foundresses of the other new congregations have learnt more and more from experience. New conditions of the order demand new regulations, yet always in the old spirit, and based on the old foundations. Internal observance stands ever the same; the order of a congregation uniting a number of houses under one general government alone asks for consideration. As the Church adapts her discipline to changed circumstances, so do the religious orders. Rigidity is not life but death.

What your wise foundress had most at heart, and most constantly prayed for, what your present superiors ponder on with great solicitude, what I desire to see, is such a form of congregational government as will leave no door open for the ape of charity to enter. Now the ape of charity is ambition. The devil of ambition has a shrewd experience of cloisters, and has brought many a foundation to the loss of its first spirit. Ambition is subtle and deceptive, at once flattering and hypocritical. A wily schemer, ambition sows insinuations, fosters divisions, and with the softest, gentlest hand, breaks the sinews and joints of discipline. Ambition has the art above all of affecting the common good, of correcting standing evils, and of simulating a great charity to all concerned.

If charity is patient for the love of eternal things, ambition can be patient for the love of transient things. If charity is benignant and kind to the poor, ambition can be affable and winning to the influential. If charity believeth all things in God, hopeth all things from God, and endureth all things for God ; ambition can believe all things of self, hope all things from self, and endure all things for self. If charity suffereth all things for the truth, ambition can suffer all things for her own vanity. The vice of ambition can so far simulate the virtue of charity as to mislead the unwary, but when we penetrate to motives, they are as distant from each other as hell is from heaven. Even the outward resemblance of ambition to charity wears a lurid bloom that reveals the deception to the humble of heart. When it has once entered into a community, who shall exorcise it ? Who shall drive this evil spirit from them who are possessed by it ?

"I see some religious," says St. Bernard, "who make me grieve ; who have despised the world only to learn greater pride in the school of humility.

They become more self-asserting than they were in
the world, and more restless in the cloister than
when they were outside of it. And, what is worse,
some of them who were contemptible enough in their
own house, will not endure contempt in the house of
God. Having never obtained any special notice
where most people get some honour, they make up
for it by seeking for honour where all honour is
despised." *

Far am I, my sisters, from saying that ambition
has hitherto found its way into this congregation.
God has kept from you the very shadow of it.
Hitherto, thanks to the form in which you have been
governed, and to the spirit which God has given you,
there has been no field for it, and no opening for its
entrance. And I have been singularly gratified in
observing how the communities have, with a beautiful simplicity of purpose, delegated their oldest
members to this chapter, as being the best witnesses of your spirit and your traditions from the
beginning.

Close the doors, my sisters, at whatever cost close
the doors, against the infernal ape that mocks
heavenly charity. Settle your rule of elections with
a special view and a keen foresight to future pos-
sibilities of abuse. Secure their being conducted
under the wisest counsel of the wisest members of
the congregation, and then will you secure the future
well-being of the whole body. You know that your
holy foundress was wont to say, and that from her
inmost conviction, that her work would stand or fall

* S. Bernard, ILom. 4, Super Miss.

R

by the principle upon which the local elections were finally determined.

You have prayed for light upon this chapter in all your communities, long and earnestly have you prayed. This is your pious contribution to its deliberations. When the work of deliberation is completed, each member of the chapter will return to her place and office, bearing with her the fruits of your common light. What is the fruit of light? St. Paul tells us that "the fruit of the light is in all goodness, and justice, and truth." And this fruit of your counsel, whether carried to the branches or remaining at the head, will enable you to illustrate what has been provided for the common good, and to make intelligible in due time to the absent what has here been regulated.

And so, my sisters, to make an end of this instruction, let us carry it all before the throne of mercy in the voice of prayer. And in the words in which Solomon asked for wisdom to guide and regulate his kingdom, according to the wisdom and equity that come from God, let us ask with equal confidence for wisdom and equity to guide this congregation of Christ's servants.

XI.

The Discourse

Delivered in the Diocesan Synod of Birmingham
of 1875.

"Then, calling together the twelve Apostles, He gave them power and authority over all devils, and to cure diseases. And He sent them to preach the kingdom of God, and to heal the sick. And He said to them : Take nothing for your journey, neither staff, nor scrip, nor bread, nor money, neither have two coats. And what-soever house you shall enter, abide there, and depart not from thence."—LUKE ix. 1-4.

VERY REV. and REV. BRETHREN,—This is the synodal gospel. The Church puts it before her pastoral clergy in all their synodal assemblies for their perpetual instruction. If you ask me why the Church selects this gospel, I must lead you back to the moment when our Lord Himself delivered it. With his rapid pencil St. Mark depicts that moment : he says that Jesus "going up into a mountain, called unto Him whom He would." As the Temple and the synagogues were consecrated to the old law, our Lord made the mountains the first temples of the new; on them He offered His most solemn prayers, there He assembled His disciples, there His greatest actions were accomplished. "And," continues St. Mark, "He made that twelve should be with Him, and that He might send them to preach. And He gave them power to heal sicknesses, and to cast out devils." Put St. Luke's report of our Lord's acts and words to St. Mark's description of the scene, and you have the first ecclesiastical synod, and He who holds it is Jesus Christ the Bishop and Shepherd of our souls. In that synod He calls His apostolic missioners, gives them their commission, and delivers to them a rule of life and conduct.

It may strike you that this rule of conduct is addressed rather to the episcopal than to the priestly order. Let me, then, direct your attention to the gospel read on the second day of a diocesan synod, as it follows in the next chapter of St. Luke. In that you will find the second synod which our Lord called together, when He appointed the seventy-two whom the priestly order unquestionably represents. To them He repeated the self-same rule of life with certain grave additions. "And after these things," says the Evangelist, "the Lord appointed also other seventy-two : and He sent them two and two before His face into every city and place whither Himself was to come. And He said to them: The harvest indeed is great, but the labourers are few. Pray ye the Lord of the harvest that He send labourers into His harvest. Go: Behold I send you as lambs among wolves. Carry neither purse, nor scrip, nor shoes ; and salute no man by the way. Into whatsoever house you enter, first say : Peace be to this house ; and if the son of peace be there, your peace shall rest upon him : but if not, it shall return to you. And in the same house remain eating and drinking such things as they have. For the labourer is worthy of his hire. Remove not from house to house. And into what city soever you enter, and they receive you, eat such things as are set before you ; and heal the sick that are therein, and say to them : The kingdom of God is come nigh unto you "* After these words our Lord portrays the terrible condition and awful punishment awaiting those who receive not His messengers, and concludes His instruction by impressing the seventy-two with the tremendous responsibility of their ministry : " He that heareth you, heareth Me ; and he that despiseth you, despiseth Me ; and he that despiseth Me, despiseth Him that sent Me."

To be sent from Christ as His missioners, yet to abide always with Him, to represent His authority and to exercise His power, is a divine commission, that in the very nature of things must presuppose a supernatural life in them who are sent. And this divine form of life our Lord delivers to His missioners conjointly with, as being morally inseparable from, their divine commission. It is the first rule of life ever divinely given to a chosen body of men ; for neither the Levites nor the prophets received any rule of the kind, however the prophets, as the preachers of the diviner life to come, may have practically foreshadowed such a rule in their lives. Like the Ten Commandments and the Lord's Prayer,

* Luke x. 1-9.

although brief in words, this rule of the missionary life is complete in substance. It stands before the rules of the religious orders, both in time, in the order of intention, and in the universality of its application. And whilst the rules of religious life contemplate the sanctification of select bodies of men within the Church, through the instrumentality of their vows and observances, this pastoral rule has for its object the conversion of the world and the building up of the Church through the holy and self-denying lives of her missioners. Through the observance of this rule the pastors exhibit Christ before they preach Him, convert them who fill the religious orders, and secure the success of the gospel they are sent to preach.

Had we received this rule like the seventy-two, from our Lord's lips into our mind, each word of it had been engraved as a law of conduct on our hearts; but grown familiar with words whose sense and application to ourselves we have perhaps imperfectly realised, we may have failed to see how truly and sharply this rule applies at every point to our own missionary calling. As an emanation of the Eternal Wisdom fitted to the ministry of the final dispensation, the principles of this rule must be unchangeable, though in that in which they cross our natural man and baffle his worldly prudence, it is obvious that the wisdom of its practice must rest on faith before it grows clear to the understanding. Were any one so weak as, before taking it on faith, to ask its demonstration, I should say to him: Look through the history of the Church, and you will have a demonstration eighteen centuries long. And in the long course of it, wherever you see this rule most closely observed to the letter, there will you see the greatest fruits of the divine ministry; the further you see this divine rule departed from, there you will see the divine ministry in its most languid and least effective condition. There you will see how, when filled with its discipline, the force of Christ's servants is multiplied. Under the influence of its observance, the Apostles, sacerdotal saints and holy missioners, with or without marked natural qualities, have planted, have built, have again and again renewed the Church of God. For this rule contains the secret of bringing home Christ to the souls of men. And if any one thinks that he knows a better way, better that way may be for some purpose of his own, but he will never beat the Eternal Wisdom in opening a path to those souls for which that Wisdom came on earth and died. And this we may take for unchangeable truth, that even when working through us as His instruments, our Lord will only enter into souls by His own rules and in His own way. It is one of His divine maxims that the disciple is not greater than his Master, but that he shall be perfect if he be as his Master.

Let us, then, examine this divine rule of missionary life and success point by point; not that we may criticise the laws of divine wisdom on which the progress of the Church is built, but that by their light we may examine and criticise ourselves. To meet, however, from the outset, that clerical temptation to casuistical criticism which so often damps and checks our more generous inspirations, let it be said at once, that when God gives us a rule whereby to do His work, however the application of its letter may alter with change of conditions, its spirit must everlastingly continue to be one and the same.

1. From the first point we learn that our Lord has chosen us "to be always with Him;" from Him to learn of what spirit we are; from Him to draw that spirit; from Him to learn how we are to represent Him to the world; from Him to understand our constant and universal dependence on God, the Father of spirits, the Father of lights and the Father of mercies; that with Him, and through Him, and for Him, we may act in all our life and ministry, always looking upon ourselves as God's instruments in the executing of those noblest and sublimest works of which the human creature is capable through the divine condescension. And as Christ Himself was the divine missioner of His Father to the world, holding Himself as nothing in Himself, but all things in the Father; so must we, who are Christ's missioners to the world, hold ourselves as in ourselves nothing, but all things in Christ. Wherefore He said, "Behold I am with you all days, even unto the end of the world."

2. From the second point we understand that Christ has sent us into the world to do His work; to preach His kingdom, to heal the souls that are sick, and sometimes even their bodies, and, as St. Matthew adds, to raise the dead to life. How marvellous a work it is to convey spiritual light into souls, and in that light the eternal truth! A soul is a centre of

life set between earth and heaven. Invisible as its
Creator, like Him spiritual, like Him mysterious, and
destined to live in His eternal presence, it is greater
than this whole material universe ; and truly may we
say that to enlighten a soul is to enlighten a world ;
and that to bring that soul to Christ is to draw a
world out of chaos into life and order.

The first duty of the missioner is to preach the
Word of God both to believers and to unbelievers.
This is his great privilege as compared with that of
the ordinary pastor, that he is not only sent to the
children of light, but to them that sit in the darkness
of error. Of this our last provincial synod reminds
us, when it says that "the missioner is sent not only
to the Catholics, but to the non-Catholics within the
sphere of his mission ; nor do we know to whom it
may please God to reveal through our voice His
saving grace."

Priests are sometimes heard to say that preaching
is a rare gift. But by the sacred mission we have
received from Christ I deny that assertion. It is
injurious to Christ to say, that having called us, and
ordained us, and sent us to preach, He has withheld
from us the gift of preaching. Rather would I believe
the laity, when, with a deeper instinct, they say that
the gift of preaching is not much cultivated among
us. At your ordination you were told that "it
behoveth the priest to preach," and the Church
addressed you in these solemn words : " Let your
teaching be the spiritual medicine of God's people.
Let the fragrance of your life delight the Church of
God ; so that by your preaching and example you

may build up that house which is the family of God."
The gift is there, or the Church would not have invoked it. The giver of the gift is the Holy Ghost, the
time of its advent was the hour of your ordination. But,
unlike the power of consecrating the sacrifice, which
is absolutely and in all respects divine, and therefore
of equal power in all, the measure of the gift of
preaching is not the same to all, but to one thus and
to another thus. Still *there* is the gift, like the gift
of any great virtue, awaiting to be cultivated; although in too many cases it is smothered by neglect,
or, like the evangelical talent, it is buried in a napkin.

The word *preaching* I take in that comprehensive
meaning in which it is used in the gospel, not as
mere pulpit declamation, but as the ministry of the
divine word on each and every occasion that may call
it forth. It comprises the delivering of God's message,
and the drawing souls to God's truth and law, whether
in the pulpit, in the confessional, in the catechetical
class, or in the household visitation, each opportunity
suggesting its own spirit and method. And this is
what St. Paul means when he says: "Preach the
word: be instant in season, out of season."

The preaching of the twelve and of the seventy-
two was in conversations with individual men, or
with a household, or with clusters of men on the
road or in the fields, or with a gathering of neigh-
bours into one house, or, as believers multiplied, in
their public assemblies. They followed the free
method of our Lord, who never let the opportunity
of delivering His truth go by. They told their
hearers of His personal character, of His life, of His

miracles, of His doctrines, of His parables, of His divine promises; they showed how in Him the prophets were fulfilled, and the Desired One given to the nations. They forgot themselves in the word of Christ, and spoke it with a simplicity like His own; they so preached because our Lord so taught them to preach. To this method succeeded the homilies of the Fathers on the Scriptures. For the most part they were not only earnest, but wonderfully simple: and yet the profoundest theology has been drawn out of those simple discourses. What was their secret? Like the apostolic men they spoke the sense of God and not their own; and that divine sense they obtained by meditating on the Holy Scriptures and the traditions of their fathers.

After the Fathers came a time when preaching was often little better than a patchwork repetition from older writers. Limbs and fragments rent from their vital centres, and piled on each other in lifeless shapes like constructed ruins, have neither spirit, sap, nor vital force. Life can only emanate from life: nor can a soul be touched except by vital power. No patching, no parroting will ever make a preacher. These are not the *veræ voces ab imo pectore*; not the tide of truth quivering with life from the living breast; not the light-bearing words imbued with the unction of the Holy Ghost, as they work through our own interior life and thought, such as even the simplest and plainest men give forth when they speak from their own devout conceptions. But the saints still carried on the true tradition of preaching.

Then came the passionate revival of pagan litera-

ture with all its pride and pomp, and with it came a
contempt for the simple ways of God's Word. Rhe-
torical self-display corrupted the evangelical simplicity
of the preacher, encumbered the divine message, profaned its purity, and dulled its spiritual edge. Still
the purer tradition of the saints and holy men of God
went on. The substantial methods of preaching may
best be learnt from St. Augustine's two masterly
books, *De Catechizandis Rudibus* and *De Doctrina
Christiana*. But if you would comprehend the deeper
mystery of the spoken word, and how the preacher's
voice but kindles the heart's attention to the voice of
the Divine Master speaking within the soul, you
must read the admirable little book by the same
great doctor which is entitled *De Magistro*.

One thing is it to have the gift of preaching,
another to bring that gift into exercise. The gift is
like the grace of any arduous virtue ; it will not come
into free, prompt, and grateful action, without dili-
gent co-operation and the right use of the proper
means. In the diversity of ministries, St. Paul places
the word of wisdom, the word of knowledge, and the
gift of prophesying, that is, of preaching, among the
principal operations of the Holy Spirit. The gift of
outward expression flows from the interior word of
wisdom and of knowledge. So it is in the natural, so
it is in the supernatural order. All spiritual operations are reflections, nearer or more remote, of the
operations of the sacred Trinity. From eternity the
Father generates the substantial expression of Himself, His Word, His well-beloved Son. In contemplating He produces His Word ; in contemplating,

the Father and the Word produce eternally the Holy Spirit. Then, for delivering this world from darkness, in the hour marked in the eternal counsel, through the operation of the Holy Spirit, the Father communicates fertility to the humble Virgin Mary, and through her produces the Word Incarnate. And as all divine ministries on earth are reflections of what is accomplished in heaven, the priests ordained by the Church through the Holy Spirit, are associated with the Divine Paternity, and through the Holy Spirit's operation have power to produce, with the Father, the Incarnate Word in the minds and hearts of men. This is the mystery of sanctification. What God does eternally in heaven, and what Mary did on earth, that the pastors of the Church through the Holy Spirit operate in souls. But to generate Christ the Incarnate Word in souls, you must be filled with Christ ; and as through contemplation in Himself, the Father generates the Eternal Word, so through contemplating Jesus Christ in yourself, in your own soul, you are made capable of communicating Him to other souls. By having Jesus Christ constantly before your eyes, making Himself man to make you partaker of His Divinity ; the Victim of men in His Passion, that He may reconcile them to God ; taking new life in His resurrection, and by His grace and Eucharist giving that new life to us redeemed, the preacher will have his breast filled with the Word of life, by which to quicken the souls of other men. Then, in His preaching, will he think more of Jesus Christ than of himself; in Christ's authority he will forget his own ; and, ascending in meditation to the bosom of the Father, there to contemplate the Divine Persons in their operations, he will come down again to spread the knowledge and love of the thrice holy God on earth.*

Of the Eternal Word you have the twofold ministry. From the Sacrifice, with great reverence, you minister that Word to souls in the communion of His Body and Blood; from your own breast you minister that Word to souls in the communion of His Truth. And to this ministry as well as to that, is a great reverence due, because in the heart we carry the light of the Word, as in the pyx the Holy Sacrament.

I still speak of God's word in all its offices and applications, as St. Paul did, when he said : " Preach the word : be instant in season, out of season ; reprove, entreat, rebuke, in all patience and doctrine." That is to say : Exert your gift with constant zeal. If that gift be of an humble order, exert your gift with that humble and patient simplicity that, in shewing less the man, shews more the virtue of Christ. Patiently feed your soul with light and doctrine ; patiently set that doctrine forth in all the moods you find will touch your hearers, and will bring them to love the truth. Obey your gift, and affect not wonders beyond your gift ; for nothing debases the word of God but the affectation of the man. The very pain that affectation inflicts, wakes up criticism in the place of devout attention. But it is the want of patient and persevering zeal to fill our own soul with living doctrine, that causes the word of God to languish, that makes so much preaching

* See the *Memorial de quelques points* of Cardinal Berulle.

defective and unfruitful, that explains the lack of conversions.

The communicating of light to souls demands one condition more, and that is the pure and sympathetic relation of the soul of the preacher with the souls of his hearers. Unless with your spirit you feel the souls that look up to you, you can never reach them with power. You must feel their wants and their aspirations, the nature of their difficulties, and the character of their temptations. Without that loving, intuitive, embracing sense of souls, which belongs to the charitable heart of the true pastor, and comes of taking interest in them, all the science of heaven and earth will not avail you to draw those souls to God with power. For the power of drawing them comes of thinking of them in God, of loving them in God, of commending them to God, and so of feeling them in God; out of which sense of souls there springs, as from a fountain, a quick sensibility of their true condition, and of their real needs, and a quick rising of the waters of life, with which to supply their wants.

The great school where we learn to know souls, and to treat them with the reverence that brings understanding, is the Confessional. In that sacred tribunal, where you sit as the father and the judge, the physician and the pastor of souls, if the penitent who pours all the miseries of his soul into yours, does not inspire you with tender compassion; if he draw not from you some brief but penetrating word to purify and deepen his contrition; if he win not from you some wise word of direction to guard him from future evil; some fortifying word to confirm his resolution; some healing word that sends the penitent away in peace and consolation; depend upon it you are neither a preacher nor a guide of souls. And the fault lies in neglect of the interior life.

Children require a careful, tender, and reverential treatment in the Confessional. But I regret to say that they are not unfrequently treated in a cursory and slovenly manner, partly from the absence of due consideration for the requirements of young souls, partly from the reckless motive of getting through with them and saving time. Yet children were our Divine Lord's predilection; He rebuked the disciples who would have kept them from Him; He said: "Suffer the little children to come unto Me, and hinder them not;" He drew them to Him with great affection; He uttered a terrible anathema on those who scandalized them. They are the hope of the Church; from their tender freshness they are more open than others to divine impressions; and what is sown in their youth grows up with their life. To plant divine things in their souls is to lay the foundation of the tradition and strength of the Church in future generations. This cursory treatment of souls is not limited to children; and yet how awful is the responsibility that God has put into our hands, whether it be of giving them light in their doubts and difficulties, or of judiciously revealing them to themselves, or of steadying and advancing them on the path of sanctity. How many souls aiming at the better things are retarded, or kept back, or left in perplexity, simply for the occasional want of a little wise and thoughtful guidance that they seek in vain! And yet, the light of the Holy Spirit is promised to all who seek it for their sacred office, and a few clear, apt, and decisive words in due season is all that is required.

I take this opportunity of saying a word to the confessors of nuns. Some of them scarcely ever speak to a nun unless in reply to a question. This is more than a mistake, it is a disqualification for the office. Religious women but seldom hear their state of life explained from the pulpit, they mostly hear the Church through the Confessional. They have their difficulties, and a wise word to them in season is always fruitful. I can assure you that they very much feel the privation of it. It should be brief and very prudent. If the confessor hesitate and halt between two opinions, he may do more harm to them than to persons less sensitive to every shadow of fault or error; he may make those scrupulous who, apart from his indiscretion, would be free from this spiritual torment. It is a grave mistake to suppose that a nun's ordinary confessor is not her director, both as to her interior, and as to the spirit of her exterior duties. He will know, of course, how to refer points of rule and discipline to the decision of her superiors, towards whom he must ever sustain the spirit of obedience and submission ; and he will be very careful how he touches the question of manifestation. Yet the confessor should understand that within recent times the Holy See has, for the present, limited the manifestation of nuns to their superioresses to external faults against the rule, and to progress in the virtues; to which effect a clause is

S

inserted in new rules when they are approved. But
this check is rather upon the right of the superioress
than upon the freedom of the nun, who may always
extend her free and spontaneous confidence to the
mother whom religion has given to her. It is obvious
that the confessor should uphold the lawful influence
of the superioress where the conscience is not committed, and should keep in view the legal maxim
that *præsumptio stat pro superiore.*

I return to preaching in its ordinary acceptation,
and to the words of St. Paul, that the gift is to be
exercised "in all patience and doctrine." Good
preaching comes from a soul that is full of good
things ; but the preacher cannot be rich in all
doctrine who does not study, reflect upon, and medi-
tate God's teachings, as the Holy Scriptures, the
Fathers, and the living Church present them to him.
Every meditation is a new possession. Tell me the
home habits of a priest, that great revealer of his
inward life, and I may fairly judge in most cases how
far he is a preacher. I do not so much ask how it
has fared with his early intellectual training, nor
whether he has a natural turn for eloquence ; these
ought to be great advantages, and spiritually used
they are ; but they may be perverted to foster con-
ceits that embarrass the pure and simple operations of the Holy Spirit.* Neither the twelve nor

* Next to cultivating a devout habit of mind and recollected manner,
Bossuet used to press the superiors of his seminary to train their pupils
in the habit of ready speaking, and of regarding the ministry of the
word as our Lord's special gift to His Church. He used to warn the
students against over-anxiety to cultivate an elegant and studied style,
bidding them rather to seek that ardent spirit of love in which they

the seventy-two were possessed of high human training, but they were filled with the word of Christ, and
with the wisdom and strength of that Holy Spirit
who reaches from end to end mightily, and disposes
of all things sweetly. And if St. Paul possessed the
higher accomplishments of his time and country, he
buried them in the Cross of his Master, and came
not " in the ostensible words of human wisdom, but
in the showing forth of the spirit and of power."
Giving themselves up to the Word of God the apostolic preachers became the transparent organs of its
utterance, moved to speak by the fiery motion of
their love towards those souls for whom Christ died.
Therefore, were they all Christ's vessels of election,
to carry His name before the Gentiles, and kings,
and the children of Israel, having much to suffer for
His sake.

After giving you the type of the true preacher, I
will give you a sketch of him who is no true preacher,
and will put it in the shape of a supposition. If the
missioner have no deep sense of his divine commission to preach the gospel ; if he be content to live on
with but few internal resources ; if he neither medi-
tate on the word of God, nor read it With reflection ;
if, from living outside himself, he have no internal
concentration ; if, with a soul thus barren from
neglect of cultivation, his love of souls has likewise
lost its energy, and so his relish for the holy work ;
if he wistfully look to a Bishop's pastoral as a relief

will find the promptings of the Holy Ghost. It is not man, he said,
who is to speak, but God in man, God alone, whose powerful grace
works through His servants.

from his own dreariness; if he repeat—I do not say
the Word of God, which cannot be too often repeated
—but if he repeat himself to weariness; if, empty
and void, his mind be like the chaos before the Holy
Spirit brooded over it; if, nevertheless, he prolong
his sapless platitudes, without salt of the new with
savour of the old, until he pall upon the people;
then, I say, he has neglected the gift of the Holy
Ghost, has done injustice to his divine commission,
and he stands blocking the way between the thirsty
souls of the people and some more faithful preacher
of the word of life.

"Preach the word; be instant. . . . in all patience." What is patience? Patience is the solid basis
of self-discipline. Patience is the virtue whereby we
hold with a constant firmness to our centre, and
refuse to be drawn away from it by any disturbing
provocation. What is that centre? That centre is
the sustaining presence and support of God within
the soul. "The Lord is my foundation and my
refuge." Our God within us is the rock of our
strength. And holding with firm endurance to that
Living Rock, by patience we refuse ourselves to all
provocation, come it from without us, or come it
from the inferior nature within us. This our Lord
would have His missioners to understand when He
said to them: "Abide in Me, and I in you." And
He completed the instruction when He said to them:
"In your patience you shall possess your souls."
But this belongs not to *extroverted* men, but to *intro-
verted* men, such as our Lord expects all His priests
to be.

Now may we see why St. Paul demands all patience in the preacher. In the first place, you cannot
command the souls of other men unless you command your own. In the second place, the preacher
is the organ of the Holy Spirit, Who descends upon
the peaceful soul and operates in the quiet soul.
"The fruit of justice is sown in peace." But you
cannot have peace without patience. Our Lord not
only gave His peace to the seventy-two, but He
commanded them to give it before all else to them
to whom they preached. But when the preacher
loses his patience, he first loses his centre, and then
his peace ; and whether to the children at their
catechism, or to the flock beneath his pulpit or to the
family in his household visit, he then puts his own
weakness in the place of God's Word, and exhibits
the earthly to them who are looking for the heavenly
man.

Let us take an example or two of this loss of patience, for they are not so scarce but that they may be
found. The proud man is easily disturbed, because
his centre is a false one. The vain man is still more
easily fretted, because his centre is outside of him,
and incessantly shifts its place. The man who loves
money has an outside centre of a yet baser description. Now preaching, as we have seen, is neither a
display of rhetoric, nor an exhibition of literature,
nor a glibness of tongue. It is not an exhibition of
the man, interposing his borrowed finery between
Christ and His people ; nor is it a display of the
human temper. And here I pause a moment : for I
have been young, and have grown old, and I under-

stand this style. It is the most undivine, the remotest from God's Spirit, the weakest—the offering of closed lips were better—the most contemptible of all styles, whether we consider its cause in the man, or its effects on the people.

The preacher is out of sorts ; or something has crossed his calmer mood ; or some vulgar emotion, born of affectation or suspicion, and unpurged by self-discipline, takes the ascendant for the time ; or, coming unprepared, he sees no clear line before him. Instead of looking calmly to God for light ; instead of holding in peaceful hope and patience to his centre, where he would certainly find some edifying word for his people ; instead of falling back as his final resource on those elementary doctrines with which he is always at home ; the preacher yields himself up to his inward provocation, nurses the sore of his wounded fancy, gives the old Adam his way, lets his warmed imagination follow her unpleasant fancies, and breaks over his congregation in a distempered fit of scolding that damages himself and damages them. If he be vain as well as weak in spirit, he will imagine he has given a powerful dis- course, and that the relief he feels after firing off his temper is a sign of the good he has accomplished. If he have spiritual sense that is lost but for the moment, he will feel shame and regret. If you consult the faces of the people as they leave the church, they seem to say : We looked for the Spirit of God, and have found the weakness of the man.

There is another form of temper that, where it exists, is more serious in its results, because it is cool,

calculating, and habitual. I speak of the habit of
wearing, scolding, or fretting the people, in season
and out of season, about money. Occasionally this
is accompanied by querulous complaints, and by
reference to personal affairs that lower the ecclesiastical dignity. I know how free the great majority
of the clergy are from anything so degrading, but I
cannot close my eyes to the exceptions, and where
this habit exists it is very desolating. As lower-
aimed minds are moved by the lower motives, I will
say at once that this is not a successful way. But to
this subject I shall return.

I must now draw your especial attention to the
duty of catechising. In my younger days the congregations were small, and the children of all classes
were catechised each Sunday afternoon at the altar
rails, in presence of the whole congregation. In
those days there were many good catechists, and the
laity took great content from this gift in their pastors.
But under our altered circumstances we have but few
good catechists. And yet this is the most imperative
as well as the most fruitful ministry of the divine
word. To make a good catechist requires as careful
preparation as to make a good preacher. To be
clear, to be simple, to speak to the point, to be able
to illustrate the truth with anecdotes and imagery
adapted to the minds of young people; to awaken
the moral sense, and to keep attention alive ; all this
demands forethought, the help of judicious reading,
and that tact and skill that come from love of the
work. Here, again, more than half the secret lies in
understanding the souls of children, whose sense of

reverence, lying deeper than their physical restlessness, is sustained by teaching them with reverence.

3. The third point of our Lord's rule to His missionaries is more complete in St Matthew: "And Jesus, seeing the multitudes, had compassion on them, because they were distressed, and lying like sheep that have no shepherd. Then He said to His disciples: The harvest indeed is great, and the labourers are few. Pray ye, therefore, the Lord of the harvest, that He send labourers into His harvest." Were our Lord to appear this moment in the midst of us, could He more perfectly describe the calamitous condition of the great majority of souls? Could He suggest a more effectual remedy than what He here suggests? " Pray ye the Lord of the harvest, that He send labourers into His harvest." To the sacerdotal order He commends this work; and to pray implies the zeal to accomplish the object of our prayer. The labourers are to seek for more labourers, to forward their vocation, to fit them for their work. Work your own field, and shepherd your own sheep, but forget not how many other fields lie uncultivated, how many other sheep lie distressed without a shepherd.

Our Lord would increase our merits on every side, and especially on that of extending His fold. He would have that love of souls that carries with it a personal interest enlarged to that more Catholic love that is untouched by personal interest. He would joyfully behold that generous spirit made our own, of which the great Shepherd of Israel set the example. When Moses had chosen the seventy elders of Israel, the Lord came down in a cloud, and took away of the spirit of Moses, and gave it to the seventy men. But when the spirit likewise rested upon Eldad and Medad, and they prophesied, it was told to Moses. And Josue, the chosen minister of Moses, said to him : " My Lord Moses, forbid them." But he said : " Why hast thou emulation for me ? O that all the people might prophesy, and that the Lord might give them His Spirit."

Beyond the solicitude to increase the number of well-trained clergy, there is another solicitude that is according to God, and that is to have co-operation in our own work. Our Lord sent forth His disciples two and two, and the Scripture says that " brother helped of brother, is as a strong city." Two are strong in mutual counsel and support, and their diversity of qualifications enables them better to meet the varied requirements of a considerable congregation. But there are some who never seem to enter into that word of Scripture : " Woe to him who is alone, for if he fall there is none to lift him up," and who from very inferior motives stave off the help of a second priest as long as possible. Then there are some whose emulation is of the kind rebuked by the great spirit of Moses, and who, forgetting the great freedom so wisely left to the faithful by the Church respecting choice of confessors, are jealous of those who, having once been their penitents, use their free right of going to other confessors. This to me is inexplicable on any principle, and cannot fail to be mischievous to souls as well as unjust.

The three first evangelical rules, on which I have

dwelt already, regard our divine commission. The five that follow, and on which I shall be brief, have respect to our personal conduct in the exercise of that commission.

4. "Behold, I send you as lambs in the midst of wolves." Short is the sentence, but how profound the instruction. The world can never be made subject to Christ by the world's temper or the world's weapons. Pride is unequal to the subjugating of pride, and temper grows more stubborn when resisted by temper. The arms of our success are not earthly, but heavenly, and God exercises His power over souls without violence; He is patient, peaceful, and long-enduring. We can only conquer the world to Christ as He Himself conquered, not by anger, but by meekness; not by overbearing, but by suffering; not by striking, but by patience. "When I am weak," says St. Paul, "then am I powerful." Our Lord bore the name of the Lamb of God to express His meek and gentle character, and it belonged to His office to bear upon Him with patience the sins of the world. He would have us understand that by the force of meekness and simplicity we overcome the proud and draw to Him the stubborn and the froward; whereas, to encounter such spirits on their own ground, is to add pride to pride, and flame to fire. It is not our spirit to call fire down from heaven, but our Lord tells us of what spirit we are; "Learn," He says, "from Me, for I am meek and humble of heart."

5. "Carry neither purse, nor scrip, nor shoes." Before He sent His disciples out to do their ministry,

our Lord planted deep in their spirit the foundation
of disinterestedness. He did not reason as a philosopher would have done; He commanded their
faith, and left His reasons to come out in the result.
He might have shown how they had to represent the
wisdom of His mode of life in their own. He might
have spoken of the repulse they must receive, should
they preach a detachment they did not practise. He
might have urged that the man of God, the prophet
of the future things, should show, by indifference to
present things, that his heart is set on high. He
might have alleged the great reason, how far more
powerful comes the gospel from the hearts of men
known to seek nothing in this world but souls, and
always souls. But in place of this pale and abstract
method of teaching, our Lord takes the practical
way, and simply tells His missioners to "take neither
purse nor scrip." At His Last Supper He put this
precept in a new light. He then asked His disciples:
"When I sent you without purse, or scrip, or shoes,
did you want anything? But they said : Nothing.
Then said He to them: But now he that hath a
purse, let him take it, and likewise a scrip: and
he that hath not, let him sell his coat, and buy
a sword." * After the manner of Jeremias † and
Ezechiel, ‡ by this strong figure our Lord showed
that searching calamities were approaching them,
that their condition was to be wholly changed, that
such persecution was impending, that, but for God's
protection, they would stand in need of every human
help and defence. After the Pentecost they under-

* Luke xxii.   † Jeremias ix. 17, 18.   ‡ Ezechiel iv. 2.

stood these words, and how God was their provider
and defender, and went forth with confidence to
preach Christ's kingdom, yet without purse, or scrip,
or sword. We must still, however, wait a moment
for the complete explanation of this rule.

6. "And salute no man by the way." The word of
the Lord hastens on to its destination. On and ever
on goes the herald of God, too earnestly impressed
with the import of his message, too conscious of the
infinite consequences depending on his diligence, to
loiter on the way. When the wounded and dying
strew the battlefield, the surgeon has no thought of
turning aside to salute his friends, he bends himself
straight on to the saving of life. When the sheep are
scattered, and stray in peril of the wolf, the shepherd
hastens in all directions to gather the sheep into the
fold. When souls are perishing, there is no time to
relax. "The command is upon God's messenger,"
says St. Ambrose, " he must not turn aside to indulge
in gossip on the way."

7. " And into whatsoever house ye shall enter, first
say : Peace be to this house ; and if the son of peace
be there, your peace shall rest upon him : but if not,
it shall return to you." This rule is extremely beautiful and efficacious. But our Lord first gives His
own peace to His missioners : "My peace I leave
you, My peace I give unto you ; not as the world
giveth it, do I give it to you." This is no mere salu-
tation of peace, such as the children of the world give
each other. It is the communication of a gift, and
that gift is peace in the conscience, tranquillity in
the soul from her harmony with the light and law

of God. After His resurrection, whenever our Lord appears anew to His disciples, He first says to them : "Peace be with you." He would have them always carry this peace in their breast, He enjoins them to communicate this peace to all who can receive it as a preparation to receive the Word of God. It was the custom of our venerated predecessor, Bishop Milner, to greet the members of each household that he visited with the apostolic blessing: "Peace be to this house." If in our household visitations we withhold from giving Christ's peace aloud, let it at least be done with inward aspiration, so to bless the Christian household, so to tone our own spirit to our ministry, so to put our own heart into its spiritual relations with the family, so to guard our nature against its levity, complying in spirit with the divine injunction. But why may this peace not be given with open voice, that the household may know they receive the blessing of him who cometh to them in the name of the Lord ?

8. "And in the same house remain eating and drinking such things as they have. For the labourer is worthy of his hire." St. Matthew puts it : "For the labourer is worthy of his meat," which seems to be the literal limitation of the text, although its spirit undoubtedly extends to all needful requirements. "Remove not from house to house. And in what city soever you enter, and they receive you, eat such things as are set before you ; and heal the sick that are therein, and say to them : The kingdom of God is come nigh unto you." We may now completely understand what our Lord means, when He says : "Take neither scrip, nor purse, nor two coats." He

would have us to live by the gospel, and receive our
provision from them to whom we minister. And for
this apostolic rule there are profounder reasons than
appear on the surface. There is no more binding
union between men than that which rests upon the
free and constant interchange of gifts that are needful
for their very life. Freely has the pastor of souls
received, freely must he give to the flock what is
needful to their spiritual life. And without contract,
bargain, or form of exchange, since there can be no
measure of proportion between things spiritual and
things temporal, the people freely offer to their pastor
the means for his earthly subsistence. " If," says St.
Paul, "we have sown unto you spiritual things, is it a
great thing if we reap of your carnal things ? "

The good shepherd expending his life for his flock,
the flock, from duty, gratitude, and devotion, support-
ing the life that is expended for them, presents one
of the most beautiful combinations in the whole
divine structure of the Church. Each party has a
work and a sacrifice in the other, and whatever is
cherished by sacrifices is dear to them who make the
sacrifice. In these obligations of mutual service, our
Lord provides the bonds of higher confidence and
closer love. But for this whole reason can there be
nothing more injurious to the filial devotion of the
people towards their spiritual father, than for him to
be constantly reproving them, and driving at them,
in ways that reveal a hankering for their money. It
makes the Church and the priesthood odious in their
eyes. It displays an utter want of spirit, sense, and
spiritual tact. Such a one will ask me—Then how am

I to live ? What am I to do ? Our Lord will tell you : "Give, and it shall be given unto you." If you are really generous to the people's spiritual wants, they will be generous to your temporal wants. Wise, prudent, and laborious priests will all tell you this. It works, as our Lord intended it should work, with the regularity of a law of nature, that if the pastor give himself heart and soul to the spiritual interests of the people, without distinction of person or class, they will never see him want. Nay, if he set himself to provide needful charities, his resources will grow in proportion. But if the people see him more zealous for money than for souls, they will close their hearts to his most passionate pleadings. Of course there are times and occasions when it becomes the pastor's duty to bring money questions before his congregation, and to do his best to succeed ; but a wise priest accomplishes this duty in the most calm, sensible, and reasonable way, be it for church, school, charity, or personal requirements. Of what he receives he keeps accurate record, and gives true account, which inspires confidence both in his disinterestedness and his management.

When our Lord tells His missioners not to go from house to house, but to abide where first they come, and to eat what is set before them, "He instructs us," says St. Ambrose, " that the teacher of God's kingdom ought to rise above the weakness of running from one house to another, indulging his levity, and seeking better fare than his home provides him with." He seems likewise to point to the disedifying practice of so frequenting other men's houses, as not to be found at home when duty calls, or the people need his service. The highest testimony I ever hear the people give of their pastor is when they say: He thinks a great deal of our souls, and very little of himself. And when that is the case, they are sure to think a great deal of him.

To show you that I have followed the track of the fathers, St. Gregory says: "Christ forbade the taking of purse or scrip, granting us our needs and nourishment from our preaching." And St. Augustine says: "He made it clear why they should carry neither purse nor scrip, not that they were not needful to maintain life, but that coming unprovided, the faithful might understand it to be their duty to provide for them who preach the gospel to them." When a house or a city received not His messengers, the one severity enjoined by our Lord was to shake the dust of the place from their feet. This was a testimony before God, and a sign to men, that they would take nothing from those who would not receive their message; they would not even hold the dust of their property in common with them.

Finally, our Lord concludes His rule by impressing on His missioners the solemn grandeur of their office, an office in which they represent to the world both Himself and His Father. "He who heareth you, heareth Me; and he who despiseth you, despiseth Me; and he who despiseth Me, despiseth Him that sent Me." If, carrying the peace of Christ in our breasts, and His living truth, we so preach, "not the word of man, but as it truly is, the Word of God," be it from the pulpit, in the catechetical class, in the

Confessional, or the household visit, if we so minister the Divine Word in the Holy Spirit as to draw many souls to Christ and the Father, then our reward will be very great. But if we neglect to foster the Word of God within us, if we slack from bringing that Word forth, if like hirelings we prove recreant to our gift, and so cause Christ to be despised in us; better were it that we had never come at the divine call, than thus to bring God's visitation instead of His blessing on His people.

The seventy-two obeyed these evangelical rules with fervour, and returned in the joy of success. But when in their joy they said: "Lord, the devils also are subject to us in Thy name," our Lord checked their joy and said to them: "Rejoice not in this, that the spirits are subject to you ; but rejoice in this, that your names are written in heaven." And looking high into the heaven, where He beheld the future reward of His faithful ministers, "in that same hour He rejoiced in the Holy Ghost, and said: I confess to Thee, O Father of heaven and earth, because Thou hast hidden these things from the wise and prudent, and hast revealed them to little ones. Yea, Father, for so it hath seemed good in Thy sight."

XII.

On the Festibal of all Saints of the Benedictine Order.

"Let us now praise men of renown, and our fathers in their generation. The Lord hath wrought great glory through His magnificence from the beginning. Such as have borne rule in their dominions, men of great power, and endued with wisdom, showing forth in the prophets the dignity of prophets, and ruling over the present people, and by strength of wisdom instructing the people in most holy words. Such as by skill sought out musical tunes, and published canticles of the Scriptures. Rich men in virtues, studying beautifulness; living at peace in their houses. All these gained glory in their generations : and were praised in their days."— ECCLESIASTICUS xliv. 1–7.

THE choirs of the Benedictine Order, my brethren, are celebrating the festival of all the saints who have borne the Benedictine name. Whether those saints be of the number known to general fame, of those less known beyond the limits of their Order, or of that multitude which is only known to God and to Heaven, we celebrate them all, we give glory to God for His magnificent work in them all, and we call upon them to help us with their prayers. It is a vast theme for an hour's discourse, and a theme that must carry us beyond the track of ordinary sermons.

The text I have read to you is the inspired description of the prophets of the Old Law, and for reasons
as beautiful as they are expressive, this commendation of the prophets is read in the Nocturnal Office
of the Benedictine Order on this Festival of its Saints,
as I proceed to show.

So many and so striking are the points of resemblance between the prophetic order of the Hebrew
Church, and the monastic orders in the Church of
Christ, that it is difficult not to conclude that the
monastical is the legitimate successor of the pro-
phetical order. But to compare them aright, the
greater prophets must be put in comparison with the
greater religious founders, and the schools of the
prophets with the monastic communities. Drawn
from the world into closer communion with God, in
rapture and in vision the great prophets contemplated the mystery of Christ to come, and portrayed
the all-saving life and death of the God-Man. They
may be truly said to have lived on Christ ere He
came into the world. They were partakers above
other men of the Eternal Word. And in the light of
that Word they were the predictors of the things
that were to come upon the world. They led
secluded and austere lives, abstracted from the ways
of the world. They were God's witnesses against
the sensuality and self-love of the world, and the
preachers of the more perfect way of God. They
drew disciples to their way of life, and formed them
into rule, and gathered them into congregations, and
gave them wisdom, and composed for them written

canticles in musical measures, with which in choirs
and processions they praised God. These are the
"sons of the prophets," or, as we now call them, the
schools of the prophets, who, like their spiritual
fathers the prophets themselves, lived secluded from
the common life of men, in ascetic piety and self-
denial, inhabiting the mountains and unfrequented
places, rudely clad in sheep-skins and in goat-skins,
and hoping for the better things to come.

King Saul meets a company of them harping and
singing their canticles, and he cannot resist the
impulse of joining in their procession and their
psalmody. In the Fourth Book of Kings we see an
assembly of fifty of them in one place, and of four
hundred in another ; and the description of the
Essenians by Josephus shows that this form of
secluded, religious life was continued in the Hebrew
Church until the destruction of Jerusalem and dis-
persion of the Jews. The contemplative order of
the Carmelites claims an actual descent from the
prophetic order founded by the prophet Elias on
Mount Carmel.

Thus far, my brethren, the resemblance between
the prophets and their disciples with the monastic
founders and their monks, is so obvious that you
must yourselves have already drawn the parallel
between them. If the prophets lived on the Eternal
Word and the Christ to come, the founders of religious life lived still more on that Eternal Word, and
on Christ Himself, whom the prophets hoped for, but
whom they possessed. Nor were such patriarchs of

religion as St. Benedict without the prophetic gift of searching the secrets of hearts, and of predicting things to come.

Another striking point of resemblance between them is this : The prophets with their schools formed no part of the ordinary ministry of the Hebrew Church. They entered not into the constitution of the sacred hierarchy as delivered to Moses. The great Hebrew legislator gives no rules respecting them or their office. As miracles are a special intervention of God above the ordinary course and law of nature, so the prophets are God's witnesses beyond the ordinary provisions of the sacerdotal ministry, and the manifestation of a special providence to meet the pressing needs and calamities of their times. Moses himself was their type ; and they not only obeyed his law, but added to it the testimony of their luminous souls, revealed its higher spirit, and called men back to its authority. Lovers of solitude, humble of heart, austere in self-denial, undaunted in courage, and strict enforcers of the divine will ; chanting ever the magnificence of God, His power, His goodness, His justice,. and His mercy ; the prophets were the highest witnesses to the sanctity of God, the rebukers by their lives of the sensuous and sinful world, and an ever-accumulating proof that God never abandons His people. To the proud and haughty oppressors of the earth they are as stern as Retribution. To the poor sorrowers and humble sufferers of calamity, they are as tender as mothers.

Can you fail, my brethren, to see that such, also, is

the character of the great monastic orders? As religious orders, they form no part of the divine plan of
the sacred ministry as constituted in apostles, bishops,
presbyters, and deacons. They come not into the
ordinary composition of the sacred hierarchy. And
yet their whole life is in the gospel, and our Divine
Lord Himself is their model, both in His life of
solitude and when surrounded by His disciples. And
the life of the first Christians in Jerusalem, when "no
one called anything his own, but all things were in
common to them," was the type of their poverty.

Like the prophets the religious founders were
raised up from time to time, when the conflicts
between the world and the Church were the most
critical; and were raised up to give light and
courage, heart and discipline, to the faithful. In
their compact strength they held the advanced posts
of the Church against her adversaries. What Samuel
and Elias, what Isaias and Jeremias, what Ezechiel
and Zacharias, with their disciples, were to the
strength and sanctification of the Hebrew Church;
that were St. Antony and St. Basil, St. Benedict
and St. Bernard, St. Dominic and St. Francis to the
Church of Christ. And forasmuch as through the
ever-blessed Mary, woman was restored to her lost
dignity and prerogatives, foreshadowed in the female
prophets of the Old Law, and as in Mary herself the
virginal type of sanctity was revealed, for which
reason, as well as her being the Virgin Mother of God,
is she "blessed among women;" therefore has the
monastic life been made illustrious, as well in the
number and greatness of the saints who have worn

the virginal veil of Mary, as in those who have worn the cowl.

The monastic orders, under the high discipline prescribed by their founders, could the world but comprehend it, are the grandest expression the world has seen of that elevation of soul to which men may ascend through the power of grace, and through the force and joy of self-sacrifice. They exhibit the strength with which the human soul can work its way from the bondage of nature to the freedom of divine love. Like the inspired prophets, they lift the soul of the law above the letter, and their own souls above the world, until its votaries stand amazed to see the peace of heart and freedom of spirit, which abstraction of life, a thing to them so dreadful, brings to men of like nature with themselves.

Like the prophets, too, in their strong contrast with the common tide of life, the genuine monks belong to the grand poetry of life. They bring heaven and earth together on the scene of human interest. Let a true monk of the old stamp come into the presence of the world, and although the artist may call him a picture, of that he is unconscious. What he makes the world conscious of is the shock his presence gives to the fashionable theories of life and happiness. How dead he is to outward things ; yet how keenly alive to things internal ! That he holds a secret, and a magnificent secret, the radiance of his features never lets us doubt. Clad in rude garments, and in meek humility, he is as firm as the living rock, and as silent. But let his charity be invoked by human need, and, like the rock struck by Moses, he can give forth the waters of life. He is John the Baptist from the desert. He is Elias fresh from conversing with God in the retirement of Horeb. As the chorus of the Greek drama came upon the scene of human passions amidst their agonies and conflicts, calm in wisdom, inspired with the supreme law that presides over human actions, interpreters of the profounder sense of the human tragedy; so from their calm contemplation looked the monks on the troubled world, revealing to its children how their restless discontent, their eager ambition, and their troubled life, come of living at cross purposes with the will of God and with His unchangeable designs. Because they looked at all things from the side of heaven, their chronicles often read as if they were the notes of angels upon human history.

With this preface I turn to the old and venerable Benedictine Order, of which I am an unworthy disciple. In happier times for religion, and those times were long, that great Order peopled the western world with saints, and founded works that were only less great than themselves. The Order had its august Patriarch, the Abraham of religious life, in St. Benedict himself. It had its great renovators in such illustrious founders as St. Odo, St. Romuald, and St. Bernard. It had its apostles, such as St. Maurus in France, St. Augustine in England, St. Boniface in Germany, and St. Amand, in Belgium; men who brought the Catholic faith to the nations through the medium of the monastic life. It had its glorious martyrs like St. Placid, St. Boniface, and St. Thomas of Canterbury. It had its canonized Pontiffs, drawn from the monastic cell to the chair of Peter, such as the two great Gregories. At the call of the Church it sent forth thousands of holy bishops, either to convert the heathen world or to shepherd the flocks of Christ. The number of holy abbots and sainted abbesses who have guided their Benedictine families with firm but gentle crosier on their way to God, almost exceeds belief. And the holy monks and nuns who, in the Benedictine vocation, have adorned the obedient life would in their numbers make a nation. All this may I with safety say, and yet not subscribe the apocryphal catalogues of Arnold Wyon, whose statements, however often repeated, have been long since chastened by the investigations of more learned monks. Yet it took the most learned monks of the learned seventeenth century, it took Mabillon and Martène, with their numerous co-operators, fifty years of life, and nine volumes in folio, to bring together the acts and lives that time has left us of the Benedictine saints known to fame, and yet this vast collection includes but the first six centuries of the Order.

The mere catalogue of these saints makes up a volume. Instead, therefore, of the impossible task of putting their lives before you, I must endeavour to find you a key to that spirit of the Order which made them saints. I wish, then, to put before you the character of that reform which St. Benedict introduced into the monastic life ; the position which he and his Order has held in the Church ; and the reason why that Order superseded the older Orders

of the West, and for so long a time universally
prevailed. To show how far the more recent Orders
have drawn profit from the Benedictine Rule would
demand a second discourse.

Like the Church herself, the monastic life came
from the East to the West. St. Benedict was by no
means the first founder of this kind of life even in
the West; whilst in the East it flourished for two
hundred years before his time. There is good reason
for believing that St. Mark the Evangelist founded
the monastic life near Alexandria, and that Philo
the Jew has described the life of his monks. At all
events, the solitudes of Egypt were peopled by the
monks of St. Antony in the third century; whilst
St. Pachomius, who wrote the first monastic rule,
could assemble five thousand monks at once from his
various monasteries in the Thebaid. In the course of
the fourth century, from the Nile in Egypt to the Tigris
in Armenia, and from the coasts of Palestine to the
mountains of Sina, all the solitudes of the East
became populous with monasteries and hermitages.
The monks sang and prayed, and worked, and meditated on God, and on eternal things. Away for ever
with the notion that they were idlers in the world,
or useless beyond themselves! They were the light
and counsel of their brethren who struggled on
towards sanctity in the world; and their labours
fed the poor of the cities. Turning from all things
else to God, the chosen among them entered more
deeply than other men into the wisdom of God.
And the profound maxims of wisdom and experience, gathered by reverential pens from their lips,

enlighten the devout souls of the Church to this day.
From their solitudes they had a great mission to the
world, not only a mission of prayer for the needs
of the world, but a great mission to edify and instruct the ages after them. The directive books of all
religious Orders glow with light from their wisdom ;
and the manuals of piety that at this day guide devout
persons living in the world are studded with their
holy maxims. The tens of thousands of devout
women, in active communities, who in these days toil
for God and for the poor, receive a great part of their
religious wisdom from the contemplative Fathers of
the Oriental deserts. Living so intimately with God,
those solitaries have been preaching the way of
perfect life to them who thirst for it, and revealing
its most perfect methods in every period of the
Church. Communities of women were not much later
in their commencement than communities of men.
The sister of St. Pachomius ruled a community of
nuns. Later on we have in Egypt what is little less
than a city of nuns. At Oxyrinchus on the Nile
there are ten thousand of them together, and their
convents are arranged in streets. They keep up their
choirs day and night without cessation. Three hundred priests minister at their altars. And it is
recorded that the streets were almost as light by
night as by day, from the number of lamps that
lighted their choirs.

Each group of monasteries had its special rule
prescribed by its founder, but Cassian tells us that
in substance they were the same, and were trace-
able to Apostolic tradition. At last, in the fourth

century, arose the Great St. Basil, who drew up a rule, so wise in its provisions that by degrees it took the place of every other Eastern rule, and has continued to be the sole rule of Eastern monastic life to this day. What St. Basil did for the Eastern Church, that, later on, St. Benedict did for the Western Church. But his time had not yet come. It was the great champion of the Divinity of Christ, it was St. Athanasius, flying from the persecution of the Arian Emperors, who first introduced the monastic system into Milan and Rome. And St. Jerome tells us that from the influence of St. Athanasius, many in his time were the monasteries in Rome of monks as well as of nuns. St. Augustine introduced the religious life into Africa, and from Africa it was carried into Spain. Coming to France we find the great monastery established by St. Martin at Tours, and from Tours St. Patrick carried the system into Ireland. And unquestionably it was to the monks of that severe Order, animated by St. Patrick, that Ireland owed its Catholic faith and education. The race of monks made the island of saints.

To be brief, St. Honoratus founded the famous monastery of Lerins, an island on the French coast, so famous for its saints and for its learning ; and the renowned Cassian, after travelling through the Oriental monasteries to gather and record their experience, ruled over ten thousand monks around Marseilles. From Ireland St. Columba brought the substance of St. Patrick's Rule into Scotland, and from Scotland it passed into England ; the monks of St. Columba, with alternating success, converted the pagan races of Great Britain to the faith, and raised many chosen souls to a high degree of sanctity, so that many of the earlier Scotch and Saxon saints are of the Rule of St. Columba. What the Irish St. Columba did for this island, that the Irish St. Columbanus did for the south-west of France, and for a part of Italy; and the Irish St. Gall for Switzerland. All these monastic rules were in vigorous action before St. Benedict arose, and were famous in their day, both for the great number of monks and nuns who lived under them, for the many saints they produced, for the nations they brought to Christ, and for their civilizing influence upon mankind.

Meanwhile the vast Roman Empire was breaking up through its own corruption, and dying in every limb. Every province of that blighted civilization was being trodden to death by wild pagan hordes, who in their barbarous strength and inexhaustible numbers rushed down, from almost unknown regions, on their destructive way. Then, for the time, sank the cause of Christ in many lands. Conversion had to be begun anew, and civilization to be re-established on a Christian basis. This mighty task was mainly committed by the Church to the monastic Orders.

Such was the state of things when in the year 480 St. Benedict was born. Sprung of a notable family, in his fourteenth year he was placed in the Roman schools. There his devout and innocent mind came first in contact with examples of licentious vice, and horrified at the spectacle, he fled away to the neighbouring mountains. In his first retreat the fame of sanctity gathered round the youth, to escape

from which he pursued his lonely way until he
reached a distance of forty miles from Rome, where
he came upon the rugged and solitary mountains
that close in upon the early course of the river Anio,
where Nero had formed the lake of Subiaco. There
he met a monk from a monastery that stood on the
lofty hill above the chasm, who gave him a religious
habit of skins, took him to a cave in the precipice
below his monastery, kept his secret, and by a rope
sent him down one-half of his daily allowance of
food. There for long years the youthful Benedict
dwelt with God alone. There, in solitude and
privation, he strove by prayer and labour to gain
abstraction of life from the outward senses, and to
quell down his nature to a state of settled recollection
and peace in God. The rude peasants mistook him
in his garment of skins for a wild beast; but he
brought them from their own wild life to the love of
Christ. As he matured in the wisdom of sanctity his
fame spread far and wide. Many persons came to
him for spiritual counsel, and among them came the
noble senators of Rome. Not a few were they who
wished to share his mode of life; and for them, he
raised twelve monasteries one after another on the
rugged flanks of the mountains looking down upon
the lake. In each of these monasteries he placed
twelve monks, and to each of them he gave an abbot.
But persecution ever attends the saints, and when he
had accomplished his work at Subiaco, bitter persecution drove him to seek another abode and another
work. He journeyed on until he ascended the lofty
summit of Mount Cassino. There he destroyed the

pagan temple of Apollo, converted the inhabitants to Christ, and raised a great monastery on the site of the destroyed temple. In the valley below his sister St. Scholastica, of whose gentle and loving firmness St. Gregory has given us such an exquisite picture, trained the first community of Benedictine nuns under his direction. And to speak in the words of Pope Urban II., " from this place there flowed out of the breast of St. Benedict the spirit of monastical religion as from the fountain of Paradise." * Here he wrote his famous rule.

And now comes the question—What was there in that rule and form of life, that gave it vigour to supersede almost every other rule of the Western Church, and that from the sixth or seventh to the thirteenth century ? When, from the beginning of the thirteenth century, new orders with new aims and purposes sprang up to meet the new requirements of the Church,—what part of their strength did they derive from the old Benedictine Rule ? In the third place, after many new orders had arisen, by what inherent force did the old Benedictine Order still continue to hold its ground ? The reply to these questions points the instruction of this discourse.

That all the older Orders had given place to the Benedictine throughout the vast Empire of Charlemagne in the eighth century, appears from the question which that Emperor put to his abbots. Remember that his empire extended from the south of Italy over France to the north of Germany. He asked the abbots whether there had ever been an-

* Bulla Urbani, ad Calc., Chron. Cassinen.

other religious Order besides that of St. Benedict, since he had heard that once there had been the Order of St. Martin of Tours. Ireland was, however, an exception. So great was the reverence and devotion of her people to St. Patrick and to his institutions, that his Rule almost exclusively held its ground until the three great Orders of friars arose in the thirteenth century. The Benedictine Rule never had much footing among the Irish people, even at the time when almost everywhere else reigned the calm mind and strong heart of St. Benedict.

Yet, if we compare his Rule with the older rules, whether of the East or West, we shall see that most of the provisions of religious life are substantially the same in them as in that of St. Benedict. The life of poverty, chastity, and obedience are in all these orders alike. In the observance of abstinence, self-denial, and austerity, the older rules are generally more sharp and stern. The laws of silence, of labour, and of obedience on the instant, are in those older Orders fully as rigorous. I will go further, and state, that some of the most important parts of St. Benedict's Rule are directly copied from the Institutes of Cassian. For example, the famous Twelve Degrees of Humility, which form the basis of the Benedictine spirit, are taken with some enlargement from Cassian's Ten Signs of Humility; yet St. Benedict has imparted to them a certain depth of power to search the soul which is peculiarly his own. Again, his direction that the private prayer of the monks be "brief and pure," is expressed in the words of Cassian. And it signifies, not only that after the divine office it be not much prolonged, but that it be aspirative and contemplative, a form of prayer in which self finds but little account. It was the method of the Fathers of the desert. Even his severe, but not too severe injunction, that murmurers and complainers shall be separated from the community and put alone, is to be found in all the religious rules before his time, from St. Pachomius to St. Columba. They had a sort of hospital into which those infected with the disease of grumbling were sent until the malady could be cured. But if the disease proved incurable, they sent the sufferer back into the world from which he brought it. With that grim humour that is so excellent a medicine for conceited imaginations, St. Columba prescribed that whatever the murmurer had used or made in the monastery should be sent out after him, lest it might communicate the infection to other monks. In these, as in most other provisions of the monastic life, St. Benedict followed the founders before him. In his humility he calls his own the least of rules for beginners; for precepts of greater perfection of life recommending the Holy Scriptures, the writings of the Catholic Fathers, and especially the Conferences and Institutes of Cassian, and the Rule of St. Basil.

In what, then, consists the superior excellence of St. Benedict's Rule? What gave it so great a position in the Church of Christ? Chiefly two things—a certain reform which one single word expresses; and a certain spirit, or soul, that pervades the body of the Rule. His great reform is expressed by the single word STABILITY. By requiring stability of life in the

U

monastery, the holy patriarch gave a solid and permanent character to the whole religious life. Other
founders had enjoined perseverance in the monastery
until death, and especially St. Basil; but St. Benedict
made it a solemn and essential part of the monastic
vow and profession. But we shall best understand
the value of enforcing the vow of stability after we
have considered the spirit of the Rule.

I scarcely know how in a few words I can describe
this spirit. The soul of every saint has a distinct and
individual character that is almost as much his own
as his personality. If in some great man of the
world we may call the unification of his complex
qualities his genius, in the saint we may call it his
inspiration. His special pursuits develop and concentrate the faculties of the man of the world; but in
the saint we have to account for the gifts of the Holy
Ghost, whose operation, as St. Paul tells us, is in one
soul one way and in another soul another. The soul
of St. Benedict has entered into his Rule, and, as St.
Gregory points out, its most conspicuous quality on
the human side is luminous discretion. His knowledge of men, of their diverse temperaments, and of
what in the service of God can be well done with
them, is only second to his knowledge of God. He
has the gift of ruling men in religion with a power
that is divinely humane. The words of his Rule are
brief and bracing; not sharp, but full of spiritual
nerve. There is an essence of prudence in them, an
oil of wisdom, an unction from the Holy One, which,
far from relaxing, acts as a tonic to the soul. The
great religious legislator is as firm in holding to God's

claims upon the man as he is considerate towards the infirmities of human nature. And nowhere is his gift of discretion more conspicuous than in the two chapters of the Rule on the abbot and his government, and the chapter on calling the brethren into counsel. So notable are they for their wisdom, that princes and generals have applied them to the conduct of states and armies.

Whatever religious observance exacts of the brethren that is hard to human nature, hard, that is to say, until fidelity to the grace of vocation makes it with time light and easy, comes from the provisions of the Rule; but in the breast of the abbot, St. Benedict has placed the kindly spirit of equity. The abbot is to bring his responsibility for each one of the brethren, with all his own actions, continually in review before the judgment-seat of God. Loving all under his charge with an equal charity, he must treat each one according to his spirit and intelligence ; to enlighten the good and holy ones with his words, but by his actions to demonstrate the way of truth to them who are obdurate of heart or dull of comprehension. Knowing how arduous and difficult is the task of governing souls, and of adapting one's self to many temperaments and different dispositions, as persons and times require, must he now appeal to love, now to fear ; at one time the strict master, at another the tender father. Severe to the proud and obstinate ; to the meek, the humble and the obedient, he is to be kind and persuasive ; to one he is gentle and bland, another he rebukes, a third he advances by encouragement. So must the abbot be ever solicitous that the brethren suffer no deterioration, and that he may witness the joy of their progressive goodness. He is never to rub too hard, lest in the effort to cleanse he break the fragile vessel. He is to remember the words of Jacob : " If I drive the flocks too fast, or too far, they will all die in one day." In taking counsel of the brethren he is to give particular attention to what the young ones say, because God often makes known to some younger one what is best to be done. And, to say the truth, their more open and simple minds are in many instances less likely to be pre-engaged with their own busy interests and foregone conclusions.

In the chapter on the order of the community, the holy patriarch makes exquisite provisions for upholding a high religious courtesy among the brethren. Whilst age, not in years but in religion, regulates precedence, the younger are to honour their elder brethren, whilst the elder are to love the younger. The elder are to address the younger monks as brothers, whilst the younger in the spirit of reverence must call the elder ones *nonnos*, as much as to say : You are greater than we are. The junior is to ask the blessing of his senior when he meets him, and when his senior enters, the junior must rise and give him his seat ; nor must he himself presume to be seated until requested by his senior to do so, that the scripture may be fulfilled : " In honour preventing one another."

Writing the life of the holy patriarch from the lips of four of his chief disciples, Pope St. Gregory the Great says, that the most authentic testimony to the

life and actions of St. Benedict is his Rule, for that
such a man could never have lived in one way and
written in another. To the admirable balance of
discretion in the Rule, the same great Pope bears
witness ; a discretion that carefully shuts the doors on
the side of evil, and opens them freely on the side
of charity. It is the wise proportioning of the divine
counsels to the capacities of the brethren that has
given to the Benedictine Order that spirit of largeness and freedom by which it has been always
distinguished, and that easy pliancy to enter upon the
great works which it has been raised up to accomplish.

But the spirit of largeness and freedom must of
necessity run to dissipation and weaken the strength
of the Order, unless it be firmly rooted upon a solid
centre. And for this the holy patriarch provides by the
vow of stability. In his chapter on the four kinds of
monks, he points to the scandals that have arisen
from the licence of passing from monastery to monastery, and from one form of religious life to another.
St. Basil before him had in his Monastical Constitutions put the point in clear and forcible terms, but
had not made stability a vow. He says : "It must be
held for certain that whosoever has been bound and
incorporated into the spiritual brotherhood cannot
be severed from it. You cannot cut a member off from
the natural body without its dying ; and the spiritual
is stronger than the natural bond. When a monk
has been incorporated into a community in the bond
of the spirit, if afterwards he sever himself from it,
he breaks the compact of which the Spirit of God is

the author, which cannot be done without incurring death of soul and loss of the grace of the Holy Spirit."

To prevent all such evils, and save the strength of the monk from being broken, St. Benedict binds his monks by the vow of stability to an irrevocable life in community, and in the community that has witnessed his training and profession. The monk is to be always a cœnobite, and ever a vital and inseparable part of the conventual body. That is to say, he is to live as he has vowed to live, in common with his brethren, as the Rule and its community life enjoin. If a monk is sent forth with a companion on any duty, they are to endeavour to time their reciting the divine office with that of the choir, and when the duty is accomplished they must return to the monastery without delay. Such is the Benedictine basis of "stability in the monastery." It has the centre of its life in the divine office of the choir, chaunted by the united brethren in the night and the seven hours of the day. This is called in the Rule "the daily duty," and "the divine work, to which nothing must be preferred." The whole stability of the monastery gravitates round the stability of the choir, each duty of which is fixed to the moment. The very heart of the Benedictine life was the prolonged praising of God by the united voices of all the brethren.

The words of the Rule ring like the bell in the lofty tower when they summon the brethren to be strenuous in this duty. Listen to the short chapter on the discipline of the Psalmody : "We believe," it says, "that

God is everywhere present, and that in every place the eyes of the Lord look through the good and the bad But especially and unhesitatingly do we believe this when we help in the divine work of praising God. Let us be always mindful, then, of what the prophet says: 'Serve ye the Lord with fear.' And again : 'Sing ye wisely.' And : 'In the sight of the angels will I sing unto Thee.' Let us therefore reflect how we ought to conduct ourselves beneath the sight of God and the angels ; and let us so stand to the psalmody that our mind may accord with our voice."

The three forces welded together on which St. Benedict built the monastic life, as on an immovable foundation, are the vow binding the monk to his monastery, the choral office, and the common life. For the monk to part from any one of these is to depart from Benedictine strength, from the very mind of St. Benedict, from the genius of the Order, and the spirit of its flourishing ages, when the Order converted whole nations to the Church. It is to slide from the rock of monastic solidity, and from that vigour of discipline in which numbers uphold each other. In the embattled army valour is contagious, and many are the men in the ranks who gather up a courage that, left to themselves, would sink into weakness.

To form saints, and to civilize mankind, have been the two great vocations of the Benedictine Order. Its stability accomplished the first of these vocations ; its free spirit and large-heartedness achieved the second. With these two arms it was fitted to embrace the changeable conditions of the world of man.

After the waves of barbarism had swept down from the
frozen North and the Steppes of Asia on the Roman
Empire, overturning both cultivation and civilization,
making a great part of Europe a desert, the Benedictines with their skilful industry restored agriculture.
They gathered peaceful populations around their
monasteries. They infused free life into the local
government of towns, drawn in great part from the
spirit of their own constitutional government. From
the municipalities the constitutional spirit passed into
the State ; but little in these days does this country
realise how much of its ancient liberties it owes to
the Benedictine Order. It gave a home in its monasteries to letters and learning when the world ceased
to care for them, and was suffering them to perish.
Education was renewed and kept up in the monastic
schools. The monks were the first craftsmen and the
chief inventors of those times. To them we owe
clocks, and windmills, and organs, and musical notes,
and lace-making, and the system of furnishing water
supplies from reservoirs to large establishments, and
numerous other inventions for the use or adornment
of life. They were great architects, and as copyists
they supplied what is now done by printing. From
their skill in building and adorning churches and
sacred books the fine arts arose anew. When printing was invented, they first introduced it into Italy
at Subiaco, and into England at Westminster Abbey.
Their monasteries were the schools of the people in
all the arts of life.

They brought into one country from another new
trees, and fruits, and vegetables, and flowers. They

studied the healing virtues of plants and minerals,
cultivated medicine, and spread the arts of healing
among the people. Their monasteries were the hos-
pitals, dispensaries, poorhouses, and schools of the
people, but not their prisons. They defended the
poor man's cause against the oppression of the powerful. They stood for the rights of the people against
the ungodly tyranny of kings and nobles, and counselled the mighty of the earth to justice and to mercy.
It was said in those days : It is good to live under
the abbot's crosier. They were the historians of their
times, and their chronicles show with what a truthful
simplicity they recorded events, and how they weighed
men of all ranks and callings in the balance of Christian equity.

From countless testimonies from the adversaries of
the Church to the services rendered by the Benedictines to mankind, I will quote but one. The following
sentences are extracted from Herder's " Philosophy of
History : "—" Every attempt to naturalize in the West
the monastic life of the East, happily for Europe, was
opposed by the climate, till the moderate Order of the
Benedictines established itself, under the favour of
Rome, on Mount Cassino. It adopted better cloth-
ing and diet than the hot and abstemious East required.
Its Rule, originally founded by a layman for the laity,
also enjoined labour, and thus it was of particular
utility in various wild and barren districts of Europe.
How many fine lands in all countries have been possessed by Benedictines, who had partly reduced them
to a state of cultivation ! In every department of
literature, too, they did all that monastic industry

could accomplish; individuals have written whole
libraries; and congregations have made it their busi-
ness to cultivate and enlighten the deserts of the literary world, by editing and illustrating numberless
works, particularly of the Middle Ages. But for the
Order of St. Benedict, probably the greater part of
the writings of antiquity would have been lost to us;
and when we come to the sainted abbots, bishops,
cardinals, and popes, the number of them taken from
this Order, and their labours, are sufficient of themselves to compose a library. Gregory the Great alone,
a Benedictine, did more than ten spiritual or temporal
sovereigns; and to this Order we are indebted also for
the preservation of the ancient Church music, which
has had so much effect on men's minds." *

From the time that St. Benedict converted the
peasants around his cave at Subiaco and on Mount
Cassino, the Benedictine Order has been missionary
as well as monastical. But until recent ages, and
mostly in this country, the reason of which I will
explain hereafter, its mission has rested on its communities, and has worked from its communities. To
convert whole nations united in rude heathen life and
manners, it required compact bodies of Christian
heroes. And the normal strength of the monk is a
corporate strength, his solidity lies in his stability.
He carries in him something beyond his individuality,
something of the joint force of his community. So
long as he lives in community, this corporate strength
overshadows him, upholds him, protects him, and

* Herder's Philosophy of History, Book 17, ch. iv., Churchill's
translation.

gives a vital animation to all his labours. When St. Placid was sent to Sicily, he went at the head of a large community, and more than thirty monks were martyred with him. When St. Maurus went on his mission to France, it was not parishes that he planted, but monasteries.

St. Augustine is sent by St. Gregory to convert our own nation to the faith. He comes with a community of forty monks, over which the Pope has made him abbot. After he is consecrated bishop, the Pope tells him to remember his monastic training, and to live with his priests in community after the example of the first Christians in Jerusalem. His disciples who are made bishops do the same; and the monastic life settled down as well in the cathedrals of England as in many of the principal churches. To the Benedictine monasteries England mainly owed her permanent conversion to Christianity, and her early civilization. Later on St. Dunstan was raised up to revive the drooping spirit of the monks, and to repair their community life. And, finally, the great Benedictine Archbishops Lanfranc and St. Anselm gave to the English branch of the Order an extension and more complete congregational unity that lasted until the violent destruction wrought by Henry VIII. and his ungodly satellites.

If from England you follow the monk St. Boniface on his mission to convert the German nation from idolatry, you will find him resting his strength upon his monasteries and convents. If from France you follow the monk St. Amand on the same errand into Belgium, with the help of St. Bavon he puts his

mission into the shape of monastic communities.
Read, in short, the annals of the Order, and you will
see in how many nations and provinces the monks in
their corporate force broke the strength of the
heathen, planted the Church on a firm foundation,
brought saints to perfection, and drove barbarism
away.

From the ninth to the twelfth century, the old
Benedictine stock put forth new branches with extraordinary vigour; each branch had its special constitutions, yet they were always firmly based upon
the ancient Rule. There arose the Cluniacs under
St. Berno, St. Odo and a whole line of saints; the
Vallombrosians under St. John Gualbert; the Camal-
dolese under St. Romuald; the Gilbertines under St.
Guilbert; and the Cistercians under St. Stephen
Harding and St. Bernard. The Order counts twelve
chief branches ingrafted on the primitive stock. The
whole Order with all its branches was estimated to
have reached throughout the world to the number
of seven and thirty thousand monasteries. And to
secure the privilege of being exclusively governed
by their own superiors, the very smallest of these
communities could not have had less than twelve
members. It is worth remarking that this number
of twelve, fixed as the lowest by the Sacred Canons
for securing exemption from ordinary episcopal
government, is precisely the number that St. Benedict placed in each of his twelve monasteries at
Subiaco.

If you would see what a great monastery of the
Middle Ages looked like, you can do so by making a

pilgrimage to the Abbey of our Lady of Einsedlin in Switzerland. It has stood for more than a thousand years. Its buildings, including the great minster church and the college with the monastery, form four quadrangles, covering fourteen acres of ground. The community still comprises three hundred monks, among whom are ninety priests. The college has three hundred students, of whom part reside in the monastery and part in the town. There are magnificent halls for the reception of princely and noble guests, and halls as spacious for hospitality to the poor. A hundred and forty thousand pilgrims flock to its sanctuary in a single year, nearly all of whom receive the sacraments at the hands of the fathers. On extraordinary occasions the town of seven thousand inhabitants lying round the monastery is not sufficient for their accommodation, and tents are erected for them in the fields. It is the centre of a great devotion that extends over all Catholic Switzerland and the bordering countries.

But a question has been waiting in your minds that I have promised to answer. The English Benedictine fathers, although trained in their monasteries to the whole conventual life, and belonging to those monasteries, are sent off from their communities to the missionary life like other missionary priests. This state of things has puzzled many persons, and especially those converts who are not versed in our past history. I proceed to explain. Critical times arise in certain portions of the Church, when that community life which in itself, as compared with life out of community, is the greater good, is made by

the sovereign authority of the Church to give place
to the greater good of the Church at large; and is
made to yield in a special manner to the saving of
souls that might otherwise perish. On this principle,
in all ages, have individual monks been called from
their monasteries by the Sovereign Pontiff to do
works or execute commissions for which they had
some special aptitude not so easily to be found elsewhere. And not merely on this principle, but on the
theological ground that the episcopal is the most
perfect spiritual state in the Church, have monks
been often drawn from their monasteries to be placed
on episcopal chairs, and from time to time on the
throne of Peter. With this light I come to the point.

When England through unheard-of treacheries lost
the Catholic faith, and the old parochial clergy were
either fallen away or extinct, the Benedictine as well
as the other English Orders had to establish their
monasteries abroad. For nigh three hundred years
a religious community could not exist upon our
soil. But the salvation of the English people, de-
frauded as they had been of their Catholic faith
after having possessed it for a thousand years, was
dear to the Church. And many souls, still clinging
to the faith under the greatest difficulties, cried out
for priests, and priests were few. It was a critical
time of most urgent need, when the salvation of
souls, which is the great good of the Church, demanded from many monks the sacrifice of the good
of community life. The missionary spirit of the
Benedictine Order had never died, and at the call of
the Sovereign Pontiff the monks came as individual

missionaries, where they could not live in monasteries. Concealing themselves as they best could, they accepted the perils of martyrdom in exchange for the happiness of life in the brotherhood. Strangely did some of their disguises strike the minds of their foreign brethren. For example, the venerable Father Augustine Baker tells us, that sitting at table once in Italy with two Italian Benedictines, he told them that in England he wore a sky-blue coat, white silk waistcoat, and a sword by his side; whereupon his Italian brethren rose up, refused to sit longer with him, and declared that a monk who did such things could not be saved. Yet this same Father Baker was one of the most devout and distinguished monks of his age. To his researches Dugdale owed much of his " Monasticon," Cressy much of his " History," and Reyner most of his "Apostolate of England." Moreover, he was a most eminent contemplative, as his life and the forty treatises on that heavenly pursuit which he left behind him bear witness to this day. Often had these missionary monks to take to the lowest disguises, changed perhaps for the gaol or the gallows. For it had been made treason in England to say mass, or to reconcile a soul to God in the religion of his ancestors. They toiled on to save the remnants of faith, to keep the lamp of the Church a-burning, and to prepare the way for better times. The reason of their long absence from community life is written in the Church preserved to us, in the centuries of toil and sufferings through which they worked to this result, and in the blood of the Benedictine martyrs. All which is the greater good.

But the change for which, with their brethren of other Orders, they toiled, is come. The Church in England has recovered her organization, and all things are hastening to recover their normal state. When their exceptional causes cease to exist, exceptional modes of action lose the reason for their existence. Wherefore the old English Orders are returning by degrees, as circumstances permit, to that conventual life which is prescribed to them by their founders, their Rules, and their traditions, as well as by the laws of the Church. And a great voice is heard speaking in accents like these : Well have you done in the past. But the past is the past : return, return, as occasion serves, return to community life. And I, from my long experience of the Church, of Religion, and of the condition of the times, am moved to say : Let that common life be in missionary priories as well as in educational priories—and you will then exhibit the strength of Benedictine stability; you will then eliminate what is weaker than conventual force; you will then, when the normal character of Benedictine life is well and widely known, grow rich in vocations; you will then knit on more strongly to the succession of saints; you will then tell with tenfold force in the Church; when the whole solidity of Benedictine observance at all times embraces every member of the Order.

Meanwhile we celebrate the saints who have made the Order great on earth and glorious in the kingdom of heaven. There you behold the blessed Rule written, not with ink on paper, but in characters of light, in the grace and celestial vision of undying spirits. What is chief in the Rule is its sense in the souls of the saints, who read so much deeper into that sense than other men. How beautiful, how numerous, how various, are those living copies of one and the same law of life! All are so much alike, yet each is so different from the other! They are like one great family, living in the same spirit on the same maxims. Each differs from each, because each separate work of grace, like each separate work of nature, is distinct and individual. And it is in the diversity rather than in the repetition of His work that God displays His magnificence. As each angel of the myriad hosts is a species, so each saint that God has glorified hath a special character. For "star differeth from star in glory;" and it is by the light of these Benedictine constellations that I must read the Rule if I am to pass with full light from its written text to its life-giving spirit. Its spiritual directions are the concentrated essence of the divine law, and the blessed counsels, in which our Lord Himself showed us the way to peace and beatitude. And what did the saints find in it but that very beatitude, worked out with wonderful patience and charity? Let me read the letter of the Rule indeed, and ponder it much and deeply in my heart; but to read it aright, let me read it through the souls of the Benedictine saints, beginning with St. Benedict and St. Scholastica. These saints were the simple-hearted monks or nuns of obedience. Or they rose to the elevation of ensanguined martyrs with golden wounds and glorious ignominies. Or they were fatherly abbots who led their conventual flocks to-

X

wards Christ, or motherly abbesses presenting chaste virgins unto their Heavenly Spouse. Or they were bishops who still wore the scapular beneath the cope. Or pontiffs who in their hearts cherished the Benedictine Rule whilst devoted to the universal care. What work is there allotted to man, from the humblest labour to the highest mental exertion, from the love that binds up a wound with tenderness to the charity that brings thousands of souls to their salvation, that they did not exercise? Wherefore let me look to them as my guides on the Benedictine path to heaven. Let me consider what they did when in positions most like to mine, and what now they would do in my position. And let me secure them as the patrons of my life before the throne of God.

THE END.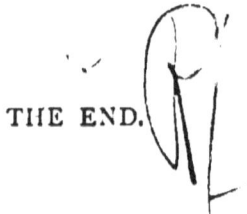

PRINTED BY BALLANTYNE, HANSON AND CO.
EDINBURGH AND LONDON

By the same Author.

Mr. Gladstone's Expostulation Unravelled. Third
Edition. Price 2s.

CONTENTS:—1. The Sources of Mr. Gladstone's Inspiration. 2. Mr. Gladstone's Objects and Motives. 3. Mr. Gladstone's Misconceptions. 4. Mr. Gladstone's "Infallibility" and the Pope's Infallibility. 5. Mr. Gladstone's "Obedience" and the Church's Obedience. 6. Mr. Gladstone's "Syllabus" and the Pope's Syllabus. 7. An Apostrophe to Mr. Gladstone.

History of the Restoration of the Catholic Hier-
archy in England. Cloth, 2s. 6d.

The Council and Papal Infallibility. Price 1s.

On the Conventual Life. Three Lectures. Cloth, 1s.

The Immaculate Conception of the Mother of God.
An Exposition. Cloth, 3s. 6d.

The Holy Mountain of La Salette. A Pilgrimage of
the Year 1854. Fifth Edition. 1s. 6d.

Sancta Sophia; or, Directions for the Prayer of Contemplation, &c. Extracted out of more than Forty Treatises written by the late Ven. Fr. F. AUGUSTIN BAKER, a Monk of the English Congregation of the Holy Order of St. Benedict; and methodically digested by the R. F. Serenus Cressy, of the same Order and Congregation. And printed at the charges of his Convent of St. Gregories in Doway. At Doway, by John Patté and Thomas Fievet. Anno D. MDCLVII. Now edited, with Preface, by Very Rev. Dom NORBERT SWEENEY, D.D., of the same Order and Congregation. 10s. 6d.

"This famous work is at last reprinted, and may take its place among the best of the modern reproductions of the standard works of our Catholic forefathers. . . . Its high character is too well known to need criticism or eulogy."—*Month.*

"We earnestly recommend this most beautiful work to all our readers. We are sure that every community will use it as a constant manual. If any persons have friends in convents, we cannot conceive a better present they can make them, or a better claim they can have on their prayers, than by providing them with a copy of 'Sancta Sophia.'"—*Weekly Register.*

"Will be welcomed by every fervent Catholic."—*Universe.*

"One of the very best of the old Anglo-Roman spiritual books."—*Church Times.*

The Spiritual Conflict and Conquest. Edited with

Preface and Notes by Canon VAUGHAN, Monk of the English
Benedictine Congregation. Reprinted from the Old English
Translation of 1652. With fine original Frontispiece reproduced
in autotype. Handsomely bound. Second Edition, with Preface
on *Meditation* and *Affective Prayer*. 8s. 6d.

"The Fifth Treatise is perhaps the best instruction in affective prayer that exists.
The 'Conquest' is more fervent and eloquent than the 'Conflict.' Page after page
reads as if St. Teresa or St. John of the Cross had written it."—*Dublin Review*.

"We thank Canon Vaughan for his valuable contribution to our ascetical library.
He has edited the book with the loving devotion of a trained disciple. Taking this
new edition as it stands, we consider it very nearly perfect; and many a devout
reader will heartily thank the editor for the beautiful and admirable book which he
has drawn out of obscurity and given once more into the hands of the public."—
Tablet.

"This golden book offers us, under a compendious form, the whole theology of
the mystical life. Canon Vaughan's notes supplement what the author has but
slightly touched upon, and so make the work a complete manual of Christian and
religious perfection."—*Weekly Register*.

"We are disposed to regard this treatise in its present complete form as decidedly
the best spiritual guide in the English language. This is very high praise, but not,
in our opinion, exaggerated."—*Catholic World* (New York).

"A book like this must be used and lived by."—*Month*.

"We cannot help the knowledge which is pressed upon us by comparison of the
immense superiority which Canon Vaughan's book has over other translations to
which we have been accustomed; and Canon Vaughan has enriched his book with
'notes' from many sources, which are scarcely, if at all, less precious than the book
itself."—*Catholic Opinion*.

"We sincerely trust that the 'Spiritual Conflict and Conquest' will speedily find
its way not only into the private oratories of the wealthy, but into the dwellings of
the middle and poorer classes of Catholic people."—*Catholic Times*.

"No other book of the type of the 'Imitatio Christi' so beautiful, and, on the
whole, so sober, as this has come in our way."—*Spectator*.

"Its aim is so pure and its expression so high, that it is impossible not to
sympathise with it. It is a book full of interest and value, and we thank Canon
Vaughan for this edition of it."—*Athenæum*.

"Canon Vaughan has edited the volume with singular ability. From his well-
written preface we have learned much of the eminent author, whose devout and
truly golden volume we respectfully and heartily commend to our readers as worthy
of a place beside the 'Imitatio Christi' and the 'Paradise of the Christian Soul.'"—
Church Herald.

"Praise by us of the original work would be needless and almost an impertinence.
It is rightly valued by devout souls in every communion. The present version is
couched in that terse, vigorous, forcible English of which those ages seem to have
possessed the secret, and whose swell and cadence delight the ear still. The editor
deserves the thanks of all for placing it within reach."—*Literary Churchman*.

"The 'Conflict and Conquest' contain much valuable teaching, and an English
priest, well taught to discern between the gold and the dross, might derive some
useful hints from them."—*Guardian*.

"It breathes a Benedictine spirit, if it is not the work of a son of St. Benedict."—
Church Review.

The Life and Labours of St. Thomas of Aquin.

By Archbishop VAUGHAN, O.S.B. Abridged and edited, with Preface, by Canon VAUGHAN, Monk of the English Benedictine Congregation. With Photographic Frontispiece of the Saint. Handsomely bound. In 1 vol. 8vo, 8s. 6d.

Chap. I. His Parents and Birth. II. St. Thomas at Monte Cassino. III. St. Thomas at Naples. IV. St. Francis and St. Dominic. V. Trials of Vocation. VI. Albertus Magnus. VII. St. Thomas at Cologne. VIII. Instruments of Knowledge. IX. Paris—The University. X. St. Thomas made Bachelor. XI. St. Thomas made Licentiate. XII. William of Saint-Amour. XIII. St. Thomas made Doctor. XIV. The Popes on St. Thomas. XV. St. Thomas and the Fathers. XVI. Tradition and Scripture. XVII. St. Thomas and Holy Scripture. XVIII. Greek Philosophers. XIX. St. Thomas and Reason. XX. St. Thomas and Faith (Part I.) XXI. St. Thomas and Faith (Part II.) XXII. Death of St. Thomas.

"Archbishop Vaughan's book is much more historical than exegetical. With wide and various erudition, that is clothed in a style of facile eloquence, he retraces the course of history and opinion for two centuries that precede and include the classic age of scholasticism. Over the whole period the archbishop passes with a light and graceful touch which leaves no part of it unadorned."—*Spectator.*

"It was a happy thought to put this excellent book within reach of the public generally. We strongly recommend it to all, no matter what their mental calibre may be, as the historical sketches with which it abounds, apart even from its scholastic worth, are quite enough to excite the interest of, and furnish much instruction to, the most casual reader."—*Tablet.*

"Archbishop Vaughan's noble work has here been admirably well condensed. Many who might shrink from attempting to master the larger work will feel grateful, we are certain, for a thoroughly readable book that has the charm as of an imaginative narrative, at the same time that it possesses no little of the value of history, and of the enthralment of biography."—*Weekly Register.*

"Though the editor has brought his volume into a space less than one-third of the original work, neither the biography of the Saint nor its near historical background have suffered in the least. On the contrary, the cutting away of remote matters leaves the towering figure of the 'Angel of the Schools' standing out with added distinctness, like a colossal monument on a level plain. Everything necessary for the proper understanding of the Saint's life and character, and of the times in which he lived and laboured, is retained."—*The Nation.*

"The work of abridgment appears to have been very judiciously executed."—*Month.*

Pax Animæ : A Short Treatise, declaring how Necessary

the Tranquillity and Peace of the Soul is, and how it may be obtained. By S. PETER ALCANTARA. Also, A Short Treatise of the Principal Virtues and Vows of Religious Persons. By Dom GERONIMO DI FERRARA. And a Rule of Life for a Person of Quality Living in the World. By the Same. From an old

English translation of 1665. Edited, in 1 vol., by Canon VAUGHAN, O.S.B. 1s. ; 6 copies, 5s. 6d. ; 50, £2, 2s.; 100, £4.

"Pax Dei quae exuperat omnem sensum custodiat corda vestra et intelligentias vestras in Christo Domino nostro."—PHILIP. iv. 7.

This golden little volume comprises three short Treatises pregnant with Divine wisdom and unction, and couched in clear strong Saxon-English. The first Treatise is suited to all Christians who are striving to lead a spiritual and interior life. The second Treatise is addressed exclusively to Religious persons, and will be found very useful to put into the hands of young persons who are thinking of joining the Religious Life. It treats of the end, obligations, and blessings of the Religious state in a manner that is at once clear, fundamental, practical, and beautiful. It is the best Treatise of its size the Editor has come across, if not absolutely the best. The third Treatise is addressed to the higher classes living in the world, and to those who have the care of a family or household, and is distinguished for its discretion, thoroughness, and spiritual insight into human nature. It is heartily recommended as a wise and safe guide.

The Spirit of Faith; or, What must I do to believe?

Five Lectures delivered in St. Peter's, Cardiff, by the Rt. Rev. Bishop HEDLEY, O.S.B. 1s. 6d.

CONTENTS :—1. Belief a Necessity. 2. The New Testament teaching as to what Faith is. 3. Prejudice as an Obstacle to Faith. 4. Wilfulness as an Obstacle to Faith. 5. Faith the Gift of Jesus Christ.

Also by the same Author.

Who is Jesus Christ? Five Lectures delivered at the

Catholic Church, Swansea. 1s. 4d.

CONTENTS :—1. The Word made Flesh. 2. Antichrists. 3. Redemption. 4. Sanctification. 5. The Abiding Presence.

"A brief but admirable summary of the Doctrine of the Incarnation."—*Weekly Register.*

"The answer to the above vital question Bishop Hedley has given with remarkable simplicity, depth, and clearness."—*Dublin Review.*

"This is the kind of writing which the age will read, because it is in its own style ; because it shows evidences of vigorous thought, and is rich in illustration and flowing with vitality. We greatly need theological and philosophical works written so as to reach the educated classes of an age which is so rich in writers of power and eloquence."—*Tablet.*

"There will be but few who cannot cull from Dr. Hedley's pages profitable instruction as well as consolation, while every one must be struck with the breadth, clearness, and aptness of the views expressed."—*Catholic Times.*

"The lectures are very clear, impressive, and satisfying. The language is simple, yet eloquent, and such as will reach the understanding of any intelligent reader. A perusal of this little work would seem to us to be a sure means of edification."—*Nation.*

"They are both theological and eloquent."—*Catholic World.*

MONASTIC GLEANINGS.

Edited by the Monks of St. Augustine's, Ramsgate.

No. 1. The Rule of our Most Holy Father, St. Benedict, Patriarch of Monks. In Latin and English. Translated by

a Monk of St. Augustine's Monastery, Ramsgate. Cloth extra, 4s.

No. 2. A Book of Spiritual Exercises, and a Direc-

tory for the Canonical Hours, written by GARCIAS CISNEROS, O.S.B., Abbot of Monserrat. Translated by a Monk of St. Augustine's Monastery, Ramsgate. [*Just ready.*

GENERAL SUMMARY :—1. The Way of Purity. 2. The Way of Enlightenment. 3. The Way of Union. 4. On Contemplation. 5. The Divine Office.

OTHER BENEDICTINE WORKS.

The Light of the Holy Spirit in the World. By Bishop HEDLEY, O.S.B. Five Lectures delivered in S. Francis Xavier's, Hereford. 1s. 6d.

The Ordinal of King Edward VI. Showing the Invalidity of Anglican Orders. By the Very Rev. PRIOR RAYNAL. O.S.B. 4s.

The Following of Christ. Translated by Father RICHARD WHYTFORD, Brigittine of Syon House, A.D. 1556. Edited with Historical Introduction. 5s.

Lectures on Catholic Faith and Practice. 3 vols. By Dom NORBERT SWEENEY, D.D., O.S.B. 6s.

Lectures on the Œcumenical Council. 5s.

Lectures on the Nature, the Grounds, and the Home of Faith. 3s. 6d.

Life and Spirit of Father Augustin Baker, O.S.B. 2s. 6d.

The Pope and the Emperor. 2s.

The Liturgical Year. By Abbot GUÉRANGER, O.S.B. Trans-lated by Dom LAURENCE SHEPHERD, O.S.B.

Advent (second edition)	6s.
Christmas (Vol. I.)	6s.
Christmas (Vol. II.)	6s.
Septuagesima	5s.
Lent	6s.
Passiontide and Holy Week	6s.
Paschal Time (Vol. I.)	5s.
Paschal Time (Vol. II.)	6s.
Paschal Time (Vol. III.)	5s.

*** Each Volume, except *Advent*, may be bought separately.

The Divine Cloud; with *Notes* and *Preface* by F. BAKER, O.S.B. Edited by Rev. H. COLLINS. 4s.

The Devotions of Dame Gertrude More, O.S.B. Edited by Rev. H. COLLINS. 1s.

The Scale of Perfection. By WALTER HILTON. Edited by Dom EPHREM GUY, O.S.B. 5s.

The Life and Revelations of S. Gertrude, O.S.B. By S. MARY CLARE of Kenmare. 7s. 6d.

The Dialogues of S. Gregory the Great, O.S.B. Edited by F. COLERIDGE. 6s.

The Prayers of SS. Gertrude and Mechtilde, O.S.B. 1s. 6d.

The Spirit of S. Gertrude. 2s. 6d.

Life of S. Benedict. By S. GREGORY the Great. Edited by Rev. H. FORMBY.

The Spiritual Works of Louis de Blois, O.S.B., Abbot of Liesse. Edited by F. BOWDEN. 3s. 6d.

A Mirror for Monks. By Abbot BLOSIUS, O.S.B. Edited by Sir JOHN DUKE COLERIDGE. 3s.

Cardinal Bona's Treatise on the Mass, and the *Divine Office.* Edited by Dom ANSELM GILLET, O.S.B. 2s. 6d.

S. Benedict's Manual. Comprising Prayers and Devotions to S. Benedict, S. Scholastica, and to all Saints of the Holy Order of S. Benedict. Compiled and Edited by Dom ALPHONSUS MORRAL, O.S.B. 3s.

Life of S. Cecilia. By Abbot GUÉRANGER, O.S.B. 6s.

The Medal and Cross of S. Benedict. By the same. 1s.

Cœlum Christianum. By Dom CŒLESTINE LEUTHNER, O.S.B. Edited by Bishop CHADWICK. 2s.

The Roman Catacombs. By Dom MAURUS WOLTER, O.S.B. Translated. 3s.

The Poor Man's Catechism. By Dom ANSELM MANNOCK, O.S.B. 1s.

The Poor Man's Controversy. By the same. 4d.

S. Anselm's Meditations. O.S.B. With *Preface* by the Cardinal Archbishop of Westminster. 5s.

The Holy Rule of S. Benedict. In Latin and English. Edited from the old English Translation of 1638, by a Monk of S. Michael's Cathedral-Priory, Hereford. [*In the Press.*

The Funeral Oration of Dom Prosper Guéranger, Abbot of Salismes. Delivered by the Bishop of Poitiers, March 4th, 1875. Translated by Dom LAURENCE SHEPHERD, O.S.B. [*In the Press.*

LONDON : BURNS & OATES,
17 & 18 PORTMAN STREET, W., AND 63 PATERNOSTER ROW, E.C.